American Crucifixion

AMERICAN CRUCIFIXION

*The Murder of Joseph Smith
and the
Fate of the Mormon Church*

ALEX BEAM

PublicAffairs
New York

PublicAffairs books are available at special discounts for bulk purchases
in the U.S. by corporations, institutions, and other organizations. For more
information, please contact the Special Markets Department at the Perseus
Books Group, 2300 Chestnut Street, Suite 200, Philadelphia, PA 19103, call
(800) 810-4145, ext. 5000, or e-mail special.markets@perseusbooks.com.

Book design by Linda Mark

A CIP catalog record for this book is available from the Library of Congress
ISBN 978-1-61039-313-3 (HC)
ISBN 978-1-61039-314-0 (EB)
First Edition

10 9 8 7 6 5 4 3 2 1

To my mother, beyond the veil

If you can imagine yourselves how the apostles and saints felt when the Savior was crucified, you can give something of a guess of how the Saints felt here when they [heard] that their Prophet and Patriarch were both Dead and murdered by a lawless mob. Never has there been such a horrible crime committed since the day Christ was Crucified . . .

—SALLY RANDALL, *writing to Mormon friends*
from Nauvoo, Illinois, July 1, 1844

CONTENTS

Contents

PART THREE

"Let us go to the far western shore / Where the blood-thirsty 'christians' will hunt us no more."

CAST OF CHARACTERS

JOSEPH SMITH JR.: thirty-eight years old, founder of the Mormon Church

EMMA HALE SMITH: thirty-nine, Joseph's first wife

LUCY MACK SMITH: Joseph's mother

HYRUM SMITH: forty-four, Joseph's older brother

WILLIAM SMITH AND SAMUEL SMITH: younger brothers

JOSEPH SMITH III: Joseph and Emma's oldest son

BRIGHAM YOUNG: head of the Quorum of the Twelve Apostles, Joseph Smith's successor as head of the church

SIDNEY RIGDON: early convert to Mormonism, orator and theologian

ORRIN PORTER ROCKWELL: aide and friend to Joseph, a frontiersman and killer, one of the church's "Avenging Angels"

WILLARD RICHARDS: Mormon church leader and Joseph's personal historian

JOHN TAYLOR: apostle, future church president

WILLIAM MARKS: Nauvoo stake (ecclesiastical district) president

HIRAM KIMBALL: wealthy Nauvoo merchant who later converted to Mormonism

HEBER KIMBALL: one of the original twelve apostles

Cast of Characters

WILLIAM LAW: prominent church member and businessman, backer of dissident newspaper *Nauvoo Expositor*

JANE LAW: William's wife

WILSON LAW: William's brother, Nauvoo Legion general, City Council chairman

CHARLES AND WILLIAM FOSTER: prominent Mormon dissidents, co-publishers of the *Nauvoo Expositor*

CHAUNCEY AND FRANCIS HIGBEE: dissident sons of a prominent church leader

THOMAS SHARP: influential anti-Mormon newspaper editor in nearby Warsaw, Illinois

GOVERNOR THOMAS FORD: "accidental governor" of Illinois who tried to mediate between the Mormons and their enemies

GOVERNOR LILBURN BOGGS: governor of Missouri, Mormon-hater, author of the 1838 anti-Mormon Extermination Order

STEPHEN DOUGLAS: influential Illinois legislator, initially pro-Mormon

"DR." ISAAC GALLAND: scalawag who sold government lands he didn't own to the Mormons

JAMES GORDON BENNETT: pro-Mormon editor of the *New York Herald*

JOHN C. BENNETT: former Nauvoo mayor, turned Mormon-hater

JAMES STRANG: Mormon prophet who attempted to take over the church after Joseph's death

PLACE NAMES

Babylon: The un-Zion, where all non-Mormons, or Gentiles, live

Caldwell County, Missouri: Scene of the 1838 anti-Mormon War

Carthage, Illinois: Hancock County seat, site of Joseph Smith's death

Montrose, Iowa: Mormon settlement on the Mississippi's west bank, in the Half-Breed Tract

Nauvoo, Hancock County, Illinois: Mormon city founded in 1839, razed by Mormon-haters in 1846

Utah Territory, the Great Salt Lake: Destination of the 1847 Mormon Trek, the religion's eventual home

Warsaw, Hancock County, Illinois: Tiny town eclipsed by more populous Nauvoo; hotbed of anti-Mormon hatred

Zion: Gathering place of the righteous, i.e., the Mormons; initially Far West, Missouri, then Nauvoo, and ultimately Salt Lake City, Utah

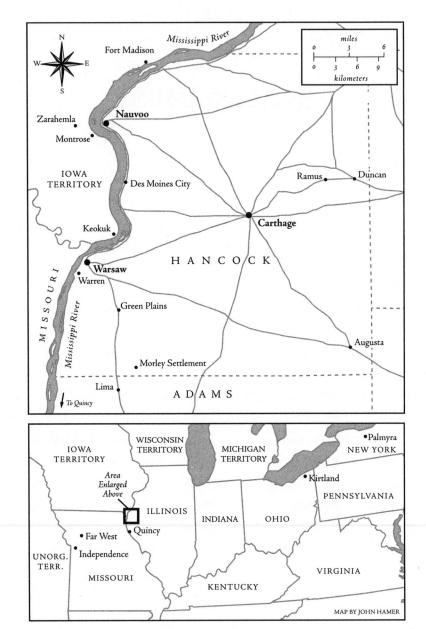

Hancock County, Illinois, 1844.

INTRODUCTION

JOSEPH SMITH THOUGHT HE WAS GIVING AMERICA TWO GREAT gifts. First, he created a new Bible, the Book of Mormon, which recounted Jesus's appearance on the North American continent. The Old Testament, the New Testament, and the New World merged into one seamless, divine narrative, handed down by Joseph. Second, he brought news of the Second Coming and a restoration of God's rule on earth. Joseph preached that a theocratic Kingdom of God would appear on American soil, possibly within his own lifetime. He had already chosen the men to administer the new, universal government.

America scorned Joseph's proffered gifts. "The whole [Book of Mormon] was a delusion," Smith's father-in-law said in an 1834 affidavit gleefully reproduced around the country. As Joseph's fame grew, his early neighbors broadcast their reminiscences of Smith and his family as a "lazy, indolent set of men." The "King, Priest and Ruler over Israel on the Earth"—a title Smith assumed in 1844—was continuously rejected by his kingdom. Smith fled the first Mormon colony in Kirtland, Ohio, under a cloud and moved his followers to Missouri.

Their new home proved even less hospitable. Within just a few years, a shooting war erupted between the Mormons and their Gentile neighbors, who chased the Latter-day Saints across the Mississippi River into

Illinois. Just six years after they settled in Illinois, the Mormons were refugees once again, this time trekking west across the Great Plains and the Rocky Mountains to their new home in Utah.

Joseph didn't live to see his people prosper in the Salt Lake Valley. He was murdered in the dusty village of Carthage, Illinois, best known then and now for its tragic role in Mormon history.

What happened? Joseph was hardly the first prophet of America's Second Great Awakening—the tide of religious fervor that washed across the country at the start of the nineteenth century—to traffic in millenarian predictions, and he wasn't the last. But he was the most successful. Converts followed him across the vast American continent, in conditions of unimaginable privation. Rich men, inspired by Joseph's biblical visions, surrendered their wealth to his fledgling church. Thousands of impoverished men and women from the British Isles crammed themselves into steamships to cross the Atlantic and half of the United States to join Joseph's flock in the American Midwest. Yet within just a few years of their arrival, their leader was dead.

Latter-day Saint historians and their Gentile colleagues have pored over many signal events in Mormon history, such as Joseph's First Vision of God, his purported discovery of the Book of Mormon, and the Saints' grueling trek to Utah. But most historians have ignored Joseph's death, known to the faithful as the "martyrdom." The church's sacred record of Doctrine and Covenants (135:1–6) reports Joseph was killed "by an armed mob—painted black—of from 150 to 200 persons," a phrase that appears in almost every high school history textbook in America. But the "mob" included a prominent newspaper editor, a state senator, a justice of the peace, two regimental military commanders, and men who just a few months before were faithful members of Joseph's church. They were a "respectable set of men," as one Carthage resident explained.

The leading citizens of southwestern Illinois could have imprisoned Joseph Smith. They could have chased him back across the Mississippi and delivered him to his old enemies in Missouri. Instead, they killed him.

Introduction

Why?

That is the story of this book.

⁑ ⁑ ⁑

JOSEPH SMITH'S DEATH WAS SUPPOSED TO "SEAL THE FATE OF Mormonism," according to the *New York Herald*, which reported that "the Latter-day Saints have seen the latter day." Quite the contrary. Joseph's death ended only the first chapter in the long chronicle of one of America's most ambitious and successful religions. Never forgetting their "prophet dear," several thousand Mormons braved the 1,300-mile overland journey to the Utah Territory. There they founded an independent republic the size of France, lived in open rebellion against the federal government for the better part of a half century, and only gradually realigned themselves with the country they held responsible for the death of their leader.

The assassination of Joseph Smith marked the beginning of the triumphal Mormon progress that continues to this day. Joseph's death did not paralyze the Mormons. Instead, it galvanized the Saints, strengthened them in their beliefs, and propelled them westward to a new, final, thriving "Zion." "The blood of the martyrs [was] indeed the seed of the church," as Joseph's nephew, church president Joseph Fielding Smith, gruesomely observed in the *Juvenile Instructor*, a Mormon children's magazine. The Saints—"perhaps the most work-addicted culture in American history," according to historian David Brion Davis—labored, they proselytized, they fought, prayed, and struggled, to erect an international Christian movement with 14 million members. That imposing edifice stands atop the modest gravestone of a thirty-eight-year-old preacher gunned down in cold blood on America's Mississippi border.

1

FLIGHT

Nauvoo, Illinois
June 23, 1844

J UST AFTER MIDNIGHT, FOUR MEN CAST A SHALLOW-BOTTOMED skiff into the roiled waters of the raging Mississippi. It had been raining for weeks. No one could remember the river this swollen, or this angry. In St. Louis, two hundred miles to the south, steamboats were boarding passengers from the second stories of flooded warehouses on Water Street. "Mississippi river very high," Joseph Smith wrote in his diary on April 25. "Higher than known by the oldest inhabitants about." Up and down the shoreline, grist mills for grinding flour had washed away; in some areas there wasn't enough to eat. In Illinois, Iowa, and Missouri, bottomland farmhouses washed into the swell, tangling their beams, joists, and window casements with uprooted trees. Flotsam smashed against the sides of the skiff, sloshing water over the gunwales.

The four Mormons from Illinois were rowing to the tiny town of Montrose a mile and a half across the river in the Iowa Territory. The US Army, homesteaders, and finally some Mormon settlers had staked out Montrose, which sat on the edge of a vast tract of real estate known as the Half-Breed Lands. Two of the passengers, Joseph Smith and his brother Hyrum, were wanted men, fleeing from writs issued by a hostile court in Carthage, the county seat of Hancock County, Illinois. They were likewise fleeing from a ragtag assemblage of town

1

militias and freebooting vigilantes gathered in Carthage, eager to bring the brothers to "justice," preferably at the end of a rope.

Orrin Porter Rockwell, a powerful, stumpish frontiersman, strained at the oars. A contemporary described him as "a shaggy and dangerous watchdog [with] the face of a mastiff and the strength of a bear." Still, Rockwell had some oddly feminine characteristics. Women noticed his "magnetic blue eyes" and delicate hands. He wore his long hair in double braids and strained not to lose his temper. When he became angry, which was often enough, his voice rose to an adolescent falsetto.

Rockwell had known Joseph since they were both young men hunting for buried treasure in rural New York. He was a celebrity on the Mississippi frontier, where he was known as the Destroying Angel of Mormon. (Joseph called him "an innocent and noble boy.") He was one of the first of the Danites, a secret Mormon vigilante force formed to protect the church from its enemies when it was headquartered in Missouri. By 1844, the Danites supposedly no longer existed, but Rockwell still had a reputation as a ferocious scrapper. He had been arrested and acquitted for the attempted assassination of Missouri governor Lilburn Boggs, who issued the famous anti-Mormon Extermination Order of 1838. Rockwell, alternately laconic and loquacious, both confessed to the crime and denied his involvement at different periods of his life. Of the Boggs shooting, he once boasted, "[I] never shot *at* anybody, if I shoot they get shot! He's still alive, ain't he?"

For many years, Rockwell served as bodyguard, barber, bootblack, and factotum to Joseph, founder of the Mormon faith, known to his followers as "the Prophet." Rockwell accompanied Joseph on his visit to Washington, DC, where Smith sought reparations for the Mormons' expulsion from Missouri from an indifferent President Martin Van Buren. In 1838, when Smith and some comrades languished for five months in a Missouri jail, Rockwell smuggled in augers to help them burrow through a wall to freedom. The walls were too thick.

Joseph and his friends were later allowed to escape, probably to spare Missouri the expense and embarrassment of an acquittal at trial.

In the early 1860s, the famous British explorer Sir Richard Burton found Rockwell herding cattle outside of Salt Lake City. "His tastes are apparently rural," the British nobleman reported, "his enemies declare that his life would not be safe in the City of the Saints." Rockwell, "tall and strong with ample leather leggings overhanging his huge spurs," carried two six-guns and treated Burton to some local firewater, or *aguacaliente.* Burton was traveling from Utah to California, and Rockwell offered some helpful tips: "Carry a double-barreled gun loaded with buck-shot . . . and never to trust to appearances in an Indian country, where the red varmint will follow a man for weeks, perhaps peering through a wisp of grass on a hill-top till the time arrives for striking the blow." "Finally, he comforted me with an assurance," Burton recalled, "that either the Indians would not attempt to attack us and our stock—ever a sore temptation to them—or that they would assault us in force and 'wipe us out.'"

Rockwell was once the subject of a famous Joseph Smith prophecy. After being released from a Missouri jail, Rockwell showed up at Smith's Nauvoo, Illinois, mansion unannounced, bedraggled, with wild, uncut hair, on Christmas Eve. Smith failed to recognize him. Finally discerning his friend, Smith declared, "I prophesy, in the name of the Lord, that you—Orrin Porter Rockwell—so long as ye shall remain loyal and true to thy faith, need fear no enemy. Cut not thy hair and no bullet or blade can harm thee." Unlike some of Smith's predictions, this one came true. After a long career as a frontier scout, Indian killer, and mountain man, the shaggy-maned Rockwell died peacefully in Salt Lake City in 1878.

Next to Rockwell, bailing furiously with his boot, sat Hyrum Smith, taller and thinner than his famous younger brother Joseph. Except for Joseph's wife, Emma, Hyrum was his brother's most trusted family member. A member of the ruling Quorum of Twelve Apostles and patriarch of the Church of Jesus Christ of Latter-day Saints, Hyrum also claimed to have witnessed Joseph's miraculous transcription of the

Book of Mormon from golden plates found near Palmyra, New York. Hyrum and several other men who later parted company with Joseph swore that his brother "had shewn unto us the plates of which hath been spoken, which have the appearance of gold; and as many of the leaves as the said Smith has translated we did handle with our hands; and we also saw the engravings thereon."

Joseph had recently entrusted Hyrum with the delicate task of explaining his revelation concerning polygamy—the necessity of marrying multiple wives—to Emma, his faithful wife of seventeen years.

"If you will write the revelation, I will take and read it to Emma," Hyrum assured his brother. "I believe I can convince her of its truth, and you will hereafter have peace."

A bemused Joseph answered that Hyrum did "not know Emma as well as I do."

The even-tempered Hyrum failed to pull off what would have been a masterstroke of diplomacy. In fact, Emma broke into a fit of rage and abused him. "Emma was very bitter and full of resentment and anger," Hyrum reported, adding that "he had never received a more severe talking to in his life."

"I told you, you didn't know Emma as well as I did," was the Prophet's quiet rejoinder after learning of the eruption.

Alongside Hyrum sat Willard Richards, a longtime church loyalist, also bailing frantically while Rockwell wrestled with the oars. Richards was huge and ungainly, weighing three hundred pounds. He was about to turn forty years old, but his fleshy face had already collapsed into jowls, and his neck was a roll of fat. He was called "Dr. Richards" because he studied and practiced herbal medicine in Massachusetts before moving west. Like Rockwell and Hyrum Smith, Richards was an intimate acquaintance of Joseph's. As the target of many lawsuits filed by a panoply of detractors, Joseph kept a meticulous record of all his daily activities; Richards was his chief scribe and recorder. Richards was also Joseph's brother-in-law. His older sister Rhoda was one of Joseph Smith's dozens of polygamous wives.

In Nauvoo, Illinois, the tightly controlled theocratic city-state that Joseph founded and ruled with a velvet fist, many other ties linked Richards with Joseph and Hyrum Smith. For instance, all three were officers in the 2,000-man Nauvoo Legion, a Mormon militia formed to defend the Saints against their enemies. Joseph, who had no military experience, was the Legion's commander in chief and assigned himself the title of lieutenant general. Smith liked to tell visitors that he was the only lieutenant general in the United States, which was true. George Washington had been the last one, and Ulysses S. Grant would be the next. Lately, Smith had taken to parading around Nauvoo in his dark blue general's uniform, with accompanying ostrich-plumed headgear.

Willard Richards and the Smiths were also members of the secret Quorum of the Anointed, one of Joseph's many overlapping councils that ruled over the 10,000 or so Saints gathered in Nauvoo. The three men had received the secret Second Anointing, a religious ritual that Joseph said would confer eternal life. All four men in the skiff were members of the Mormons' secret Council of Fifty. Joseph appointed the Fifty, whose membership was unknown to Nauvoo's citizens at large, to be the core of the world's government when Christ returned to earth. "The whole of America is Zion itself from north to south," Joseph thundered at a speech in April. At a secret Fifty meeting, Smith "suffered himself to be ordained a king, to reign over the House of Israel forever." The Council of Fifty explored the possibility of annexing Texas, restive under Spanish rule, and also Oregon, jointly administered with the queen of England, into a putative Mormon empire. To this end, Smith and the Fifty asked the US Congress for permission to raise a filibustering army of 100,000 men. That request was politely ignored.

Richards and the Smith brothers shared another secret in Zion, albeit a poorly kept one: They all had multiple wives. Richards had sealed himself to four different women. Hyrum Smith, who violently opposed the doctrine of "plural marriage" when Joseph first described it to him in 1843, later took three wives. Smith himself had between thirty-three and forty-eight wives, depending on who was counting.

The fourth man bobbing on the waves of the swollen river was thirty-eight-year-old Joseph Smith—prophet, seer, and revelator, the president of the High Priesthood, candidate for the presidency of the United States, king of the Kingdom of God, commander in chief of the armies of Israel, judge, mayor, architect, recorder of deeds, postmaster, hotel operator, steamboat owner, and husband, many times over. Born in Vermont, Smith was a far cry from the stereotypical New England man of God. "People coming to Nauvoo expected to find a kind of John the Baptist, but they found a very jolly prophet," a convert remembered. "He used to laugh from the crown of his head to the soles of his feet, it shook every bit of flesh in him."

He was no hair-shirted prophet. Joseph, reared on subsistence farms, scorned the pious pharisees of the preaching profession. "I love that man better who swears a stream as long as my arm and [is attentive to] administering to the poor and dividing his substance, than the long smoothed faced hypocrites," he told the Saints in 1843. Perhaps Mormons were supposed to shun alcohol, as prescribed by the revelation known as the Word of Wisdom, but Joseph didn't. When he heard that some of the "brethren" had been drinking whiskey, "I investigated the case," he reported. "Satisfied that no evil had been done," Joseph "gave them a couple of dollars with directions to replenish the bottle to stimulate them in the fatigues of their sleepless journey."

A very jolly prophet, to be sure.

Smith was a gregarious, articulate man, six feet tall and solidly built, with a long nose, a slightly receding hairline, and riveting blue eyes. He had a chipped front tooth, and sometimes a slight whistle crept into his speech. Like the barely noticeable verbal fluting, Joseph also had a hard-to-detect limp, the vestige of a grisly childhood leg operation. An innovative surgeon removed nine infected bone fragments from the seven-year-old Joseph's lower leg, without benefit of anesthesia. The normal treatment for serious bone abscesses was amputation, which Joseph refused.

Essentially unlettered, he was a charismatic speaker capable of exerting extraordinary suasion on his audiences. Brigham Young proclaimed himself mesmerized when he first heard Joseph preach. "He took heaven, figuratively speaking, and brought it down to earth" was Young's famous observation. Joseph taught that a restoration of Bible times was happening *now*, in nineteenth-century North America, and that his adherents were saints, as Luke and Paul called Jesus's followers in the New Testament.

Joseph hadn't limited himself to transcribing the wondrous Book of Mormon. He likewise undertook to retranslate the Old and New Testaments of the Bible, adding or expunging passages that he deemed to have been mistranslated or suppressed by corrupt church fathers. (He deleted the Song of Solomon, dismissing the sensuous text as "not Inspired Writing.") Most notably, Smith added fourteen chapters to the Book of Genesis, and wrote himself into the narrative:

> A seer will I raise up out of the fruit of thy loins . . . bringing them to a knowledge of their fathers in the latter days; and also to the knowledge of my covenants, saith the Lord.
>
> And that seer will I bless, and they that seek to destroy him shall be confounded . . . and his name shall be called Joseph.

If Smith indulged in megalomania, he came by it honestly. From his humble beginnings as a diviner and scryer—a person who sees miraculous occurrences through translucent "seer" stones—in upstate New York, he had accomplished the work of several lifetimes. There were plenty of millenarian preachers with apocalyptic scenarios spinning their tales in northern New York's "burned-over district" when Smith launched his career. Charles Grandison Finney, who became one of Smith's detractors, claimed to have entertained Jesus Christ in his law office. The Campbellites, the Millerites, the Rappites; by 1844, they were mostly forgotten. "I am the only man that has ever been able to keep a whole church together since the days of Adam," Smith bragged to his followers just a month before this parlous river crossing. "A large majority of the whole have stood by me. Neither Paul, John, Peter, nor Jesus ever did it. The followers of Jesus ran away from Him; but the Latter-day Saints never ran away from me yet."

Increasingly alienated from the US government, Smith now envisioned himself as the spiritual monarch of his putative Kingdom of God. "I am above the kingdoms of the world, I have no laws," he said. A devoted follower of Jesus Christ, Smith had been comparing himself to Mohammed, the warrior-prophet of Islam. To the world, Smith's recently announced campaign for the US presidency seemed quixotic at best. But not to Joseph. "When I look into the Eastern papers and see how popular I am, I am afraid I shall be President," he proclaimed.

☥ ☥ ☥

FOR THE SEVENTH TIME IN HIS SHORT LIFE, SMITH WAS FLEEING justice. He had been tarred and feathered, tried, jailed, and exiled. A furious mob in Hiram, Ohio, once ordered Dr. Dennison, a local doctor, to castrate him. But Dennison, who by coincidence had attended baby Joseph's delivery into the world in Vermont, couldn't bring himself to do it. A virulent Mormon-hater, Dennison did try to force a vial of deadly nitric acid down Joseph's throat. That explained the broken tooth, sheared off in Dennison's botched murder attempt. Joseph was once condemned to death and saved by a militia commander who refused to carry out the spurious execution order.

Joseph and his people were no strangers to biblical flights. They escaped their first settlement in Ohio just ahead of furious citizens who had lost money in a dubious Mormon banking venture. Reestablished in Missouri, the Mormons were chased eastward across the Mississippi in the winter of 1838, into Illinois. Just four years later, Joseph was on the run again from Missouri lawmen, hiding on the Mississippi shoreline and spending many nights in leaky skiffs much like the one he was now riding through the summer storm.

After each setback, Smith successfully led his flock to a new town, to a new state, to new strengths and to greater prosperity. The Mormons' theology, which places Smith's revelations on an equal footing with the Bible, was controversial, but their social ethic was not. Firmly committed to their co-religionists and to their families, the Mormons embraced hard work. One of their symbols, borrowed from Freemasonry, was the beehive. They endured unimaginable hardships and thrived wherever they put down roots.

Compared with his previous legal scrapes, the most recent charges against Smith must have seemed innocuous. Three weeks before this flight to Iowa, a Carthage magistrate accused the Smith brothers of inciting a riot, and of breaching the First Amendment's guarantee of a free press. Smith had indeed demanded the destruction of Nauvoo's sole opposition newspaper, the *Expositor*, at a public meeting, calling the broadsheet "a greater nuisance than a dead carcass." As mayor, he ordered the city marshal to destroy the paper's printing press, and as Lieutenant General Smith, he instructed the Nauvoo Legion to help. Illinois governor Thomas Ford, who fancied himself a skillful intermediary between the politically powerful Mormons and their many enemies in the state, had promised Smith safe passage to Carthage. But Joseph feared the shadowy, marauding Illinois militiamen who despised the Mormon religion, hated the Saints' anti-slavery politics, reviled them as Indian lovers, and equated polygamy with orgiastic excess.

Just a few days earlier, Smith's mortal enemy, the firebrand newspaper editor Thomas Sharp, wrote that "we would not be surprised to hear of [Smith's] death by violent means in a short time. He has deadly enemies—men whose wrongs have maddened them—and who are prepared at all times to avenge themselves."

Pitching to and fro on the stormy waves, peering westward to discern the far bank, Joseph believed that he was fleeing for his life. He was right.

Nauvoo Temple

PART ONE

"In Illinois we've found a safe retreat . . ."

2

KING JOSEPH

This Joe Smith must be set down as an extraordinary character, a prophet-hero, as Carlyle might call him. It is no small thing, in the blaze of this nineteenth century, to give to men a new revelation, found a new religion, establish new forms of worship, to build a city, and make proselytes in two hemispheres. Yet all this has been done by Joe Smith, and that against every sort of opposition, ridicule and persecution.

—*New York Sun, 1843*

JOSEPH SMITH IN 1844 WAS A MAN AT THE HEIGHT OF HIS powers. He was a national celebrity, perhaps more notorious than famous, but a figure of renown nonetheless. Ten years earlier, Ohio newspaper editor Eber Howe dredged up rumors, innuendos, wild stories, and half truths—a half truth is half true, remember—about Joseph's early years as a prophet in upstate New York and published them in *Mormonism Unvailed*. The book, which found a wide audience, portrayed Joseph as a cynical and unscrupulous treasure hunter who had plagiarized the Book of Mormon from a rival divine and published it in

1830. Damningly, Howe included an affidavit from Joseph's father-in-law, who "considered the whole of it," meaning the Book of Mormon, "a delusion, and advised them to abandon it."

In 1842, Smith's former first counselor and apostate extraordinaire, John C. Bennett, published *The History of the Saints: or, An Exposé of Joe Smith and Mormonism*, filled with lurid tales of plural wifery, killing, and blasphemy, all of it laid at the feet of "Holy Joe, and his Danite band of murderers." But Smith was a hard man to bring down. By the spring of 1844, Bennett was back at work on the poultry essays that would gain him some culinary fame—he was a determined champion of the Plymouth Rock hen—and Joseph was ruling a city of 10,000 people and corresponding with the rulers of France, Russia, Great Britain, and the United States.

Joseph Smith had been tested, and he had prevailed. In the spring of 1844, he delivered a sermon at an outdoor stand before an audience of several thousand Saints. He called out his detractors: "Come on! ye prosecutors! ye false swearers! All hell, boil over! Ye burning mountains, roll down your lava! For I will come out on the top at last. I have more to boast of than ever any man had."

Ɨ Ɨ Ɨ

JOSEPH SMITH WAS BORN INTO A HUMBLE FARMING FAMILY IN Sharon, Vermont, in 1805. Crop failures and business reverses plunged the Smiths into debt, and Joseph Smith Sr. took his wife and four children westward to Palmyra, New York, to make a new start. Life was better there. Everyone in the family worked, either clearing land, sewing small baskets for sale, planting corn, or baking cakes to sell to travelers navigating the nearby Erie Canal. Several hostile memoirists berate young Joseph as an idler, but it is hard to imagine that anyone could have been idle in a family now numbering eight, struggling to survive on newly cleared land purchased with loans the Smiths could barely afford.

Joseph embarked on his unusual religious inquiries when he was barely an adolescent. Although the details of his meetings with angels and heavenly spirits changed considerably over the years, the core story remained the same. As a young boy, he said, he had noticed the multiplicity of churches. In tiny Palmyra alone, there were four denominations—Presbyterian, Quaker, Methodist, and Baptist. Joseph said he asked in private prayer, *Which religion is true?* The answer came when he was fourteen. Jesus Christ and his Heavenly Father appeared to him in a vision and promised to explain the tenets of true belief.

Encounters with the godhead were not rare in early nineteenth-century America, and they were not so uncommon in western New York. America was experiencing the Second Great Awakening, a breakout period of radical, passionate rethinking of traditional Christian worship. The twenty-four United States had reinvented the Old World, and American ministers and prophets were revivifying the old religions. The energy and novelty of the New World prompted many to dream of a radical new world order, highlighted by the Second Coming of Christ. New doctrine was everywhere. Ann Lee's Shakers had established a Lake Ontario beachhead just thirty miles from the Smiths' Palmyra home. The Shakers danced feverishly, practiced celibacy, and worshipped Lee as the reincarnation of Christ. Just twenty-five miles to the south, another striking woman, Jemima Wilkinson, claimed to be the risen Christ. Although she could neither read nor write, Wilkinson recited the Bible by heart, occasionally aided by her sidekick, Elijah. The Baptist farmer William Miller had plenty of followers in northwestern New York, which became known as the "burned-over district" because the hot fires of religious revivalism swept through so often. ("A mad mix of doctrines and preachers," critic Harold Bloom has called it.) Miller predicted that Jesus would return to America in 1843, then revamped his prediction to 1844, and so on.

Nor was meeting Jesus a unique occurrence in that time and place. Sixteen-year-old Elias Smith (no relation to Joseph) met "the Lamb upon Mt. Sion" in the woods near his Woodstock, Vermont, home. John

Thompson, a teacher at Palmyra Academy, saw Christ descend from the sky "in a glare of brightness exceeding tenfold the brilliancy of the meridian Sun." Pamphleteer Asa Wild of Amsterdam, New York, spoke with "the awful and glorious majesty of the Great Jehovah" and learned "that every denomination of professing Christians had become extremely corrupt," news akin to the divine message received by Joseph Smith.

As Joseph matured into his middle and late teens, his religious curiosity melded with a collection of hobbies that became his vocation: dowsing, gold digging, treasure hunting, and "scrying." These pursuits were related, and all semilegitimate at the time. A dowser looks for underground water aquifers, often using the tools of superstition, for example, a branch from a witch hazel tree. A talented dowser or treasure hunter might stare through a translucent rock, or peep stone, to identify underground pockets of water, or hidden Indian relics, or buried gold. Staring through the peep stone was scrying, from the word *descry*, meaning to perceive or reveal.

As a teenager, Joseph gained a reputation as someone with reliable powers of necromancy and intuition. Impressed by his talent, a local farmer hired Joseph to travel with him to Pennsylvania to search for a lost Spanish silver mine. In Harmony, Pennsylvania, Joseph and his employer boarded for a few weeks with a famous hunter named Isaac Hale. Smith and Hale never hit it off. Hale reviled the money-digging expedition, describing his lodger as "a careless young man—not very well educated and saucy and insolent." Hale's recollection was doubtless colored by Joseph's abduction of his tall, attractive daughter Emma. The young couple fell in love and fled Harmony to secretly marry in New York and live with Joseph's family.

A few months before Joseph's eighteenth birthday, the parallel strands of his life—his religious bent and his relentless search for treasure—came together. As he later explained, an angel named Moroni, "glorious beyond description," cloaked in "a loose robe of most exquisite whiteness," appeared to him one night and told him where to find a book, "written upon gold plates . . . giving an account of the former inhabitants of this con-

Joseph and the angel
Moroni meeting in
the woods.
*Credit: LDS Church
History Library*

tinent [with] the fullness of the everlasting Gospel contained in it."
This was the Book of Mormon, which Joseph would have to translate
using two seer stones, like peep stones, that Moroni said he would find
buried with the golden tablets.

Sure enough, Joseph found a box with the tablets and the translating device, known as the Urim and Thummim, in a trench on the hill
Cumorah, just south of Palmyra. Joseph, and Joseph alone, touched
the uncovered tablets and saw the "reformed Egyptian" hieroglyphs
imprinted on them. He assured Emma that it would be certain death
for her or other family members to see them. Nonetheless, Emma was
allowed to participate, as his first scribe, or recorder. Joseph described
himself as "unlearned," and he never claimed to have translated the

sacred text. The text came from God, speaking through Joseph while he stared at the hidden plates, wrapped in a tablecloth. Sometimes he read the revealed text from the Urim and Thummim, placed in a hat.

At first, Emma took dictation in their tiny home. But a prosperous local convert, Martin Harris, soon supplanted her, separated from Joseph by a blanket suspended from a string. A schoolteacher convert named Oliver Cowdery eventually joined them. Although Harris and Cowdery would swear to be original "witnesses" of the Book of Mormon, they claimed to have been shown the gold plates in an angelic vision, not by Joseph. When he had completed the translation, Joseph explained that Moroni had taken the plates back to heaven.

Joseph's "golden bible" first came off the printing press in 1830, six hundred pages long. In prose redolent of the popular King James Version of the Bible, the Book of Mormon related a tale omitted from the Old and New Testaments, the story of the 1,000-year conflict between two tribes of ancient Israel, the Nephites and the Lamanites. The two tribes had relocated to the American continent. The Nephites struggled to walk in the way of the Lord; the idolatrous Lamanites, less so. After centuries of near-constant warfare, a vast army of Lamanites exterminated the Nephites at the final battle of Cumorah. Tens of thousands died, but the Nephite leader, whose name was Mormon, and his son Moroni survived. Knowing he was to be killed, Mormon handed the golden plates, with the record of their righteous but doomed civilization, to Moroni, who expanded on the account, added commentary, and buried the tablets in hopes of a future discovery. When Joseph unearthed them, history was fulfilled.

The Book of Mormon caught on slowly at first. It made few claims as a literary work, with wooden and oft-repetitive prose, starting almost every other paragraph with the stock phrase, "It came to pass. . . ." If Joseph Smith had left out that one phrase, Mark Twain noted, "his Bible would have been only a pamphlet." Twain had little use for Joseph's creation, which he called a "curiosity . . . stupid and tiresome to read. It's smooched from the New Testament and no credit given. It is such a pretentious affair and yet so slow, so sleepy, such an insipid mess of inspiration. It is chloroform in print."

But the text transported the Bible story onto the American continent, reassuring its readers that they, too lived in a Holy Land. The Lamanites lived on, Joseph preached, as American aborigines, or Native Americans. Ever hopeful of converting the ancient Lamanites and restoring them to primacy on the American continent, the Mormons generally treated the Indians with respect, far from the norm on the Mississippi frontier, or anywhere else in the country.

In the Book of Mormon, Jesus visits America after his crucifixion. In the Gospel of John, Jesus tells his disciples in Jerusalem, "And other sheep I have, which are not of this fold." He repeats these words, and a great deal of other New Testament scripture, in two sermons to the Nephites at Bountiful, an ancient city somewhere in the Americas.

The Book of Mormon offered proof that God was speaking to nineteenth-century Americans through his prophet Joseph Smith. While Smith and Cowdery were taking a break from translating, the two men said they encountered John the Baptist when walking in the woods alongside the Susquehanna River in Harmony. John said he would confer the power of the Old Testament priesthood upon the two men, allowing them to baptize converts. John asked them to baptize each other, and they did. Two weeks after the Book of Mormon was published, Joseph announced to his tiny flock, primarily close friends and family members, that he had assumed the title "Seer, a Translator, a Prophet, an Apostle of Jesus Christ, and Elder of the Church through the will of God the Father, and the grace of your Lord Jesus Christ" (Doctrine and Covenants 21:1). On April 6, 1830, he announced the formation of the Church of Christ, which grew within a few weeks to forty members. Converts came from evangelical Methodism, and from the followers of evangelist Alexander Campbell, who, like Joseph, was preaching a primitive Christianity, calling for a restoration of Christ's church on earth, in anticipation of the Second Coming.

In a series of revelations, Joseph began to assemble a rudimentary theology. Men could aspire to two successive levels of priesthood, or holy rank. Women could not. The church would be a lay church, administered by male members. There would be no professional clergy. Like many evangelical Christians, the Mormons believed they were living in the latter days of history, before the return of Christ. History was thought to be 6,000 years old, with each millennium corresponding to one day of the Genesis creation story. The upcoming seventh millennium, due in 1900, would be the "day of rest," that is, the restoration of God's kingdom on earth. In 1835, Joseph offhandedly remarked that "fifty-six years should wind up the scene," implying that Christ would return to earth in 1891. The New Testament often called Christ's followers "saints," and Smith quickly adopted other biblical titles for his co-religionists. His lay leaders became deacons, elders, and bishops, and he eventually appointed twelve apostles from among his most loyal followers.

In its formative years, Joseph's church tried to distinguish itself from the roiling flotsam of wild religious euphoria sweeping the nation. Unlike many of the fiery, condemnatory evangelical creeds, his church promised near-universal salvation and taught that mortal sins are not punished forever. All persons, except a very few "sons of perdition," could expect eternal life in one of three degrees of glory: the celestial, terrestrial, or "telestial" kingdoms. Telestial was a neologism coined for the part of heaven reserved for Gentiles and other nonbelievers.

The Saints helped the Saints; that was a core tenet of Joseph's religion. In response to a revelation concerning Enoch, a grandson of Adam and Eve, Joseph encouraged his flock to "consecrate" all their property to the church, which in turn redistributed the collective wealth to families in need. This was pure communism, and it benefited many Mormons who followed Joseph to his first religious base in Kirtland, Ohio, having left their belongings behind them. By 1844, in Nauvoo—Joseph's "Zion" on the banks of the Mississippi—Joseph had abandoned the law of consecration but had substituted tithing in its place. Observant Mormons agreed to donate one-tenth of their goods or services to the bishop's storehouse for redistribution to the needy. Joseph often staked newly arrived families to (cramped) living quarters, a house plot, a larder full of supplies, or a portion of a working garden. Converts understood that their fellow Mormons would help them get on their feet, which partially explained the Saints' missionary successes.

By 1844, at least 25,000 men and women in America and Europe had joined Joseph's church, just fourteen years after its founding. Over 10,000 of them migrated to Nauvoo. Between 2,000 and 3,000 of them braved an Atlantic crossing and then journeyed 850 miles from New Orleans up the Mississippi to gather with their fellow Saints. Joseph's outriders were fabulously successful in recruiting converts to the new religion, especially in the poverty-stricken industrial cities of the British Isles.

The church was very much a work in progress, and many of its core rituals and beliefs, such as the multilayered Mormon heaven, polygamy, the multiplicity of gods, and the baptism of the dead, emerged in the early 1840s. Joseph's early followers were asked to believe that the Book of Mormon was the true word of God, and that Joseph was a true prophet. Dozens, and then hundreds, and by 1844, many thousands of men and women believed just that.

⁂

PEOPLE FOLLOWED JOSEPH SMITH PARTLY BECAUSE GOD TALKED to Joseph, but also because Joseph talked to them. He didn't claim to be a full-time preacher; "A prophet was a prophet only when he was acting as such," he told two Saints visiting Illinois from Michigan. When off duty, as it were, he generally acted like a charming and gregarious mayor and innkeeper, just two of the many roles he played in Nauvoo, "the city of Joseph."

When Brigham Young and his brother Joseph traveled 325 miles to meet Joseph Smith, they expected "to find him in his sanctum dispensing spiritual blessings and directions [about] how to build the Zion of God on earth," Joseph Young reported. Instead, they found Smith in the forest, chopping wood. The men shook hands, then all of them chopped and loaded wood together.

According to another story, when Joseph first arrived in Kirtland, Ohio, he had no place to stay. So he directed his sleigh to the front door of a general store owned by two Saints, whom he knew only by name. Joseph bounded up the front steps and thrust his hand across the store counter.

"Newel K. Whitney! Thou art the man!" he shouted, as if he had known Whitney all his life.

"You have the advantage of me," the bemused Whitney replied. "I could not call you by name, as you have me."

"I am Joseph, the Prophet," said the smiling stranger. "You've prayed me here; now what do you want of me?"

Joseph ended up lodging with the Whitneys for several weeks, and the family remained devoted to him for the rest of their lives. They followed Joseph west to Nauvoo, where Newell became a bishop. His daughter Sarah Ann, who was six years old when Joseph came bounding up her father's steps, would eventually become Joseph Smith's sixteenth wife. She was "the first woman ever given in plural marriage by or with the consent of both parents," according to her mother.

A glance at Joseph's diary for February 20, 1843, provides a window into his variegated life. He spent some of that morning drawing, and sawing, chopping and splitting wood with "about 70 of the brethren" who were tithing their services to the Prophet. "The day was spent by them in much pleasantry, good humor, and feeling," he reported. The snow had melted, so no one could go sledding.

Then Joseph devoted two hours to "reciting in German" before he oversaw Nauvoo court proceedings in the upstairs office of his redbrick store. Joseph was both mayor and chief justice in Nauvoo. There was a lawsuit to adjudicate, and a theft. While supervising the court, Joseph looked out the window and spotted two boys fighting with clubs in front of a nearby tavern. "The Mayor saw it and ran over immediately," his journal records, "caught one of the boys and stopped him and then the other." Joseph chided the bystanders for not breaking up the fight, and then walked back to his store. His final message to the two young miscreants: "No body is allowed to fight in this city but me."

Not everyone succumbed to Joseph's bumptious self-absorption. "His whole theme was himself," reported Pittsburgh editor David White, who visited Joseph at the Nauvoo Mansion in 1843: "The prophet ran on, talking incessantly." That same year, Charlotte Haven, a young Gentile woman from Portsmouth, New Hampshire, attended one of Joseph's speeches. She "had expected to be overwhelmed by his discourse" but found him to be "a great egotist and boaster . . . his language and manner were the coarsest possible." A month later, Charlotte visited the Smiths at home. "He talked incessantly about himself, and remarked that he was 'a giant, physically and mentally,'" Haven told her mother. "I did not change my opinion about him, but suppose that he has some good traits," she concluded. "They say he is very kind-hearted, and always ready to give shelter and help to the needy."

Benjamin Franklin Morris, a Congregationalist minister in nearby Warsaw, Illinois, found Joseph to be both awe-inspiring and detestable. "The power of Smith over his followers is incredible," he wrote in a letter to his church brethren in New York.

He has unlimited influence and his declarations are as the authority and influence of the world of God itself. He is a complete despot, and does as he pleases with his people.

Some people consider him a great man; I do not. He is not possessed of a single element of greatness, except his greatness in vice and blasphemy. He is a compound of ignorance, vanity, arrogance, coarseness and stupidity and vulgarity.

Joseph had an operatic personality. He embraced and exploited strong confederates, but he could be unsentimental when it came time to discard them. Typically, his anger flared hot and faded quickly; he often welcomed reprobates back into the fold. For instance, it was a major coup when Joseph converted the urbane and erudite Campbellite preacher Sidney Rigdon to his cause, because Rigdon's entire congregation followed him, doubling the size of Joseph's tiny church in 1830. Joseph admired Rigdon, famed for his fiery, revivalist preaching, and often deferred to the older man on theological questions or when it came time to deliver an important speech. The two men shared a famous 1832 vision, staring into the sky for over an hour while receiving a revelation of the three-tiered stratification of heaven. But when Rigdon defied him later that summer, Joseph unhesitatingly "disfellowshipped" him as his first counselor in the First Presidency, the church leadership triumvirate. Twenty-two days later, Joseph readmitted Rigdon to the high priesthood, declaring that "he has repented like Peter of old."

In the early years of the church, almost every one of his close confidants apostasized, usually in a dramatic falling-out with the Prophet. For instance, all three of the original Book of Mormon "witnesses" left the church. Three of the eight additional witnesses recruited by Joseph were also excommunicated. (Three others were family members.) Practically every major church leader, except for Brigham Young, broke with Joseph at one time or another, but, as with Rigdon, Joseph often welcomed them back with open arms. Apostle Orson Hyde was excommunicated in May 1839 and restored to the church in October. When Joseph made advances to Orson Pratt's wife while his loyal apostle was proselytizing in England, the Quorum of the Twelve Apostles excommunicated both Pratts for kicking up a fuss. The church reembraced them a few weeks later.

Joseph was all too human and made few pretensions to the contrary, Brigham Young insisted. "He had all the weaknesses a man could have when the vision was not upon him, when he was left to himself," Young said. Young urged the Saints to bind themselves to Joseph's revelatory doctrine, not necessarily to the man:

He may get drunk every day of his life, sleep with his neighbor's wife every night, run horses and gamble, I do not care anything about that, for I never embrace any man in my faith. But the doctrine he has produced will save you and me and the whole world; and if you can find fault with that, find it.

〖 〖 〖

IN NAUVOO, SMITH COMPLETELY REMADE HIS RELIGION. IN AN 1840 funeral sermon, he announced the new ritual of the baptism of the dead, apparently intended as a response to Paul's line in 1 Corinthians: "Else what shall they do which are baptized for the dead, if the dead rise not at all?" The baptisms started immediately, in the river. "Since this order has been preached here, the waters have been continually troubled," Vilate Kimball wrote to her husband Heber; "Sometimes from eight to ten Elders in the river at a time baptizing."

In May 1843, the young Gentile Charlotte Haven reported seeing two elders standing in the icy-cold Mississippi, immersing a crowd of Saints "as fast as they could come down the bank." A bystander explained the new doctrine to her. "So these poor mortals in ice-cold water were releasing their ancestors and relatives from purgatory!" Haven remarked. "You can imagine our surprise when the name George Washington was called." Benjamin Franklin, the Marquis de Lafayette, John Adams, Thomas Jefferson, and the deceased explorer Zebulon Pike also found new life in the turbid waters lapping up on Nauvoo. (Washington, along with Christopher Columbus and the signers of the Declaration of Independence, were later rebaptized in Utah.)

Around the time that the mass baptisms were ramping up, Joseph embraced Freemasonry, with a passion. There are plenty of reasons he would have *opposed* Masonry. Upstate New York, where he lived until age twenty-four, was a hotbed of anti-Masonry. The European fraternal order, which had established a beachhead in the New World during the eighteenth century, was widely denounced as a shadowy, atheistic cabal aimed at creating a secret world government. William Morgan, famous for publishing the Masons' secret codes and rituals in the widely disseminated 1826 book *Illusions of Masonry,* lived in Batavia, New York, and was supposedly drowned by hostile Masons in the Niagara River. (In a curious twist of fate, his widow, Lucinda, became one of Joseph's first plural wives.) New York even had its own anti-Masonic political party, which fielded a presidential candidate in 1831. The Book of Mormon, wholly composed in upstate New York, repeatedly condemned the "abominations" of secret societies, with "their secret signs and their secret words . . . [that] they might murder, and plunder, and steal, and commit whoredoms" (Helaman 6:22).

On the other hand, Joseph's father and brother Hyrum were Masons, as were several other prominent Saints. It was hard not to notice that almost everyone who was anyone in southwestern Illinois—the lawyers, judges, and leading businessmen—were also Masons. So, with considerable fanfare, Joseph became an entered apprentice mason on March 15, 1842. After obtaining a waiver from the usual twenty-eight-day waiting period, he attained two higher degrees the following day. To celebrate, 3,000 Saints joined Master Mason Joseph Smith in triumphal procession from the redbrick store to the grove at the base of the temple bluff. "Universal satisfaction manifested," Joseph noted in his personal journal.

Joseph quickly added several hundred Mormons to the Masonic membership rolls, outnumbering and infuriating the other lodges in Illinois. But the Masonic connection left a much more significant mark on Mormonism. Just two months after undergoing the secret Masonic admission rite, Joseph introduced a new, secret "priesthood endowment" ritual that would become mandatory for all male Saints intending to become or remain church members in good standing. In the multipurpose second-floor meeting room above his redbrick store in the center of Nauvoo, Joseph endowed his brother Hyrum, his second counselor William Law, Brigham Young, Heber Kimball, Newell Whitney, Willard Richards, and three other men with the new priesthood powers. The elaborate rite closely resembled the induction ceremony for third-degree masons, which Joseph had undergone just two months previously. "We were washed and anointed," Brigham Young recalled, "and had our garments placed upon us and received our New Name."

> Then after this we went into the large room over the store in Nauvoo. Joseph divided upon the room the best he could, hung up the veil, marked it, gave us our instructions as we passed along from one department to another, giving us signs, tokens, penalties with the key words pertaining to those signs.

The postulants donned a special white garment that bore the Masonic symbols of the square and compass on the breast, and two symbolic slashes at the abdomen and knee. The slash across the belly represented the disemboweling that would result if anyone betrayed the ritual secrets. Then the candidates witnessed an allegorical play not unlike the Old Testament drama acted out by Masons. The Masons tell the story of a noble architect, Hiram Abiff, who is murdered for refusing to disclose the order's secret codes and passwords. The Mormons instead acted out the Creation scene from Genesis. In the maiden production for the first endowed priests, Joseph played God, Hyrum acted the part of Christ, and Joseph's ghostwriter, the former newspaper editor W. W. Phelps, crawled around the store on his stomach, playing the evil serpent. After being expelled from the Garden of Eden, the participants put on tiny aprons, similar to the Masons', and learned the codes and passwords, called keys and tokens, that would eventually admit them to heaven. Joseph quickly integrated other Masonic symbols, such as the all-seeing eye, into Mormon iconography.

Word soon leaked out that Joseph had adapted and perverted the centuries-old Masonic ritual for his own ends. The Illinois Masons accused him of freighting religion into the secular rite and embarked on a successful crusade to close the Mormon lodges in Nauvoo and in the Mormon settlement in Montrose, Iowa. Joseph angrily denied copying the Freemasons' ritual and insisted that God had revealed the endowment rites to him many years previously. The Mormons' rite antedated the Masons' bastardized version, he insisted. "Masonry has its origin in the Priesthood" was the party line parroted by Willard Richards. "There is a similarity of priesthood in masonry," the equally loyal Heber Kimball explained in an 1842 letter. "Brother Joseph says masonry was taken from priesthood but has become degenerated."

Why did Joseph co-opt these Masonic rites? The answer is: secrecy. "The secret of masonry is to keep a secret," Joseph observed, and in the last few years of his life, he had many secrets to keep. Polygamy was a secret doctrine. Barely a year after creating the priesthood endowment ritual, Joseph introduced another, more secret ritual called the Second Anointing, which guaranteed the nineteen couples who received the special blessing a "calling and election sure"—a clear path to eternal life at the time of the exaltation, or the Second Coming. The Kingdom of God, which Joseph created in the spring of 1844, was a secret plan for world government. Its formal name was "The Kingdom of God and His Laws with the Keys and powers thereof and judgement in the hands of his servants, Ahman Christ."

If one sentence could describe the last few months of Joseph's life it would be: Wait, there is more. In April 1844, he preached the most famous sermon of his life, what some regard as one of the most famous sermons ever preached in America. As if on a whim, Joseph turned nearly 2,000 years of Christian belief on its head at a funeral service for his loyal colleague King Follett. Joseph had laid the groundwork for a new world order, and for the foundational ritual for his entire church, but that was in secret. Now, speaking in Nauvoo's East Grove, under a massive canopy of elm and chestnut trees, he unpacked some of the most radical Christian doctrine ever preached on the American continent. He spoke for two hours, shouting against a heavy wind. The following day, he lost his voice.

Joseph started out with his boldest statement: "We suppose that God was God from eternity," he shouted. "I will refute that idea. God that sits enthroned is a man like one of yourselves."

> It is the first principle to know. We may converse with him and that he once was a man like us. God was once as one of us and was on a planet as Jesus was in the flesh. I defy all hell and earth to refute it.

Joseph referred to gods in the plural, because he explained that gods evolved from men and were not created ex nihilo, out of nothing. The raw material of godhead was a form of free intelligence that preexisted our creation. From intelligence, God became a man, then perfected himself to become a god. So did Jesus Christ. And so, Joseph said, can you. "You have got to learn how to be a god yourself in order to save yourself," he proclaimed,

> —to be priests and kings as all Gods have done—by going from a small degree to another—from exaltation to exaltation—till they are able to sit in glory as with those who sit enthroned.

This became the "doctrine of eternal progression," the Mormons' supremely optimistic belief in the perfectibility of men and women living on earth. Joseph freed his followers from the strictures of predestination and the inevitability of sin. This was Joseph's final, grandiose gift of hope to his people—and yet another nail in his coffin. In one long, loud sermon, he had dynamited the entire Christian cosmology, the underpinnings of every credal prayer to have emerged in the previous 2,000 years. Joseph's former counselor William Law immediately organized a breakaway church, condemning Joseph as a fallen prophet. Joseph was preaching "some of the most blasphemous doctrines . . . ever heard of," Law said. Not only polygamy, but also the teaching that there are "other gods as far above our God as he is."

JOSEPH SMITH LED AN EVENTFUL LIFE, BUT THE SPRING OF 1844 seemed particularly crowded with historic undertakings. Most noticeably, he had decided to run for president, as the candidate of his newly created National Reform Party. Outside of Illinois, his candidacy was treated as a joke. "A New Candidate in the Field! Stand out of the way—all small fry!" *Niles' National Register* smirked. Even Joseph's first choice as vice president, who could not accept because he was born in Ireland, called the campaign a "wild goose chase."

Smith's platform was an olio of Whig and Democratic ideas. His call for a national bank and a "judicious tariff" scheme came straight from the Whig playbook. Like the Democrats, he urged expanding the union by annexing Texas and Oregon. Other ideas were very much his own. Joseph wanted to eliminate slavery and compensate slave owners with the revenues from the sale of public lands. He wanted to do away with military court-martials and called for the abolition of most prisons. According to the church newspaper, Joseph would "petition your state legislature to pardon every convict in their several penitentiaries: blessing them as they go, and saying to them in the name of the Lord, *go thy way and sin no more.*"

In the Mormon echo chamber of Nauvoo, where the church controlled the only two newspapers, the Saints took his foray into national politics quite seriously. At a mass electoral meeting, some Saints claimed the church had 200,000 communicants in the United States—about ten times the actual number—and could control 500,000 votes. "General Smith is the greatest statesman of the 19 century," Willard Richards opined. "Then why should not the nation secure to themselves his superior talents?" The church-controlled *Nauvoo Neighbor* published a poll conducted on board a steamboat, headlined, "Hurrah for the General!"

General Joseph Smith, the acknowledged modern Prophet, has got them all in the rear; and from the common mode of testing the success of candidates for the Presidency, to wit, by steamboat elections, he (Smith) will beat all the other aspirants to that office two to one. We learn from the polls of the steamboat Osprey, on her last trip to this city, that the vote stood for General Joseph Smith, 20 gents and 5 ladies; Henry Clay, 16 gents and 4 ladies; Van Buren, 7 gents and 0 ladies.

The *Neighbor* refrained from publishing a different steamboat sounding, taken aboard the paddle wheeler *Die Vernon*. In that survey, Joseph received six votes, to Henry Clay's fifty-eight.

Joseph was serious. In 1844, presidential candidates didn't campaign. Instead, they sent surrogates around the country to promulgate their ideas. So Smith sent ten of the twelve apostles to the hinterlands to boom his candidacy, as well as over two hundred other "volunteers." The previous year, Joseph had written letters to five of the national candidates, presenting them with his oft-repeated political litmus test: what can you do for the Mormons? (Joseph neglected to write to John Tyler, perhaps assuming he would lose, and to James K. Polk, the eventual winner.) Specifically, he asked the same question he had posed to President Van Buren and the Illinois congressional delegation when he visited Washington, DC, in 1839: can you get us reparations for our dispossessed property in Missouri? The Saints claimed over $2 million in lost land and chattel, following the brief "Mormon War," which resulted in their expulsion to Illinois. Two of the five candidates ignored his letter, and the other three gave Joseph the brush-off. He was incensed. When John C. Calhoun reiterated the conventional wisdom, that the Mormons would have to seek redress in Missouri, not in Washington, Smith lashed out at the two-time cabinet secretary. "The noble Senator of South Carolina says the power of the Federal government is *so limited and specific that it has no jurisdiction of the case!*" Joseph answered Calhoun. "What think ye of *imperium in imperio* [an empire within the empire]?"

The words call attention to themselves, because Joseph had begun to think of his "theodemocracy" of Nauvoo in imperial terms.

He dispatched an expedition to Texas, still in the throes of its grand territorial struggle with Mexico, to learn if the Saints could found their own country in the vast, sparsely inhabited tableland between the Nueces and the Rio Grande Rivers. Texas president Sam Houston liked the idea, but cooler heads warned Joseph that his people would find themselves smack in the middle of the shooting war between Texas and Mexico. At the same time, Joseph petitioned Congress for permission to raise a federal army of 100,000 men to guarantee the safety of settlers streaming into New Mexico, Texas, upper California, and Oregon. The same document asked Congress to arrest and imprison anyone who "shall hinder or molest the said Joseph Smith from executing his designs." These démarches were ignored, but they fed preexisting fears of a vast, Mormon land grab beyond the western edge of the United States. *New York Herald* editor James Gordon Bennett, a fan of Joseph's, said he wouldn't be "surprised if Joe Smith were made governor of a new religious territory in the west." "One day," he wrote, Smith might "control the whole valley of the Mississippi, from the peaks of the Alleghanies to the pinnacles of the Rocky Mountains."

Smith had grander plans. In March 1844, he created the secret Council of Fifty to rule over the still-secret Kingdom of God. (Joseph called the Fifty "the Lyceum" in his diary.) Its purpose was clear: to govern the entire world, irrespective of existing laws and sovereignties, after the coming of Christ. In April, the Fifty appointed Joseph Smith "King, Priest and Ruler over Israel on the Earth." As Joseph had been hinting for many years, the laws of this world were moot and no longer applied to the great Mormon endeavor. "When I speak of a government, I mean what I say," first counselor Rigdon explained to the Mormon faithful. "I mean a government that shall rule over temporal and spiritual affairs . . . The kingdom of God does not interfere with the laws of the land, but keeps itself by its own laws."

The plan was for Joseph to claim the presidency, if not in 1844 then in a subsequent election, and lay the foundations for a world government to greet the returning Christ. Apostles Lyman Wight and Heber Kimball declared to Joseph: "You are bound to be the President of the United States on 4 March 1845 and that you are already president pro tem of the world." Joseph called the Fifty the world's "living Constitution," in part because it confided few of its actions to paper. Its activities were secret, and its members often called it the "Ytfif" in their diaries. The Council of Fifty's records remain closed to this day.

The world government idea possessed a kind of manic intensity, and Joseph pursued it to the hilt. In his capacity as a putative head of state, he appointed ambassadors to England, France, and Russia. The choices were far from gratuitous. France and England were eager to meddle in Mexican affairs and were pressing their interests with both the Texan and Mexican republics. The United States and England were jointly administering Oregon for the moment, but Joseph and others realized that their fragile alliance would never survive America's aggressive push to the Pacific. Likewise, Russia had Great Power interests from Alaska south to California.

To the tsar, Joseph was flogging his friend Uriah Brown's groundbreaking military invention, the flame-throwing vessel. Brown had tried, in vain, to interest Congress in his dragonlike contraption, which he claimed could "destroy an army or navy." Now Joseph was sounding out the Russians about this curious weapon so powerful that it might usher in a new era of world peace. Joseph "thought that the Lord had designed the apparatus for some more magnificent purpose than the defense of nations." He cryptically explained that the mission to Saint Petersburg involved "some of the most important things concerning the advancement and building up of the kingdom of God in the last days, which cannot be explained at this time."[*]

---

[*] The maddeningly unreliable spy and freebooter Joseph Jackson met Uriah Brown in Nauvoo, where the inventor laid out Smith's plan for world domination. "[Smith's] real object" in selling the "steam fire-ship" to the tsar, Jackson explained, "was to form a league for the overthrow of the powers that be. Now this may seem too ridiculous for any man to believe possible; nevertheless, no one acquainted with the excessive vanity of Joe Smith, will doubt but that he in reality believed that he could form even so preposterous a union."

He also noted that such far-flung expeditions are "attended with much expense," and that "all those who feel disposed to bestow according as God has blessed them shall receive the blessings of Israel's God, and tenfold shall be added unto them." In other words, the trip needed a sponsor.

Joseph envisioned the Mormons expanding westward, and he wanted his voice heard in capitals other than Washington, where he had experienced painful rebuffs. His diplomatic maneuvers emanating from a tiny Illinois town—not even a county seat!—seemed absurd, at first blush. But Joseph Smith and his disciple Brigham Young correctly sensed that vast tracts of the American West were up for grabs. The Spanish and French colonial empires had either quit the continent or were retreating. Texas, which encompassed much of the Southwest, and California, which meant most of the territory along the West Coast, and Oregon, which included all of today's Pacific Northwest, had yet to organize themselves into stable, independent republics or states. Perhaps Joseph's reach exceeded his grasp, but less than ten years later, Brigham Young declared himself the ruler of Deseret, a Rocky Mountain empire that sprawled across the territory of five present-day states. It was no crime to dream big dreams, and in his heady last few years on earth, Joseph Smith did just that.

3

ZION, ILLINOIS

In Illinois we've found a safe retreat,
A home, a shelter from oppressions dire;
Where we can worship God as we think right,
And mobbers come not to disturb our peace;
Where we can live and hope for better days,
Enjoy again our liberty, our rights:
That social intercourse which freedom grants,
And charity requires of man to man.

—*Unattributed poem published in the Mormon
newspaper* Times and Seasons, *April 15, 1841*

THE CHURCH OF JESUS CHRIST OF LATTER-DAY SAINTS, organized during a prayer meeting on a central New York farm in 1830, was a storm-tossed religion. Joseph Smith "gathered" his hundred or so Saints in Kirtland, Ohio, in the early 1830s, where missionary work soon swelled the Mormons' ranks. Pursuant to a revelation, Joseph sent Saints westward to simultaneously settle in Missouri, which he believed to be the site of the biblical Garden of Eden, or Zion. Joseph's Mormon beliefs often sprang full-grown from the Old Testament. The Saints were the people of Israel; Zion was their promised land, and the rest of America was Babylon, inhabited by the churchless Gentiles.

By 1838, the Saints found themselves unwelcome in Kirtland. The nationwide financial Panic of 1837 had wiped out their oddball financial institution, the "Kirtland Safety Society Anti-Banking Company," impoverishing Gentile and Mormon investors alike. The decidedly unsafe Safety Society had declared itself a non-bank because Ohio refused to charter a real Mormon bank. The society ran out of money within three weeks of its founding. The self-styled prophet fled Kirtland in the dead of night, pointing his horse west to Missouri.

The Saints fared little better in their new home. Within just a few years, the devout, industrious Mormons, almost all of them from anti-slavery New England states, had alienated their new Southern neighbors. (The Missouri Compromise of 1820 preserved its status as a slave state.) Heeding Joseph's call, members of the rapidly growing church were gathering in Missouri, and the hordes of new immigrant voters were threatening to take over several counties from the old settlers. The Missourians pleaded with their governor to halt Mormon immigration, and vigilantes drove home the message by raiding Mormon ranches and settlements.

When nonviolent resistance proved futile, the Saints stopped turning the other cheek. To counter the "mobocrats," the Mormons organized the Danite guerrilla force, named for a prophecy in the Book of Daniel that "the saints shall take the kingdom, and possess the kingdom, for ever and ever." Under attack from marauders and night riders, the Danites returned violence for violence, matching their tormentors burned hay rick for burned hay rick, and rustled cattle herd for rustled cattle herd. The excitable Sidney Rigdon preached a sermon on July 4, 1838, rallying the Saints to "a war of extermination" against their enemies. (In the early nineteenth century, "extermination" meant to expel, not necessarily to annihilate.) Four months later, Missouri governor Lilburn Boggs issued his infamous Extermination Order, directed against Missouri's Mormons. A short, bloody, three-month-long war ensued, with casualties on both sides. A ghastly atrocity—the massacre and mutilation of seventeen defense-less Mormons, including two children, trapped inside a blacksmith shop at Haun's Mill—effectively ended the Mormon War, which the Mormons could never have hoped to win.

The Missourians clapped the Mormon leaders, including Rigdon and Joseph Smith, in jail, and observed a brief cease-fire that allowed the Saints to flee across the frozen Mississippi River to Illinois. There, the residents of Quincy, a commercial port, and other Illinois towns graciously received the bedraggled refugees, whom they viewed as vic-tims of coarse Missouri bigotry. Illinois residents were quick to believe the worst about the "pukes," their unflattering epithet for the Missouri-ans. "The citizens responded to the call and donated liberally," recalled Wandle Mace, a prosperous Mormon who had relocated his family from New York. He reported that citizens filled "a large canoe with flour, pork, coffee, sugar, boots, shoes and clothing, the merchants vie-ing [*sic*]with each other as to which could be the most liberal," and sent it across the river, to an encampment of freezing Mormon refugees.

Accepting handouts was hardly the Mormons' style; more than provisions, they desperately needed a new home. Sensing an opportu-nity, the New York Land Company's "Dr." Isaac Galland quickly found his way to the bedraggled Saints.

Galland, who had neither medical training nor legal education—he also claimed to be a lawyer—had likewise not studied for the ministry, although he did occasionally mount the pulpit on both sides of the Mississippi. He was a charming scalawag, a convicted horse thief and counterfeiter who had abandoned three wives in different parts of the country. Newspaper editor Thomas Gregg once recalled meeting "that dark-eyed, dark-hued, inexplicable, incomprehensible, unfathomable man, Dr. Isaac Galland—whom no man could see through." When he ran for Congress in 1834, Galland made light of his checkered reputa-tion. "I've been found guilty of almost everything except hog stealing," he said, "and I never owned a hog."

The New York Land Company and Galland had acquired some claims on a huge block of Iowa real estate called the Half-Breed Tract. In an 1824 treaty, Congress had set aside the 186 square miles to be settled by the mixed-blood descendants of the Sauk (also known as the Sac) and Fox Indian tribes. Legitimate claimants were hard to find, and an army of swindlers and con men descended upon the open prairie, where the lots were the subject of near-constant litigation.

Galland and his employer had sufficient claim to convince Joseph Smith to negotiate a land purchase from his jail cell in, of all places, Liberty, Missouri. In 1839, Smith bought 20,000 acres of land on the Iowa shore of the Mississippi as well as 700 acres in the center of a town across the river called Commerce, Illinois. Galland was a scamp and Commerce was a swamp, with one stone house and five other structures nearby. But the site had promise. The broad limestone flat sat in the middle of a sweeping, graceful horseshoe bend in the river, giving the town waterfront access on its southern, western, and northern borders. Moving east, there was plenty of room to grow, especially toward a line of bluffs and higher ground rising to the fertile prairie beyond.

"No man of understanding can come up the Mississippi without being filled with wonder and astonishment," the Englishman John Needham wrote to his parents in Yorkshire, in 1843.

> Just where Nauvoo stands, the river turns in the shape of a horse shoe, the river going three parts around the city. From rising ground in Nauvoo we have a splendid sight of the country on the other side of the river, which is very pleasant.

Galland's claims may have been shaky—instead of selling the Mormons property deeds, he sold them stock in landholding companies—but his terms were alluring. Joseph paid Galland $2 an acre for the vast tracts, with payments stretched out over twenty years. Galland charged no interest. Small wonder that Smith hailed Galland as "the honored instrument the Lord used to prepare a home for us" and heartily embraced the old horse thief's brief conversion to the Church of Latter-day Saints.

Joseph had employed a Hebrew tutor in Ohio and renamed Commerce "Nauvoo," a word with Old Testament roots that he said "signifies a beautiful situation, or place, carrying with it, also, the idea of *rest.*"

"The place was literally a wilderness," Joseph commented in the church history that he dictated to a rotating group of scribes: "The land was mostly covered with trees and bushes, and much of it was so wet that it was with the utmost difficulty that a footman could get through, and totally impossible for teams."

Joseph further noted that Commerce was "unhealthy." In fact, it was pestilential. Malaria was not uncommon in the Mississippi Valley, and when the Mormons started to arrive in the summer and fall of 1839, the disease struck in full force. The ague, or the "spotted fever," attacked almost every arriving family, including Joseph's. His father died, and so did his twenty-six-year-old brother, Don Carlos, as well as one of his scribes. To ensure that they were consuming boiled water, the Mormons drank teas and coffee, a technical violation of Joseph's Word of Wisdom, the guide to personal conduct that counseled the Saints to abjure alcohol and "hot drinks." The mortality rate in Nauvoo was double that of Illinois, and of the United States. So many immigrants perished that the Saints arranged a mass funeral service for their dead.

While his flock waged a life-and-death struggle with the malarial lowland he had chosen, Smith and his lieutenants worked hard to build up the hoped-for Mormon sanctuary on the Mississippi. By digging a channel along the base of the higher ground, the Mormons successfully drained the swamp. Soon the lowland acreage became dry and fertile. Joseph envisaged a town at the base of the Nauvoo peninsula, and saw plenty of open space for farms to the north and east. On the high land overlooking the peninsula, Joseph planned to build a magnificent white-limestone temple, larger and grander than the landmark the Mormons had erected in Kirtland, Ohio. This was a cornerstone of Zion, Smith declared, and the Saints and all would-be Saints had an obligation to come to Nauvoo:

> We may soon expect to see flocking to this place people of every land; the polished European; the degraded Hottentot, and the shivering Laplanders; persons of all languages and of every color who shall with us worship in His holy temple.

Galland was either a tremendous cynic, a bitter realist, or a combination of the two. He may have swindled the Mormons more than once. His land claims in Iowa proved to be vaporous, and when Joseph sent him east to convince Mormons there to help pay off the Nauvoo debt, Galland returned empty-handed. Galland predicted that the Mormons would stay in Nauvoo "until they again acquire a sufficient quantity of 'honey comb' to induce the surrounding thieves to rob them again, at which time they will no doubt have to renounce their religion, or submit to a repetition of similar acts of violence and outrage." He would prove to be partially correct.

I I I

SOUTHWESTERN ILLINOIS WAS A WOOLLY PART OF THE WORLD. For starters, the state was flat broke. Illinois had bankrupted itself investing in public works projects such as canals, roads, and railways that were never built. Illinois's state bank stopped redeeming currency for gold or silver in 1840, and state bonds were trading for 33 cents on the dollar. No one had money. There was no national currency, and the economies of towns such Quincy and Nauvoo subsisted on scrip, IOU's, barter, and the occasional gold or silver coin. Counterfeiting was rife, and continually bedeviled Nauvoo.

In his *History of Illinois,* Governor Thomas Ford noted that the southern part of the state had attracted immigrants from Kentucky and Tennessee likely to be poor because they didn't own slaves, which were banned from Illinois's free soil. "The wealthy immigrant from the slave States rarely came here," Ford wrote. But that is not to say that Illinois extended its arms to black people. The legislature resolutely vowed to enforce fugitive slave laws, to ensure that Southerners' "property" found no shelter in its borders. As in many parts of the United States, abolitionists were held in low regard. Congregationalists in Warsaw, Illinois, barely twenty miles from Nauvoo, dismissed their first minister in 1839 when they learned that he was active in the anti-slavery movement.

An Easterner by birth who lived much of his life in upstate Springfield and Peoria, Governor Ford ungenerously characterized his southern Illinois neighbors as "unambitious of wealth, and great lovers of ease and social enjoyment." The Southerners in turn despised their northern counterparts, whom they called Yankees, even though they had little idea what the name meant. They thought a "genuine Yankee was a close, miserly, dishonest, selfish getter of money, void of generosity, hospitality, or any of the kindlier feelings of human nature," Ford wrote.

In downstate Illinois, to be "Yankeed" meant to be cheated. Southern Illinois legislators even opposed the Lake Michigan–to–Illinois River canal that made Chicago's fortune, because they feared it would bring more New Englanders into their ambit. Northern Illinois residents viewed the typical downstater as "a long, lank, lean, lazy, and ignorant animal, but little in advance of the savage state; one who was content to squat in a log-cabin, with a large family of ill-fed and ill-clothed, idle, ignorant children."

The settled United States ended at Illinois's western border, and the frontier was a dangerous place. As elsewhere in Andrew Jackson's America—Jackson was still alive, although his presidency ended in 1837—the rule of law was theoretical at best. "Each state has the unquestionable right to regulate its own internal concerns according to its own pleasure," Jackson proclaimed in his Farewell Message to the

American people. In his valedictory, just as he had during his presidency, Jackson championed the doctrine of popular sovereignty, which allowed each state to sort out their affairs more or less as it wished.* Across the land, laws became tools of popular will, of whim, or of local bigotry. The sophisticated Manhattan businessman, mayor, and diarist Philip Hone called popular sovereignty "the abominable doctrine . . . viz, that the people are to be governed by the law just so long as it pleases them."

Rural Illinois, too, was a part of America where people made their own laws. The year before the Mormons came to Hancock County, a young Illinois legislator named Abraham Lincoln called mob violence the greatest threat to the young body politic. He decried "the increasing disregard of law which pervades the country; the growing disposition to substitute the wild and furious passions in lieu of the sober judgment of courts. . . ." If the American experiment were to perish, he continued, it would die from within: "If destruction be our lot, we ourselves must be its author and finisher. As a nation of freemen, we [will] live through all time, or die by suicide."

In the early decades of the nineteenth century, so-called banditti ruled several Illinois counties, in some cases locked in perpetual wars with citizen militias, vigilantes, or self-appointed "regulators," who took it upon themselves to enforce the law. Property disputes over inadequately surveyed claims often ended in violence or lynchings, or both. The state's most famous banditti were the Driscolls, a family of notorious horse thieves and murderers who terrorized Ogle County, north of Nauvoo, for most of 1841. The governor urged local citizens to bring the Driscoll gang to heel. However, the regulators' first captain resigned when his grist mill was burned to the ground, and his horse tortured and killed. The Driscolls shot his successor after Sunday church services, in front of his wife and children. Finally, a posse of three hundred armed citizens showed up at the Driscolls' farm and arrested the paterfamilias and two of his four outlaw sons. It was far from clear that

---

* Joseph Smith called Jackson "the acme of American glory," in large part because he approved of Jackson's brutal Indian removal policies.

the old man and the two sons had carried out the Sunday shooting, but the time had long passed for legal niceties. A quick, al fresco trial ensued. The county sheriff requested custody of the accused but was ignored.

One son, Pierce, walked free. Father John and his son William were condemned to hang. "We would rather be shot," John Driscoll said. Honoring his request, the one-hundred-odd regulators present divided themselves into two massive firing squads. After shooting the father, who proclaimed his innocence, they showed William the body. "Would you like to confess now?" the mob asked. William admitted that he had murdered several men, albeit not the men he had been convicted of killing. He followed his father to the grave. The Driscolls "were fired upon by the whole company present, that there might be none who could be legal witnesses of the bloody deed," wrote Thomas Ford, who noted that "these terrible measures put an end to the ascendancy of rogues in Ogle county."

Eventually, the state tried a hundred men for the Driscoll murders. They were all acquitted, thanks to a clever maneuver by their defense attorney. The lawyer ensured that everyone present at the group execution was indicted for the murders. As defendants, they weren't required to testify against themselves, and the only other eyewitnesses to the killings were dead. In his state history, Ford never mentioned that he was the complaisant judge who presided over the mass acquittal of the vigilantes.

Ϊ Ϊ Ϊ

UPON ARRIVING IN NAUVOO, THE MORMONS' FIRST ORDER OF business was to seek a city charter from the state legislature. Partly, they wanted to protect themselves; the Saints sought to create a legally organized militia, to supplant the Danite guerilla force. To ensure the future of their nascent city-state, the Mormons wanted to legitimize their way of life in Illinois.

The result, approved by acclamation in 1840 by a legislature that included the young Lincoln (his future rival, the brash attorney

Stephen Douglas, was already Illinois's secretary of state), was the Nauvoo Charter, soon to become a controversial document. But it wasn't controversial at the time. State senator Sidney Little, who represented neighboring McDonough County, duly noted the "extraordinary militia clause," although he deemed it "harmless." By the end of 1840, Nauvoo had about 2,400 new residents, and its own mini-constitution that enabled Joseph Smith to regulate Mormon life pretty much as he pleased.

The charter had three primary provisions. First, it created the Nauvoo Legion. Whereas most militias assembled their citizen soldiers from counties, or groups of counties, Nauvoo was the rare town to have its own fighting force. The charter explained that the Legion would operate independently of other militias, which reported to the governor as commander in chief. The Legion was a local police force, "at the disposal of the mayor in executing the laws and ordinances of the city corporation." Joseph Smith was Nauvoo's mayor from January 1842 until June 1844.

Second, the charter also created a University of Nauvoo, which never came into being. Like the notoriously over-officered Legion, however, the university did boast seventy-seven administrators, and again imitating the Legion, it reveled in ceremony. Although it never granted an actual degree, it did issue honorary degrees to two prominent newspaper editors—John Wentworth of the *Chicago Democrat* and James Gordon Bennett of the *New York Herald*—for printing favorable articles about the Saints. The repugnant Bennett, known as "His Satanic Majesty," was perhaps the nation's most powerful newspaper editor, and a Joseph Smith fan.

But the charter's third and most controversial provision was its distinctive court system, which effectively merged the executive and judicial branches of local government. As mayor, Joseph sat on the City Council and also served as chief justice of the municipal court. The associate justices were the City Council members and four aldermen. The mayor had "exclusive jurisdiction in all cases arising under the ordinances of the corporation" and reviewed all lower court decisions rendered by magistrates or justices of the peace. With very rare exceptions, all city councilmen, justices, and aldermen were Mormons. Because the charter required the Saints to obey the constitutions of both Illinois and the United States, litigants could theoretically appeal Nauvoo decisions to the state circuit court in Carthage, about twenty miles to the east. But the church frowned on appeals to Gentile justice, which they disdained as "lawing before the world."

Joseph's court arrogated to itself a broad power of habeas corpus, "in all cases arising under the ordinances of the City Council." In its common law origins, habeas corpus ("surrender the body") protected individuals from capricious imprisonment by state or local authorities. In Nauvoo, it was enforced indiscriminately to ensure that most Mormons could never be tried by an outside court. Although often used to protect Joseph from the many writs and summonses flying about him, the law likewise meant that a lapsed Saint charged with cattle thieving in neighboring Adams County could go free in Nauvoo, and generally did. After their Missouri experiences, the Saints craved safety above all, and sought legal, military, and political autarky to ensure that they alone could control their destiny in Illinois. The state granted them those rights; whether the Saints could preserve them would be another question entirely.

Ɏ Ɏ Ɏ

FROM 1839 TO 1842, NAUVOO'S POPULATION DOUBLED EACH YEAR. We were "growing like a mushroom (as it were, by magic)," bishop George Miller later wrote. By 1844, Nauvoo had swelled to over 10,000 residents. Although censuses were unreliable, some considered it to be the largest city in Illinois, bigger than the just-founded Chicago. Filling the peninsula created by the bend in the river, the town was laid out on a perpendicular grid. Each house lot was an acre, a half acre, or a quarter acre, with pockets of density on the south bank, near the first

A bucolic view of Nauvoo, Illinois, as seen from the Mississippi
River's Iowa shoreline. The nearly competed Nauvoo Temple,
lacking its steeple, is visible on the hill overlooking the town.
Credit: Utah State Historical Society

settlement, and on the cooler high ground near the temple site. House
owners tended gardens and nursed orchards and farm animals in their
backyards. In five years, the cluster of grim, weather-whipped log cab-
ins had become a bona fide small city.

The town boasted two sawmills, a flour mill, a foundry, and a brew-
ery. There was also a brick factory, a tannery, a bookbindery, a match
factory, and innumerable craftsmen, for example, weavers, wagoners,
cordwainers, and the like. By way of culture, Nauvoo had a zoo, a lyceum, three brass bands, and four taverns. (It was not until 1902 that
alcohol consumption by observant Mormons was categorically forbidden.) Many residents, like Smith himself, had homes in the thickly
settled town center and also owned farms outside the city.

Manufacturing never took hold in Nauvoo, to the Saints' chagrin.
But there was commerce aplenty. The Mississippi steamboat era was

in full swing, and the church owned two paddle wheelers, often used to ferry arriving Saints upriver from New Orleans. There were four landing slips in Nauvoo, and in the summer as many as ten boats a week stopped by, often filled with tourists and day-trippers eager to catch a glimpse of the exotic Mormons. ("We are a curiosity, ain't we?" Brigham Young once remarked.) But profitable trade eluded the Saints, who proved to be net importers of such everyday staples as wheat, corn, pork, sugar, coffee, tea, printed cloth, coal, and other household supplies. Prices were high, as high as in large Eastern cities like New York and Boston.

Nauvoo's spiritual and geographic center of gravity was Joseph Smith himself. The town radiated outward from the tiny, riverside homestead he occupied in early 1839. Just across the street he built his two-story redbrick store, which was the Saints' commercial and religious epicenter for many years. Joseph dispensed plots of land and even large cash loans from the store's second-floor office, and for several years he ran a general store below. Under Joseph's hand, the business quickly went bankrupt. He transferred ownership to more capable hands and tried to liquidate over $70,000 in debts using the new bankruptcy laws of 1842. As Brigham Young once joked about the Prophet's lack of business acumen: "Joseph was a first-rate fellow with [his customers], provided he would never ask them to pay him."

Joseph set to work on other building projects, including a (never-completed) tourist hotel, and a sacred temple on Nauvoo's high ground. The temple would remain under construction during Joseph's lifetime. Only the huge baptismal font in the basement, a twenty foot by twenty foot laver supported by twelve gigantic oxen—supposedly the same design as the "molten sea" in King Solomon's temple in Jerusalem—was available to him for baptizing new Saints. Joseph first introduced followers to his new, secret temple rituals inside the store. He used canvas curtains to cordon off the second-floor meeting space into the rooms that would later become constituent parts of every Mormon temple in the world. Workmen painted a pastoral mural in the corner of one room and arranged cedar boughs, evergreens, and olive branches to resemble the Garden of Eden, the locus of Joseph's endowment rite.

Like many of the uninitiated, church member Ebenezer Robinson was curious about the secret rituals administered upstairs in the store. But participants could not describe them, under penalty of death. A nonplussed Robinson once spotted Apostle John Taylor standing at the top of the stairway to the second floor, with a sword in hand, wearing a turban and a white robe. Robinson correctly surmised that Taylor was acting in the sacred endowment rite, representing "the cherubims and flaming sword which was placed at the east of the Garden of Eden, to guard the tree of life."

Joseph also administered the new, secret rite of the Second Anointing for chosen couples upstairs at the store. He sealed polygamous marriages in the second-floor office, never revealing them to the Saints at large. Smith and Brigham Young kept coded records of these events, sometimes using pseudonyms. In his diary, Smith occasionally called himself "Baurak Ale." To record his marriages, Young might write "saw E. Partridge," a code which meant "[s]ealed [a]nd [w] ed Emily Partridge," or "ME L. Beaman," which would mean "married for eternity Louisa Beaman." One of Joseph's plural wives, Willard Richards's sister Rhoda, lived in the store, which was also the site of Brigham Young's soon-to-be-famous, botched seduction of British teenager Martha Brotherton.

I I I

JOSEPH WORKED IN THE STORE, AND AFTER 1843 HE LIVED IN THE stately Nauvoo Mansion, a two-story L-shaped building at the intersection of Sidney (as in Rigdon) and Main Streets. The mansion had seventeen rooms, many of them rented out to tourists or transients, and boasted the largest stable in Illinois, a brick structure large enough to hold seventy-five horses. There was a cannon mounted in the front

Joseph Smith, Emma Smith, and Joseph's mother,
Lucy Mack Smith, who lived with them in Nauvoo.
Credit: Utah State Historical Society

yard, and the premises were often under guard, as Joseph feared process servers or Missouri bounty hunters invading his home.

Joseph and Emma employed considerable live-in help: an African American washerwoman named Jane Manning and a cook, as well as serving girls to help in the dining room. (Manning, who would later join the Mormon migration to Utah, was one of about forty free blacks living in Nauvoo.) At banquets, it was not uncommon for Joseph and Emma to help serve guests themselves, aided by the young women domiciled at the Nauvoo Mansion. The mansion girls performed household chores in return for room and board. The teenage women—Sarah and Maria Lawrence, Emily and Eliza Partridge, and Lucy Walker—proved to be a temptation too great for Joseph to resist. Having covertly introduced his revelation on polygamous marriage in 1843, he ended up marrying them all, and the ensuing opéra bouffe opening and closing of bedroom doors tormented his long-suffering wife Emma.

The mansion was Emma's home, too, and in addition to being a hotel, it was where she raised her four children, one of them an adopted daughter. Her oldest son, Joseph, a small boy during the Nauvoo years, remembered her traveling to St. Louis to buy furniture, curtains, linen, and dishes for the newly opened mansion. "When she returned," her son wrote, "Mother found installed in the keeping-room of the hotel . . . a fully equipped tavern bar, and Porter Rockwell in charge as tender."

She sent Joseph III to find his father. "Joseph," she asked her husband. "What is the meaning of that bar in this house?"

Joseph explained that his friend had just been freed from a Missouri jail, and planned to open up a combination bar and barber shop across the street. The mansion tavern arrangement was purely temporary, he said.

It proved to be very temporary indeed. "How does it look for the spiritual head of a religious body to be keeping a hotel in which a room is fitted out as a liquor-selling establishment?" Emma asked. "Either that bar goes out of the house, or we will!"

Inside both his homes, first in the rustic log cabin and then at the Nauvoo Mansion, Joseph installed hiding places to provide refuge from unwanted visitors. In his first house, there was a hinged portion of the staircase leading to the cellar. Lifting the trick stairs led to "a vaulted place . . . large enough for a couple of people to occupy, either sitting or lying down, affording a degree of comfort for a stay of long or short duration as necessary," Joseph Smith III recalled. The mansion had a garret apartment accessible from a false-backed closet built flush to one of the chimneys. If one pulled down a rack of clothespins on the back of the closet, a small staircase leading to the attic came into view. Joseph III remembered when some "so-called officials from Missouri seeking to arrest [his father] on trumped-up charges" dropped by the family home, unannounced. "Suddenly, Father and the friend who was with him disappeared," the son remembered, "and when the men came in they found the household quietly engaged in its customary affairs.

Questioned, Mother said her husband had been there a little while before but was not there then. She invited them in to assure themselves of the fact. They made a thorough search but failed to find him.

Young Joseph, who could not have been more than ten years old at the time, confessed that he was "puzzled" by his father's disappearance. Later, he understood that his father had melted away to the third-floor oubliette. "The suspicions of the manhunters were disarmed, and they went off about their business, leaving Father and his friend to breathe freely again."

ꟾ ꟾ ꟾ

WHEN HE FOUND THE TIME, JOSEPH WELCOMED VISITORS AND curiosity seekers to his "heavenly city," often escorting them up Hyde Street—most of the boulevards bore the names of prominent Saints— to his mother's home. Lucy Mack Smith, now in her sixties, controlled access to a collection of Egyptian mummies and scrolls renowned up and down the Mississippi and even further afield. There was a sign nailed to a board in front of Mrs. Smith's house:

EGYPTIAN MUMMIES EXHIBITED,
AND ANCIENT RECORDS EXPLAINED.
PRICE TWENTY-FIVE CENTS.

The mummies and the papyri, or "ancient records" were a highlight of any Nauvoo tour. Joseph sometimes told visitors that his mother had purchased the collection for $6,000. In fact, he had bought them himself for $2,400 from an itinerant showman who brought his artifacts to Kirtland, Ohio, in 1833. The mummies, "frightfully disfigured, and, in fact, most disgusting relics of mortality," according to the visiting Anglican minister Henry Caswall, were apparently genuine. Their identities, as the Smiths explained them, were probably spurious.

After leading Charlotte Haven, a visitor from Portsmouth, New Hampshire, "up a short, narrow stairway to a low dark room under a roof," Mrs. Smith held her candle up to a row of yellowing corpses. Lucy introduced her desiccated charges as the Egyptian "King Onitus and his

51

royal household:" two wives, and the daughter of a fellow king. (Joseph told visitors the king was "Pharaoh Necho.") For Charlotte, Mrs. Smith brandished what "seemed to be a club wrapped in a dark cloth, and said 'This is the leg of Pharaoh's daughter, the one that saved Moses.'" To yet another visitor, the young Eudocia Baldwin, Mrs. Smith ("a trim looking old lady in black silk gown and white cap and kerchief") introduced the mummies as "the old King Pharaoh of the Exodus himself, with wife and daughter." "My Son Joseph Smith has recently received a revelation from the Lord in regard to these people and times," Mrs. Smith said, "and *he* has told these things to *me*."

The papyri were equally problematic. Joseph claimed the hieroglyphics were handwritten by Abraham, "the father of the faithful," and bore the signatures of Moses and his older brother, Aaron. With the aid of God and a white seer stone, Joseph translated the papyri into the Book of Abraham, which purported to be a source for the Book of Genesis. His mother said the hieroglyphic scrolls were "the writing of Abraham and Isaac, written in Hebrew and Sanscrit." Charlotte Haven pointed to a drawing of Eve being tempted by a snake standing on two legs. "But serpents don't have legs," the young woman remarked.

"They did before the Fall," Lucy shot back.

Like the mummies, the papyri also appeared to be genuine Egyptian funerary relics. But they were not the "lost" book of Abraham, and they did not help explain the origins of the Negro race, as Joseph claimed. The scrolls cost the Mormons much future vexation, as they reinforced the prevalent racist doctrine that African Americans were descendants of the cursed Canaanites, the children of Noah's son Ham.

In the 1960s, a Metropolitan Museum of Art expert uncharitably characterized Joseph's translation of the scrolls as "a farrago of nonsense from beginning to end."

‡ ‡ ‡

Zion, Illinois

ON MAY 15, 1844, AS HE OFTEN DID, JOSEPH SPENT THE DAY WITH two eminent visitors who hopped off the steamboat to catch a glimpse of the "bourgeois Mohammed." The day-trippers were the young Bostonians Charles Francis Adams and Josiah Quincy, one the son of former president John Quincy Adams, and the other a future mayor of Boston. They intended "to see for ourselves the result of the singular political system which had been fastened upon Christianity," Quincy later wrote.

Joseph was at the top of his game. He showed them the Egyptian mummies and insisted they tip his mother a quarter-dollar for the pleasure. He bragged about his extensive knowledge of ancient languages ("his miraculous gift of understanding all languages"), and of course escorted his guests to the Nauvoo Temple, "the grotesque structure on the hill," as Quincy called it. With the Bostonians trotting behind him, Joseph roamed his domain like a feudal lord, bantering with a stonecutter at the temple, engaging in an impromptu debate with a visiting Methodist preacher, even rousting female visitors from the mansion in full view of his visitors.

Not for one second did Joseph sound like a man facing uprisings both inside and outside his Mormon kingdom. Quite the contrary, he waxed on endlessly about national politics, and about his personal quest for the presidency. Quincy tried to ask a serious question: "Is it possible that you have too much power to be safely trusted to one man?"

"In your hands, or that of any other person," Joseph answered, "so much power would, no doubt, be dangerous. I am the only man in the world it would be safe to trust with it. Remember,"—Quincy noted that these last few words "were spoken in a rich, comical aside"—"I am a prophet!"

4

EVERYBODY HATES
THE MORMONS

Their manners, customs, religion and all, are more
obnoxious to our citizens than those of the Indians,
and they can never live among us in peace. The rifle
will settle the quarrel.

—The Missouri Commercial Appeal, editorial

TUESDAY, APRIL 6, 1841, WAS A HOLIDAY IN NAUVOO. ON A
clear and balmy spring morning, the Church of Jesus Christ of
Latter-day Saints was celebrating its eleventh birthday. Businesses and
city offices were closed. The wharves and river landing points were
busier than usual, as Gentiles assembled from up and down the Mississippi Valley to watch the promised pageantry. The Mormons were
also celebrating a milestone in their spiritual journeys from New York,
Ohio, Missouri, and in many cases the British Isles: the laying of the
cornerstone of the Nauvoo Temple, to be built on a hill overlooking the
town center and the dark, glistening river beyond. The temple would
be the crown jewel of Joseph's new Zion. Once completed, it would

provide the sacred space necessary for administering the endowments, priesthood ritual, baptisms, and marriage-sealing ceremonies central to the Saints' spiritual lives. The church expected every resident of Nauvoo to donate time and money to constructing the temple. Joseph carefully monitored temple tithing, quick to accuse better-off Saints of stinting on their sacred obligations.

The Saints had erected a magnificent sandstone temple in Kirtland, Ohio, the scene of many legendary events. At its dedication in 1836, Joseph Smith reported that "the sound of a rushing mighty wind" filled the building. The congregation began speaking in tongues, and Joseph "beheld the Temple was filled with angels." Hearing the strange noises, people from the neighborhood ran to the temple and saw "a bright light like a pillar of fire" shooting up from the central spire. It was inside the Kirtland temple that Joseph reported meeting with Jesus, Moses, and the prophet Elijah, who shared revelations concerning the direction of the church.

In the dawn hours at Nauvoo, 650 soldiers of the Nauvoo Legion formed ranks at the town's parade grounds, just below the temple site. An estimated 8,000 onlookers, Saints and strangers, packed the streets. At 7:30 a.m., artillery fire announced the arrival of Legion generals Wilson Law and Joseph's brother, Don Carlos Smith. Promptly at 9:30 a.m., heralded by a single cannon blast, Lieutenant General Joseph Smith rode in on his white charger. In martial mode, Smith traveled with a personal staff of fifteen Legionnaires, which included two cavalry colonels and a third officer responsible for Joseph's personal bodyguard of twelve infantry captains. Some of the thousands of onlookers came just to see the Prophet's storied uniform, custom designed by his personal tailor, John Bills, who advertised "all kinds of military coats made according to the latest pattern." Joseph favored a cerulean officer's tailcoat, dripping with weighty gold braid and epaulettes, topped off with a black cockade chapeau that was adorned with a black ostrich feather. As accoutrements, he wore black leather riding boots, white gloves, a golden campaign sash, and a four-foot-long, leather-handled, forged cavalry saber. On the reviewing grounds, Joseph carried a tin speaking trumpet, to amplify his orders.

"The several companies presented a beautiful and interesting spectacle," reported onlooker Wandle Mace. "The rich and costly dresses of the officers would have become a Bonaparte or a Washington." Norton Jacobs recalled that "many strange murmurs ran through the waving throng to see the prophet, the master spirit of the glittering scene, mount a scaffold at the south-east corner in full military costume, accompanied by many of his fellow officers and friends."

The ranking officers' wives followed them onto the parade grounds, seated in an elaborate carriage. Emma Smith, sporting a black cap with a black ostrich plume, and dressed in a tight-fitting habit adorned with gold buttons, entered riding sidesaddle on her horse Charlie. In front of the reviewing stand, she presented Joseph with a twenty-six-star, handcrafted silk American flag, sewn for the occasion by the ladies of Nauvoo. Then the officers, the honored guests, and the twenty members of the Legion marching band assembled for the procession to the temple site. Joseph had assigned special places on the reviewing stand to the Sauk Indian chief Keokuk and his entourage, who had crossed over from Iowa to partake in the festivities. "Smith had always shown great favor to these red men and encouraged them to be on friendly terms with him," noted young William Baldwin, a visitor from Carthage, who spotted the towering, "dusky" Keokuk in Nauvoo that day. "He had constant communication with them and may have looked forward in imagination to some time when they would become valuable allies." ("I am a son of the Great Spirit," Keokuk once told Joseph, adding that "I have a Book of Mormon at my wigwam that you gave me many moons ago.") Ladies and gentlemen of the local gentry marched in double file behind the honored guests. Above them waved the individual flags of each Legion company, flapping on poles topped with carved wooden eagles, as well as the Illinois flag, the American flag, and the unforgettable standard belonging to William Pitt's brass band: a five foot by four foot banner depicting a single, huge all-seeing eye of God, observing the proceedings.

At the temple site, construction workers lowered each of the four cornerstones into place separately, accompanied by a special blessing from a church leader. Like most public events in Nauvoo, the ceremony occasioned a poem, this one springing from the pen of Hosea Stout, a particularly militant member of Joseph's bodyguard:

> 'Tis now the sixth of April in Eighteen Forty-One,
> Eleven years exactly since the Church of Christ begun;
> And then all men did hate us, our numbers being few,
> But now we've honor, power, we've a Legion of Nauvoo . . .
>
> Our "Legion" is all powerful, t'is warlike, brave and grand,
> E're long t'will prove a terror to Boggs and all his clan,
> T'is peaceable and harmless to all who come to view
> Or have a mind to settle in the City of Nauvoo . . .
>
> Our Legion is commanded by men of great renown,
> Our foes, in vain may threaten, in vain may on us frown,
> Our chief commander's Joseph, he well knows what to do,
> Because he is a prophet in the Legion of Nauvoo.

The Mormon newspaper *Times and Seasons*, edited by Joseph's brother Don Carlos Smith, hailed the day as a mammoth success:

We never witnessed a more imposing spectacle than was presented on this occasion. . . . Such an almost countless multitude of people, moving in harmony, in friendship, in dignity, told with a voice not easily misunderstood, that they were a people of intelligence and virtue, and order; in short, that they were saints.

And they behaved like saints, too. The editor made special mention of his "happiness . . . that we heard no obscene or profane language; neither saw we any one intoxicated. Can the same be said of a similar assemblage in any other city in the Union?" he asked.

> Thank God, that the intoxicating beverage, that bane of humanity in these last days, that—what shall we call it? Devil? is becoming a stranger in Nauvoo.

꽃 꽃 꽃

ONE OF CHIEF KEOKUK'S FELLOW DIGNITARIES WAS THE STRIPLING owner of the only newspaper in Hancock County not under Mormon control—Thomas Sharp, the twenty-two-year-old editor of the War-saw *Signal*. Sharp, a recent arrival in Illinois, had purchased the *Western World*, renamed it, and set off to make a name for himself in the public affairs of the day. His only competition, the Saints' official organ, the *Times and Seasons*, trafficked in upbeat news about the Mormons' social and economic progress, and in grim reports of tidal waves, earthquakes, and floods that augured the approaching End Times.

The son of a well-to-do Methodist minister, Sharp grew up in Pennsylvania and studied law at Dickinson College. He came west to make his fortune at the bar. He practiced briefly in Quincy, but a chronic hearing problem limited his effectiveness in the courtroom. In September 1840, he traveled north to Warsaw, a small (population 500) Mississippi river town located just south of the Des Moines rapids. Warsaw had about ten stores, two taverns, two steam mills, one doctor, a printing plant, and one lawyer already in business. The town did have enviable commercial prospects. Just to its north, the Des Moines River linked Illinois with the interior of the vast Iowa Territory and the largely uncharted West. On the Illinois side of the river, a railway line could theoretically connect Warsaw to a town above the Des Moines rapids and open up transport to northern Illinois and Wisconsin. Tiny Warsaw—previously named Fort Edwards, and then Spunky Point— was undergoing an image upgrade, much to the consternation of its most famous son, John Hay, the former Warsaw *Signal* delivery boy, who would grow up to become Abraham Lincoln's personal secretary and later, secretary of state. "I lived at Spunky Point on the Mississippi river," Hay later wrote,

> so named because some Indian rode by Fort Edwards on a spunky horse. This is a graphic and characteristic title of geographical significance, but some idiots just before I was born, who had read Miss Porter's novel "Thaddeus of Warsaw," thought Warsaw would be more genteel, so we are Nicodemussed [reduced by timidity] into nothingness for the rest of time.
>
> I hope every man who is engaged in this outrage is called Smith in heaven.

The novice newspaper owner Sharp declared his ambition "to please ourselves, pursuing an independent and unyielding course; on the one hand battling with tyranny in all its forms . . . and on the other uphold- ing the high and lofty principles of republicanism and equal rights." Like many prominent Illinois citizens, including Abraham Lincoln, Sharp was active in his local Washingtonian Society, which inveighed against alcohol and all "intoxicating drinks."

Like the Signal's previous owner, Sharp had no strong opinions about the Mormons, who were flooding into Nauvoo, just eighteen miles north of Warsaw. He noted the legislature's passage of the liberal Nauvoo Charter with equanimity. Just a few days later, Sharp editori- alized on Joseph's call to the world's Mormons to "gather" in Nauvoo. "Whatever may be thought of the tenets of this sect," Sharp wrote in a January, 20, 1840, editorial, "it is certainly an imposing spectacle to wit- ness the moral power which in so short a period they have exerted. . . .

Already in obedience to this call, thousands have left their homes in Europe, and thousands are now preparing to leave and take up residence in a far distant land." He called the Mormons "that persecuted people" and even mentioned that he had been accused of partiality to the Saints.

Sharp and Joseph Smith had never met, but Joseph certainly appreciated the power of a favorable press. He invited Sharp to the April 6 celebration, saving him a seat on the reviewing platform, and assigned him a groom to care for his horse. The groom, Norton Jacobs, later regretted waiting on "the mean hypocritical human." Like Keokuk and many others, Sharp enjoyed a turkey dinner that Joseph laid on for his special guests at the Nauvoo Mansion.

Perhaps it was something he ate. "I believe [Sharp] here imbibed that spirit of rancor which since has been so freely manifested against the Saints," Jacobs wrote, "for he envied that majesty and magnanimity which he had not the honesty and courage to emulate." Whatever the case, by the late spring of 1841, after seeing the serried ranks of Joseph's military might on the Nauvoo parade ground, Sharp turned against the Saints, with a vengeance.

The young Thomas Sharp would prove to be a formidable enemy. He was intelligent, eloquent, and seemingly tireless in his efforts to blacken the name of Joseph Smith and his followers. He carefully monitored the Saints' newspapers and apparently had some informants in Nauvoo. Within just a few months, he became a determined, professional Mormon-hater. "He was more dreaded and hated by the whole Mormon tribe than any other anti-Mormon in the county," Sharp's contemporary, editor Thomas Gregg recalled.

> The editorials of the *Signal* were extensively copied into other papers throughout the country, and from their pugnacious and violent character, people at a distance were led to believe that "Old Tom Sharp" was a perfect walking arsenal, his person bristling with Bowie knives and pistols. Who would rather fight than eat.

In reality, Gregg insisted that Sharp was a "mild-mannered, good natured and rather conservative individual."

Sharp first criticized the Mormons, gently, in a lengthy dispatch one month after the Saints' parade. He reported, perhaps correctly, that "great dissatisfaction exists at Nauvoo amongst those who have lately arrived from England." Then Sharp offered a broader critique of the Saints' political ambitions in Illinois. The Mormons, he opined, had stepped "beyond the proper sphere of religious denomination and become a political body." Sharp insisted that he honored the Saints' religious beliefs but was "bound to oppose the concentration of political power in a religious body, or in the hands of a few individuals."

Joseph overreacted, immediately firing off this brief note to "Sharp, Editor of the Warsaw *Signal*":

Nauvoo, Ill., May 26, 1841

Sir—
You will discontinue my paper—its contents are calculated to pollute me, and to patronize the filthy sheet—that tissue of lies—that sink of iniquity—is disgraceful to any moral man.

Yours, with utter contempt.

Joseph Smith

P.S. Please publish the above in your contemptible paper.

Of course, Sharp did publish the note, under the headline

HIGHLY IMPORTANT!
A New Revelation from Joe Smith, the Mormon Prophet

Smith had unwisely picked the proverbial fight with a man who bought printer's ink by the barrel. Sharp never stinted on sarcasm and mockery where Joseph was concerned, inevitably referring to Smith as

"His Holiness" and characterizing every communication from Nauvoo as a "revelation." As one of his many pranks, Sharp pulled Smith's old subscription request form from the *Western World*'s files. According to Sharp, the Prophet still owed the paper $3.00 in unpaid fees:

> Come, Josey, fork over and for mercy's sake don't get a revelation that it is not to be paid. For if thou dost, we will send a prophet after thee mightier than thou.

Sharp quickly revisited the events of April 6, after the *Times and Seasons* accused him of repaying the Saints' "hospitality and kindness" with "baseness." "It does make us feel right bad," Sharp shot back, "that we have been so ungrateful to the Mormon brotherhood.

> Just think, reader!—after having been invited to Nauvoo on the 6 of April, by the Mayor of the city. . . . After having ridden to the Temple on that great day, in presence of assembled thousands, by the side of the Holy prophet—after supping with the Prophet, and eating heartily of his stall-fed turkey. . . .

Sharp introduced a theme that would dominate his anti-Mormon rhetoric for several years: the Saints' militarism, so blatantly on display at the Legion parade: "How *military* these people are becoming," Sharp wrote:

> Every thing they say or do seems to breathe the spirit of military tactics. Their *prophet* appears on all great occasions in his splendid regimental dress, signs his name Lieutenant General, and more titles are to be found in the Nauvoo Legion than any one book on military tactics can produce. . . .

Reporting the Legion's weekly maneuvers in the center of Nauvoo, Sharp concluded: "Truly *fighting* must be a part of the creed of these Saints!"

What motivated Sharp to hector the Mormons so relentlessly for six long years, until he and his confederates succeeded in driving the Saints out of Illinois? The Mormons' ostentatious militarism probably shocked him, as he wrote. He repeatedly assailed the notion that a religion should have its own army. Furthermore, Sharp was one of the first to realize that the Saints' rapid immigration into Nauvoo had created a powerful voting bloc, capable of ruling the county. "If Joe Smith is to control the majority of votes in our county, are we not, in effect, the subject of a despot?" Sharp wrote. "Might we not as well be serfs to the Autocrat of Russia?" "We ask the independent citizens of this county and this state *to wake up from their slumber* . . . to put down this foul and unholy attempt to *enslave* them." He called Mormonism "a power in league with the Prince of Darkness, not inferior to the Spanish Inquisition in its capacity for secrecy and intrigue."

Never underestimate the craven opportunism of the newspaper owner. "Mormon Joe and his Danite seraglio" provided great copy, and plenty of it. When Sharp wasn't busy reporting, and often distorting, the goings-on in Nauvoo, he printed long swaths of text drawn from the anti-Mormon well. Several newspapers in New York and Pennsylvania were serializing wild tales of Joe Smith's necromancy and plural wifery, retailed by money-hungry apostates, and Sharp delightedly reprinted any anti-Mormon trumpery, real or imagined. His readers lapped it up. Like journalists before and after him, Sharp knew how to milk a good story. When the Warsaw *Signal* finally ceased publication in 1846, Sharp admitted that "our cause against the Mormons has kept us in business."

With Sharp riding high, Joseph's younger brother William entered the fray. William was bad seed, needlessly combative and possessed of exceedingly poor judgment. (William once said his older brother Joseph "ought to have been hung up by the neck years ago.") He saw that Sharp was landing some haymakers and influencing public opinion well beyond the confines of tiny Warsaw and Hancock County. William believed that his brother Don Carlos's *Times and Seasons* lacked the stomach to fight toe-to-toe with Sharp, so he launched a newspaper with the express purpose of parrying the thrusts of the downstate newspaper tyro.

On April 16, 1842, William published the first issue of the Nauvoo *Wasp*, to combat "the shafts of slander . . . foul calumnies, and base misrepresentations" appearing in journals like the *Signal*. The *Wasp* vowed "to convey correct information to the world and thereby disabuse the public mind as to the many slanders that are constantly perpetrated against us." In the very first issue, William published a brief item headlined "Nose-ology," about one "Thom-ASS C. Sharp:"

> the length of his snout is said to be in the exact proportion of seven to one compared with his intellectual faculties, having upon its convex surface well developed bumps.

According to William, Sharp's nose deformations betrayed many dark traits, including "Anti-Mormonitiveness."

But William was wielding a knife at a gun fight. "We have received the first number of a new six by nine, recently started at Nauvoo, yclept '*The Wasp*,'" Sharp informed his readers:

> Of the "varmint" itself we have nothing to say, further than that the title is perfect *misnomer*. If it had been called *Pole Cat*, its name would then have corresponded perfectly with the character of its contents. It is needless to inform our readers that we don't fight with such animals—nature having given them a decided advantage.

Joseph quickly realized that William needed adult supervision, and cut short his brother's tenure at the *Wasp*. The Mormon leadership disavowed the "stinging" nature of William's commentary and announced a new, irenic moniker for the weekly tabloid: "The Dove of the West." The dove never flew. Instead, it became the *Nauvoo Neighbor*, a somewhat folksier version of the *Times and Seasons*, and Joseph appointed the so-bersided Apostle John Taylor as the new editor.

‡ ‡ ‡

UNFORTUNATELY FOR THE SAINTS, SHARP DIDN'T LIMIT HIS involvement with the Mormons to sarcastic spitballing. In July 1841, he queried his readers: "I ask you candidly, fellow citizens, if there is not need of an anti-Mormon Party in this county?" It was not a rhetorical question. Sharp was the driving force behind a countywide anti-Mormon convention that met in Warsaw, where Hancock's "old settlers" tried to woo political candidates who would agree not to kow-tow to the ever-increasing Mormon vote. "Old settlers," or "old citizens," as they called themselves, was a relative term. Carthage, the county seat, was established in 1833, and the town of Warsaw was laid out in 1834. Illinois had been a state for barely twenty-five years. Almost to a man, the Mormons' opponents were new settlers, like Sharp himself, who was born in New Jersey. Businessman Mark Aldrich, who would become a prominent anti-Mormon agitator, built the second house erected in Warsaw, just eight years before the Mormons arrived. William Grover, who declared himself to be the "governor" of the "Warsaw Legislature," an ersatz anti-Mormon civic organization, was born in New York, and so on.

The anti-Mormon party never really became a political organization, because Illinois already had two vigorous political parties, the Democrats and the Whigs. The post–Andrew Jackson Illinois Democrats represented the radical populist wing of the party, branded "locofocos" for their supposed impulsiveness (a locofoco was a sulfur match), and shared the votes in Hancock County and the surrounding areas with the more staid Whigs. The Democrats held the balance of power statewide, but the Whigs generally won Hancock County elections. The populist Democrats were pro-immigration free traders, anti–federal government and opposed to ambitious, federally funded public works. The Democrats favored states' rights and America's rapid westward expansion. The Whigs were the ideological heirs of Alexander Hamilton's Federalists, favoring a national bank and a strong national currency. They waxed more cautious about widening the borders of the ever-growing union. In the large East Coast cities, interparty animus was real and sometimes spilled over into violence. In Illinois party politics, though, cooler heads generally prevailed.

Joseph Smith liked to say that he had no politics: "We care not a fig for *Whig* or *Democrat*, they are both alike to us," he declared at the end of 1841. "We shall go for our *friends*, our TRIED FRIENDS, and the cause of *human liberty*, which is the cause of God." Smith favored whichever party seemed most likely to help the Mormons strengthen their hand in Nauvoo, or advance their case for reparations from Missouri. It was assumed that he hated Democrats; after all, it was the Democratic governor of Missouri, Lilburn Boggs, who signed the 1838 anti-Mormon Extermination Order. When Joseph traveled to Washington in 1840 to ask Democratic president Martin Van Buren to make good the Mormons' enormous property losses in Missouri, Van Buren brushed him off, twice. "He is not as fit as my dog for the chair of state," was Joseph's famous assessment of Van Buren, "for my dog will make an effort to protect his abused and insulted master, while the present chief magistrate will not so much as lift his finger" to help citizens of the United States. Furthermore, it was Governor Boggs's Democrat successor, Thomas Reynolds, who kept sending lawmen across the Mississippi to extradite Joseph Smith, for crimes he may or may not have committed. In 1840, the Nauvoo Saints voted Whig and helped swing Hancock County to William Henry Harrison, who became the ninth president of the United States.

But party lines meant little to Smith. He liked his friends more. Illinois state senator Stephen Douglas once helped Joseph out of a legal jam, and Joseph swung toward Douglas's Democrats in the state elections of 1842. As Joseph voted, so voted the 2,000 or so eligible Saints who accepted his word as gospel. Eager to attract new residents, Illinois had liberal alien suffrage laws, which allowed white males to vote almost immediately after arriving in the state.

A notorious example of the Mormons' mercurial political alliances, and one that earned them lasting enemies, occurred in mid-1843. Missouri governor Reynolds had issued a warrant for Joseph's arrest, averring that he had escaped their Liberty jail in 1838. (In fact, he had been allowed to go free, for expediency's sake.) Two deputies masquerading as Mormon elders hunted Joseph down and locked him in an upstairs room in a tavern in Dixon's Ferry, Illinois, where he and Emma were visiting relatives upstate. The Missourians hoped to spirit Smith across the river without benefit of counsel, but the leather-lunged Joseph started to plead his case with the local citizenry from the pulpit of his second-story bedroom. Soon the Illinois crowd was cursing the "damned infernal pukes" and "nigger drivers" from Missouri and insisting that Joseph be allowed to consult with a lawyer.

It so happened that Cyrus Walker, "the greatest criminal lawyer in that part of Illinois," was litigating in the neighborhood, and he also happened to be running for Congress. He "told me that he could not find time to be my lawyer unless I could promise him my vote," Joseph explained. Illinois had just been redistricted, and Walker knew that the votes at Joseph's command would pick the congressman from the Hancock County area. Joseph gave his word, and Walker exulted: "I am now sure of my election," he boasted, "as Joseph Smith has promised me his vote, and I am going to defend him."

Walker performed his legal magic, and soon Joseph reentered Nauvoo at the head of a half-mile-long triumphal procession, with the Legion band playing "Hail Columbia," and his lawyer at his side. That evening, Joseph threw open the doors of his Nauvoo Mansion and laid out a huge banquet for all concerned. The perfidious Missouri sheriffs "were seated at the head of [the table] and served with the utmost kindness by Mrs. Smith in person," a guest reported.

At a mass meeting in the "grove," an open public area beneath the Temple hill, Joseph lauded Walker in front of thousands of his co-religionists. "I understand the gospel and you do not," Smith proclaimed. "You understand the quackery of law, and I do not."

With the August election just a few weeks away, Joseph made an unfortunate discovery. His brother Hyrum had been serving in the Illinois legislature and had promised the Mormon votes to the Democratic candidate, Joseph Hoge. Both Walker and Hoge spent the campaign's final days electioneering in Nauvoo, and the situation turned awkward. The secular *Nauvoo Neighbor* suggested that the Saints vote in a unanimous bloc, further recommending that they vote for Hoge. Then God intervened. On Saturday evening, just two days before the election, Hyrum Smith rose to address the Saints in the grove and made a startling announcement: He "knew from knowledge that would not be doubted, from evidences that never fail, that Mr. Hoge was the man." Hyrum raised both arms and brandished a yellow ballot printed on wrapping paper. "Those that vote this ticket, this flesh colored ticket, the Democratic ticket, shall be blessed," he declared. "Those who do not shall be accursed. Thus saith the Lord."

William Law, one of Joseph's two counselors in the First Presidency, questioned Hyrum's vision. Law told the assembled Saints he was certain that Joseph wanted Walker for the congressional seat and that "the prophet was more likely to know the mind of the Lord on the subject than the patriarch." This was a rare public feud in the top echelon of the church leadership. Law, Taylor, and Hyrum were all apostles, and also members of the secret Council of Fifty. Law was effectively third in command to Joseph, and Hyrum was the church patriarch, a nebulous leadership post previously held by the men's father, Joseph Smith Sr. The Prophet would have to be heard from, and soon.

The next day, on the eve of the election, Joseph allowed Apostle Parley Pratt to deliver the Sunday sermon. Then Smith approached the stand and told the Saints he would talk about the election. "I am above the kingdoms of the world, for I have no laws," he announced. "I am not come to tell you to vote this way, that way or the other."

William Law was wrong, he said. "I never authorized him to tell my private feelings."

Joseph praised Cyrus Walker in a backhanded manner and told the Saints that he intended to vote for his lawyer. But "Brother Hyrum tells me this morning that he has had a testimony to the effect it would be better for the people to vote for Hoge; and I never knew Hyrum to say he ever had a revelation and it failed. Let God speak and all men hold their peace." Joseph offered the Saints a choice, to vote for his lawyer or to follow the will of God.

The results were foreordained. Hoge won election from Illinois's newly created Sixth Congressional District by 474 votes. An estimated 3,000 Mormons voted for him. The Whigs were apoplectic, but the Democrats had learned a lesson, too. The Mormons would promise both sides their votes, then throw the election in the direction they chose at the eleventh hour. The anti-Mormon party was back in business, and a meeting attended by 200 old settlers in Carthage shortly after the election condemned Joseph, the "pretended prophet" and "dangerous individual . . . claiming to set aside, by his vile and blasphemous lies, all those moral and religious institutions which have been established by the Bible." This "modern Caligula . . . [has] been able to place himself at the head of a numerous horde, either equally reckless and unprincipled as himself, or else made his pliant tools by the most absurd credulity that has astonished the world since its foundation." The settlers resolved never to vote for a political candidate who "truckled" to the Saints, and to resist Mormon domination of Hancock's political affairs, "forcibly, if we must." Some of the members of the "correspondence committees" tasked with monitoring the Mormons' behavior would soon enter the annals of Latter-day Saints history: Mark Aldrich; Colonel Levi Williams; Franklin Worrell; Captain Robert F. Smith, and the settlers' ubiquitous mouthpiece, Thomas Sharp.

By the fall of 1843, the Saints had almost exhausted their small reservoir of goodwill in southwestern Illinois. Just four years before, the residents of Quincy had opened their arms and their homes to the refugee Saints, fleeing the Missouri oppression. Three years earlier, the legislature's Whigs and Democrats had unanimously approved the Nauvoo Charter, which granted the Saints quasi-independent status within Illinois borders. Now the worm had turned. "From this time forth," Governor Thomas Ford wrote in his *History of Illinois,* "the Whigs generally, and a part of the Democrats, determined upon driving the Mormons out of the state."

In 1843, Joseph vowed that the Mormons would remain neutral in the country's next major political confrontation, the presidential election of 1844. Then he announced his own quixotic presidential candidacy, guaranteeing that neither major party need bother wooing the Saints' votes. It was a strategy for near-total isolation, and it succeeded all too well.

☽ ☽ ☽

IN A SHORT SPACE OF TIME, THE MORMONS HAD BECOME POLITICAL orphans. They were religious pariahs as well. Southwestern Illinois was not a churchy part of the world: "The minister of the gospel has had to contend with foul mouthed Atheism and rabid infidelity," one visiting Presbyterian reported. "The church has not only been asleep, but it really seems as if they designed to keep their spiritual eyes shut forever." Still, Christians such as they were in Hancock County viewed the Mormons as craven heretics. The "Golden Bible," the far-fetched tales of the Plains Indians as ancient Lamanites, and the rumors of serial wifery, waxed too exotic for workaday Christians. "I presume Nauvoo is as perfect a sink of debauchery and every species of abomination as ever were Sodom and Nineveh," the Presbyterian missionary Reverend William M. King wrote to his colleagues at the American Home Missionary Society in New York. Writing to the society from Warsaw, missionary Reverend Benjamin Franklin Morris complained, "We are surrounded by the delusion of Mormonism . . . the frogs of Egypt are literally covering the whole land."

"Mormonism is exerting a great and pernicious influence in this county," he continued.

> Here is the seat of the Beast and the false prophet. Here are 15,000 souls deluded and under the absolute dominion of Joe Smith. They have unlimited belief in his prophecies; and no prophecy however absurd and preposterous can dissipate the dreadful delusions that cover their minds.
>
> The old citizens are under great excitement. We are on the eve of an outbreak and I should not be surprised to see very soon the scenes of Missouri enacted anew. What is to be the finale of this chief of all modern humbugs I know not.

Jonathan Turner, a Presbyterian divine in Jacksonville, Illinois, published a lengthy attack in his *Mormonism in All Ages* in 1842, branding the Saints "the most dangerous and virulent enemies to our political and religious purity, and our social and civil peace, that now exist in the Union."

It's far from clear if the Mormon-haters ever read the Book of Mormon or understood much about the Saints' beliefs. But they knew what they didn't like. Editor Gregg, who briefly took over Sharp's newspaper in 1843, fretted that "the pretended prophet" Smith, using "vile and blasphemous lies," would remove "all those moral and religious institutions which have been established by men, as the only means of maintaining those social blessings which are so indispensably necessary for our happiness." Reporting on a well-attended "anti-Mormon convention" in Carthage in September 1843, Gregg asserted that it was time "to take a firm and decided stand against the high pretension and base designs of this latter-day would-be Mahomet."

One controversial element of Mormon doctrine gained notoriety in Hancock County: the Saints' penchant for "consecrated thieving."

This murky doctrine, repeatedly denied by Joseph Smith and others, purportedly allowed Mormons to steal from Gentiles. There was a material incentive; the Mormons believed that Missouri had stripped them of almost $3 million worth of land and property during the 1839 expulsion. They were nearly destitute upon arriving in Nauvoo, and the Gentiles owed them. There was also a dubious spiritual imperative. Stolen goods were said to be "consecrated" if a certain portion—one quarter, or one-third—was donated to the Nauvoo Temple construction fund. "To take from the Gentiles [is] no sin," Joseph told Justus Morse in 1838. Morse reported Smith's policy, that

> the Church should "suck the milk of the Gentiles," that we had been injured by the mob in Missouri . . . but should we get caught in this work . . . to swear to a lie, to do so, and to do it with such positiveness and assurance that no one would question our testimony.

Any time a Hancock County farmer lost a horse, or a heifer, or a valuable farm tool, he blamed Mormon thieves. Sometimes he was right. In 1840, church leaders dissolved the entire stake in nearby Ramus, Illinois, and excommunicated the bishop, the first counselor, and a captain in the Nauvoo Legion for stealing. A few years later, these men rejoined the church, which never spoke with one voice on the question of thievery. In 1843, Joseph condemned stealing at a church conference. "I despise a thief above ground," he preached. "He would betray me if he could get the opportunity. If I were the biggest rogue in the world, he would steal my horse when I wanted to run away." But many Gentiles thought Joseph turned a blind eye to Saintly thieves. Apostle Orson Hyde famously remarked that he "would never institute a trial against a brother for stealing from the Gentiles."

Similarly, accusations of counterfeiting dogged the Saints in Nauvoo. Two members of Joseph's secret Council of Fifty had experience in "bogus making." Edward Bonney, a distant relation of Billy the Kid, "was not averse to passing the 'long green' of counterfeit bills when it suited his purpose," according to one biographer. New York state was pursuing Fifty member Marinus Eaton on counterfeiting charges. Eaton served as a personal aide to Joseph Smith, alongside Joseph Jackson, whose "principal business" was "trying to make bogus," according to Hyrum Smith. Jackson, a provocateur with complicated allegiances—he alternately claimed to be a Catholic priest and a Missouri spy—wrote a memoir claiming that he and Joseph Smith made bogus on the second floor of the Old Homestead, Smith's first log cabin home in Nauvoo. Jackson wrote that Smith imported a $200 German press from St. Louis, which resulted in "an excellent specimen of base coin produced." Jackson reported that Joseph, aided by ten of the twelve apostles, fabricated about $350,000 worth of false coin, half of which they spent in Hancock County, and half of which they sent east to finance church purchases.

The truth is elusive. But it hardly mattered; as the years progressed, Hancock County husbandmen found plenty of reasons to dislike the Mormons, and they added thievery, often alleged, more rarely proved, to the list. Governor Thomas Ford thought the accusations sprang from prejudice. "I have investigated the charge of promiscuous stealing and find it to be greatly exaggerated," he reported to the legislature in December 1844. "I could not ascertain that there were a greater proportion of thieves in that community than any other of the same number of inhabitants."

There is no denying, however, that the Mormons made powerful economic enemies in Hancock County. Partly by chance and partly by design, Joseph had chosen a remote, undeveloped corner of Illinois to build his new Zion. Neither Warsaw nor Carthage had more than five hundred inhabitants, and neither was thriving economically. By the sweat of Mormon brows, Nauvoo had transformed itself from an uninhabited malarial swamp into a city with several thousand citizens within three years. The population quickly grew to 5,000, and then to over 10,000 by 1844. With Joseph's call for the Saints to "gather in Zion," his town was gaining a thousand new residents a year, while the populations of Warsaw and Carthage remained stagnant. Hancock County wasn't participating in Nauvoo's mini-economic boom and was unlikely to benefit in the future. Warsaw enjoyed a modest business in trans-shipping goods overland for merchants chary of entrusting their goods to the roiling waters of the nearby Des Moines rapids. But the more prosperous Nauvoo was weaning Mississippi ferry traffic from Warsaw, and the Mormons were talking about building a dam, and even a railroad, that would make Nauvoo the central trans-shipment port for merchants hoping to skirt the rapids.

Competing with the Saints was hard work. Mormons preferred to do business with other Mormons, and, like other New World sectarians, they equated material success with spiritual achievement. "We cannot talk about spiritual things without connecting with them temporal things, neither can we talk about temporal things without connecting spiritual things with them," Brigham Young explained. "They are inseparably connected. . . . We, as Latter-day Saints, really expect, look for and we will not be satisfied with anything short of being governed and controlled by the word of the Lord in all our acts, both spiritual and temporal." Orson Hyde, an apostle like Brigham, put the matter more succinctly: "When we descend to the matter of dollars and cents, it is also spiritual."

As Nauvoo's prospects brightened and grew, Warsaw's future was dimming. Likewise, Nauvoo's autonomous civil government obviated the need for the county seat in Carthage. Joseph was running the Mormons' Registry of Deeds out of his redbrick store. He told his followers that their weddings and births didn't need to be recorded with the state, and practically all of Nauvoo's legal business cycled through its own courts, established by the legislature's generous charter. Unitarian missionary George Moore noted disapprovingly that the Saints sometimes conducted marriage ceremonies in the middle of the frozen Mississippi, outside of Illinois, to avoid paying fees to Carthage's county court.

Nauvoo ground its own flour, milled its own lumber, raised its own food in the vast farms that stretched several miles into the countryside, and imported anything it needed through its many municipally owned wharves. At one point, Joseph even owned shares in two paddle-wheeled steamers, which figured among his unsuccessful investments. Fatefully, Smith bought a part interest in a steamboat being sold by a young Army Corps of Engineers lieutenant named Robert E. Lee, who had been dredging the Mississippi rapids near Nauvoo. One of Smith's partners in the deal was Robert F. Smith, who, along with Joseph, became the target of a federal bankruptcy claim when two pilots hired by the Mormons wrecked the boat on the upper Mississippi. A resentful Robert F. Smith would reappear in Joseph's life, in the dual role of magistrate and militia captain overseeing the Prophet's fate in the Carthage jail.

Egged on by local speculators, Joseph plunged the Saints into another dubious investment scheme that would have dire consequences for the Mormons. As happened several times during his stay in Illinois, Joseph befriended a lawyer who helped him out of a jam. In 1841, Calvin Warren, aided by a silver-tongued attorney named Orville H. Browning, managed to free Joseph from a Missouri arrest warrant served in Illinois. (The judge who released Joseph was a rising star in Illinois politics, Stephen Douglas. Smith befriended him, too.)

After Warren collected his substantial $250 fee, he pitched Joseph a real estate deal: Warren's friend Mark Aldrich, one of the four original developers of Warsaw, owned a mile-square tract of land south of the city ideal for Mormon settlement. Aldrich and Warren, working with Brigham Young and Willard Richards, arranged for 204 Mormon immigrants to settle on lots in a new town to be called Warren. Editor Sharp, normally a booster of all things Warsaw, couldn't resist the opportunity to take a poke at Smith. His newspaper had been running a series of articles written by a former resident of Palmyra, New York, detailing Joseph's inglorious past as a treasure hunter—a "money-digger," Sharp called him. "We have not heard what name Joe intends to give to the new city," the Warsaw *Signal* opined, "but we would call it 'MONEY-DIGGERSVILLE'—quite a mouthful, but still symphonious."

Sharp loved to accuse the Mormons of questionable business practices and outright thievery. With wagonloads of "red-hot Mormons" closing in on Warsaw, he predicted, the price of locks for doors and windows would skyrocket.

When the British Mormon leader Joseph Fielding settled his flock in Warren, problems arose. He reported that Aldrich and Warren's partner was price gouging the Saints on flour sales, even selling them mill sweepings at exorbitant markups. The rents were rising even as the Saints were moving in, and the Mormons were forbidden from collecting wood in the area. When Joseph heard the complaints, he immediately recalled the English Saints to Nauvoo. Not long after, Aldrich and Warren demanded an audience with the Prophet, and laid out their case. Warren said he would go broke if the Saints backed out of the deal and offered "liberal benefits" to lure the Mormons back. But Joseph responded with a tirade, damning Warsaw and its noxious citizens to hell. "I prophesied in the name of the Lord, that the first thing toward building up Warsaw was to break it down, to break down them that are there," Joseph thundered, "and to let Sharp publish what he pleases and go to the devil, and the more lies he prints the sooner he will get through." He predicted that Warsaw would never prosper until "capitalists from the Eastern States, say from Pennsylvania" introduced rational business practices to the downstate backwater. Perhaps his remarks were calculated to offend. Southern Illinois residents despised Yankee meddlers of all stripes and colors.

As a result of the Warren debacle, both Aldrich and attorney Warren declared bankruptcy. (Warren was a bankruptcy specialist, whom Joseph had retained in an earlier, unsuccessful effort to make his general store's indebtedness disappear.) But both men would be heard from again, as stalwart, fanatical Joseph Smith–haters who changed the course of Mormon history.

5

POLYGAMY AND ITS DISCONTENTS

That which is wrong under one circumstance, may be, and often is, right under another.

—Joseph Smith, letter to Nancy Rigdon, April 1844

I N 1830, MARY ELIZABETH ROLLINS WAS A PRETTY, PRECOCIOUS twelve-year-old girl living with her aunt and uncle in Kirtland, Ohio. Her father had perished in a shipwreck on Lake Ontario when she was two years old. Mary and her mother went to live with her uncle Sidney Gilbert, an early convert to Joseph Smith's new religion. Soon the mother and daughter became Saints, baptized in a stream near their home.

Visiting a neighbor's house, Mary spotted a rare Book of Mormon. Only a few hundred copies had been printed, mostly reserved for the use of missionaries wending their way around the northeastern United States. Mary begged to borrow the book for an evening. In her autobiography, she reported that she and the Gilberts savored the "Golden Bible" until late at night. She woke up early and memorized the first verse of Nephi, the first book in the Mormon bible: "I, Nephi, have been born of goodly parents. . . ."

When she returned the book early the next morning, her neighbor chided her. "I guess you did not read much in it."

"Actually, I read quite a lot," she insisted.

"I don't believe you can tell me one word of it," the skeptical man replied.

"I then repeated the first verse, also the outlines of the history of Nephi," Mary remembered.

"Child, take this book home and finish it," her neighbor replied. "I can wait."

Soon afterward, Joseph Smith himself settled in Kirtland and paid a call on the Gilberts. He spotted the Book of Mormon and asked who had been reading it. Everyone, the Gilberts replied, even our twelve-year-old niece.

"Where is your niece?" Joseph asked.

"I was sent for," Mary later wrote, "and when he saw me, he looked at me so earnestly, I felt almost afraid and I thought, 'He can read my every thought,' and I thought how blue his eyes were. After a moment he came and put his hands on my head and gave me a great Blessing and made me a present of the Book."

Just a few days later Mary and her mother attended an evening prayer gathering with other Saints at Joseph's house. Mary watched the proceedings from a corner, sitting on a plank suspended between two boxes. After some prayers and hymn-singing, Smith suddenly froze.

"His countenance Shone," Mary recalled, and seemed almost transparent.

It seems as though the solemnity of Eternity rested upon all of us. He seemed almost transfixed, he was looking ahead and his face outshone the candle which was on a shelf just behind him. He looked as though a searchlight was inside his face and shining through every pore. I could not take my eyes from his face.

"Who do you suppose has been in your midst this night?" Smith asked.

"An angel?" one of the faithful suggested.

Then Martin Harris, who financed the printing of the Book of Mormon, prostrated himself in front of Joseph, grabbing the Prophet's leg. "I know," Harris said. "Jesus Christ was here."

"That is right," Smith testified, "Brethren, our Saviour has been in Your Midst, and talked with me face to face.

> He has commanded me to seal you up unto Everlasting life, and he has given you *all* to be with me, in his kingdom, even as he is in the Father's kingdom. And he has commanded me to say unto you, that when you are tempted of Satan, to say get thee behind me Satan, for my salvation is secure.

"I felt he was talking to the Lord and the power rested upon us all," Mary wrote.

Mary Rollins's life continued to be eventful. Possessed of the gift of tongues, she sometimes interpreted Indian languages and even engaged in religious prophecy, which occasionally set her at odds with her Mormon elders. She was a talented seamstress. When she and the Gilberts followed the Saints to Missouri, the newly elected lieutenant governor, Lilburn Boggs, asked her to help tailor a formal suit for his inauguration. Impressed by Mary and her work, Boggs tried to convince her to leave the church and join his family. Four years later, Boggs would issue the Extermination Order that would send Mary and thousands of Saints fleeing for their lives across the frozen Mississippi river.

In 1839, Mary, her Gentile husband, Adam Lightner, and their two young children did indeed flee Missouri and settle not far from Nauvoo. Lightner suffered business reverses and had trouble earning a living. Mary taught art to young children, including to Joseph Smith's adopted daughter Julia. She was living with her family in a tiny dwelling near the

Nauvoo Mansion when Smith first asked her to marry him in early 1842.

Mary was twenty-three years old, married, and pregnant with her third child. Joseph was thirty-six years old, the father of four children and, unbeknownst to Mary and almost every other member of his church, was husband to eight wives, including Emma, the mother of his children.

Joseph explained to Mary, as he would to many other women, that an angel of the Lord had revealed the doctrine of plural marriage to him three times since 1834. Naturally, he had at first found the teaching shocking and repugnant. On the final visit, the angel, brandishing a sword, "said I was to obey that principle or he would slay me."

Joseph told Mary that the two of them had already been together, that "I was created for him before the foundation of the Earth was laid." He further explained—and he would repeat this to many women—that God had granted him eternal life. "I know that I shall be saved in the Kingdom of God," he said. "I have the oath of God upon it and God cannot lie." Furthermore, his wives and children would be granted salvation with him at the end of time.

Mary worshipped the Prophet, but she had doubts about this new revelation. If you saw an angel, she asked, why didn't I? And how do you know the angel came from heaven? Perhaps Satan sent one of *his* angels? Mary said she would accept this new teaching only if an angel came to *her*. That will doubtless happen, Joseph said. And in the meantime, please don't repeat this conversation to anyone.

I wouldn't dream of it, Mary answered: "I shall never tell a mortal I had such a talk from a married man!"

Mary prayed as Joseph counseled her, and one night, she reported that "a Personage stood in front of the Bed looking at me.

Its clothes were whiter than anything I had ever seen, I could look at its Person, but when I saw its face so bright, and more beautiful than any Earthly Being Could be, and those eyes pearcing me through, and through, I could not endure it, it seemed as if I must die with fear, I fell back in Bed and Covered up my head.

Mary shared the bedroom with her mother and her aunt, who also saw "a figure in white robes pass from our bed to my mother's bed and pass out of the window."

This was the sign, Mary concluded. In February 1842, on the second floor of Smith's redbrick general store, Brigham Young sealed Mary and Joseph as husband and wife for "time, and all Eternity." She was told to remain married to Adam Lightner, who was out of town on business.

I I I

SECURE ATOP HIS INDEPENDENT CITY-STATE, JOSEPH SMITH WAS boldly re-creating the Mormon religion. He had introduced the doctrine of baptism of the dead, ensuring that the Saints' forbears—and ultimately the nations of Gentiles—would be prepared to greet Jesus Christ in the glory of the Second Coming. He had refined and formalized the endowment ritual required for men and women to enter the Mormon priesthood, borrowing heavily from his new enthusiasm for Freemasonry. The King Follett sermon shook the theological foundations of his own church, announcing the doctrine of plural gods, and of the humanity of the Christian God. But the most controversial new teaching, which Smith insisted was a very old teaching, firmly rooted in the Old Testament experience, was polygamy, the doctrine of plural wives.

From the moment he received his first revelation, Joseph never wavered from his insistence that Mormonism was a *restoration* of the original church of Jesus Christ, and of the Old Testament prophets. Thus Joseph styled himself to be a prophet, aided on earth by twelve apostles. All Old and New Testament teachings, along with the Book

83

of Mormon, were true, Joseph said. According to him, the established churches had distorted and polluted God's messages over time. Joseph knew the Bible backward and forward and often mentioned the multiple wives of such Old Testament figures as Abraham, Jacob, Moses, and King David. The great Hebrew king was said to have had over twenty wives and concubines, and his son Solomon had "seven hundred wives, princesses, and three hundred concubines," according to 1 Kings 11:3. In the original polygamy revelation of 1831, God reminded Smith that "David also received many wives and concubines, and also Solomon and Moses my servants . . . from the beginning of creation until this time; and in nothing did they sin." In a separate revelation the same year, God suggested that the Mormons might convert the Native Americans, supposedly descendants of the Book of Mormon's Lamanites, through polygamous intermarriage:

> For it is my will, that in time, ye should take unto you wives of the Lamanites and Nephites, that their posterity may become white, delightsome and Just, for even now their females are more virtuous than the gentiles.

Although a few Mormons did marry Native American women later in the century, the revelation—which the church never published—went unfulfilled.

Joseph received so many revelations that they inevitably conflicted. The Lord did advise him, just as he had counseled Moses in the Ten Commandments, to "love thy wife with all thy heart, and cleave unto her and none else"(Doctrine and Covenants 42:22). And it could hardly go unnoticed that the Book of Mormon, which Joseph compiled before 1831, condemned polygamy, in two passages from the Book of Jacob. The dissolute Nephites

> began to grow hard in their hearts and indulge themselves somewhat in wicked practices, such as like unto David of old desiring many wives and concubines, and also Solomon, his son (Jacob 1:15).

In Jacob 2, the Lord speaks even more directly, noting that "David and Solomon truly had many wives and concubines, which thing was abominable before me." "Nephite Men Should Have Only One Wife" the book sternly warns, and God speaks yet again on this subject to his people:

> For there shall not be any man among you save have it be one wife; and concubines he shall have none. For I, the Lord God, delight in the chastity of women and whoredoms are an abomination before me (Jacob 2:27–28).

In the same chapter, the Lord makes the ambiguous statement, "For if I will raise up seed unto me, I will command my people; otherwise they shall hearken unto these things." For decades, Joseph and other apologists for Mormon polygamy claimed they were "raising up seed" to their Lord, his previous strictures notwithstanding. In a famous letter to nineteen-year-old Nancy Rigdon, who repelled his advances, Joseph simply explained that "whatever God requires is right," and he was the one entrusted to interpret God's intentions: "That which is wrong under one circumstance, may be, and often is, right under another."

Joseph had been confiding his thoughts about plural marriage to his most trusted confederates throughout the 1830s. It seems that Joseph was practicing polygamy without benefit of clergy during that time. "Joseph's name was connected with scandalous relations with two or three families," according to his friend Benjamin Winchester. "There was a good deal of scandal prevalent among a number of the Saints concerning Joseph's licentious conduct, this more especially among the women." In 1835, rumors of Mormon polygamy were so intense that the Saints' general assembly issued a statement asserting, "Inasmuch as this church of Christ has been reproached with the crime of fornication, and polygamy; we declare that we believe, that one man should have one wife; and one woman but one husband." The Saints adopted the measure while Joseph was absent on a missionary trip to Michigan.

It is possible that he married his first "celestial wife" in 1838, although his first recorded plural marriage took place in 1841. Joseph shrouded polygamy in great secrecy, for several obvious reasons. Not only was the practice morally shocking and contradicted by passages in both the New Testament and the Book of Mormon, it was also illegal in Illinois. Nonetheless, defectors and apostates were reporting Joseph's scandalous views to the world. "Old Joe's Mormon seraglio" quickly became a stock phrase in the nation's newspapers, despite the Saints' heated denials.

Polygamy was not an idea that occurred to Joseph alone. Utopian ideologue John Humphrey Noyes had been propagandizing free love during the 1830s and introduced a system of "complex marriage" at his upstate New York Oneida colony in 1848. At Oneida, all men and women were married to each other, and exclusive attachments were forbidden. It was Noyes who famously observed that "there is no more reason why sexual intercourse should be restricted by law than why eating and drinking should be." There is no evidence that Noyes and Smith ever met, although it seems likely they would have known about each other from the popular press. Smith *did* meet the notorious Robert Matthews, who claimed to be the reincarnation of the disciple Matthew, returned to earth "to establish a community of property, and of wives." After a short prison stint, Matthews showed up on Joseph's doorstep in Kirtland, Ohio, masquerading as "Joshua the Jewish Minister." After forty-eight hours of intense discussions, Joseph decided that "Joshua's" doctrine "was of the Devil," and he escorted him out of town.

Smith definitely knew about Jacob Cochran's doctrine of spiritual wifery at his Saco, Maine, colony, because the Mormons had tried to convert the Cochranites. Future apostle and polygamist Orson Hyde visited a Cochranite community in 1832 and reported on their "wonderful lustful spirit,

> . . . because they believe in a "plurality of wives" which they call spiritual wives, knowing them not after the flesh but after the spirit, but by the *appearance they know one another after the flesh.*

In 1841, Joseph discussed polygamy with his Apostles, and the doctrine was formally recorded, albeit secretly, in July of 1843. In the revelation, God invoked the names of the Old Testament polygamists, and continued: "Verily I say unto you, my servant Joseph, that whatsoever you give on earth, and to whomsoever you give any one on earth, by my word and according to my law, it shall be visited with blessings." In the next to last verse of the lengthy revelation, God invoked the "law of Sarah," an insidious stricture for women who didn't want to share their husbands. If a wife refused to consent to polygamy, the revelation instructed, the husband no longer needed her assent to take on other wives.

God also included a special message for "mine handmaid Emma," whom he correctly imagined might greet the new doctrine with muted enthusiasm:

> And I command mine handmaid, Emma Smith, to abide and cleave unto my servant Joseph, and to none else. But if she will not abide this commandment she shall be destroyed, saith the Lord; for I am the Lord thy God, and will destroy her if she abide not in my law (Doctrine and Covenants 132:54).

A decade earlier, God had issued a revelation, through Joseph, that Emma should "murmur not because of the things which thou hast not seen, for they are withheld from thee and from the world" (Doctrine and Covenants 25:4).

God might well worry that Emma would "murmur" against polygamy. Joseph's scribe William Clayton wrote down the polygamy revelation sentence by sentence in the Prophet's second-floor office of the redbrick store, while Smith dictated. (The revelation was hardly news to Clayton; Joseph had urged him to marry his first plural wife earlier in the year.) Joseph's brother Hyrum was the only other person in the small room. The men realized that someone would have to show the text to Joseph's wife.

"If you will write the revelation, I will take and read it to Emma," Hyrum assured his brother. "I believe I can convince her of its truth, and you will hereafter have peace."

Hyrum's mission failed utterly. Returning from his audience with Emma at the Mansion, he announced that "I have never received a more severe talking to in my life. Emma is very bitter and full of resentment and anger."

Emma "did not believe a word" of the revelation, Clayton wrote in his diary, noting that she destroyed the text Hyrum had handed her.

Emma hated polygamy all her life, even though there were moments when she reconciled herself to the new theology. For instance, in a gesture that must have tried her soul, she allowed Joseph to marry two pairs of young sisters who lived in the mansion with the Smiths: Emily and Eliza Partridge, and Sarah and Maria Lawrence. Joseph thanked Emma profusely, never informing her that he had in fact married the Partridge sisters two months beforehand, or that he already had sixteen other wives. Right after the marriage ceremony, Emma "was more bitter in her feelings than ever before, if possible," Emily Partridge recounted, "and before the day was over she turned around and repented what she had done." Emma "kept close watch on us," Partridge added. "If we were missing for a few minutes and Joseph was not at home the house was searched from top to bottom and if we were not found the neighborhood was searched until we were found."

Within just a few months, Emma threatened that "blood would flow" if the marriages were not undone, and the sister wives were evicted. Joseph sheepishly arranged for the girls to board elsewhere in Nauvoo. William Clayton reported that Emma was threatening to sue for divorce, an untenable proposition for Joseph. Despite her many humiliations, Emma remained the "Elect Lady" of the Latter-day Saints and was quite popular among the Mormon rank and file. She was a principal player in the brief history of the Mormon Church. Joseph often mentioned that the angel Moroni refused to show him the golden plates until Joseph was married, and that Moroni specified Emma Hale as the desired spouse. Emma was Joseph's first scribe and an early and ardent believer in the plates ("I felt of the plates as they lay on the table," she later told her oldest son) and in the doctrine of the newly restored gospel.

During his nine-month-long jail term in Liberty, Missouri, Joseph and Emma exchanged tender letters. She visited her husband three times, with their children, before being forced to flee Missouri for Illinois. Rather than risk a messy break with his wife of seventeen years, Joseph generally assuaged Emma's public demands and did his best to conduct his private life in private.

In a famous incident, Emma is supposed to have surprised Joseph and another mansion lodger, the raven-haired poetess Eliza Snow, kissing on a second-floor landing. With her children begging her not to harm "Aunt Eliza," Emma grabbed Snow by the hair, then threw her down the stairs and out into the street. Snow was said to have suffered a miscarriage as a result. The tale looms large for the Saints because Snow became the poet laureate of Mormon culture, and a grande dame in the Saints' new Zion of Salt Lake City. A plural widow of Joseph Smith, she married his successor, Brigham Young, and outlived him by a decade. Snow never spoke of the stairway incident, confirming only that she had been the Prophet's wife and lover.

A Gentile visitor from Carthage, while paying a call on Emma, innocently inquired, "Mrs. Smith, where does your church get the doctrine of spiritual wives?"

Emma's face flushed scarlet, the guest reported, and her eyes blazed with fury. "Straight from hell, madam."

꠸ ꠸ ꠸

EMMA SMITH'S HORRIFIED REACTION TO POLYGAMY WAS THE RULE, not the exception, among the devout Saints. Joseph's brother Don Carlos said, "Any man who will teach and practice the doctrine of spiritual wifery will go to hell; I don't care if it is my brother Joseph." Brigham Young, doggedly loyal to Joseph and his teachings, said that learning about plural marriage "was the first time in my life that I desired the grave." Apostle John Taylor called plural marriage "an appalling thing to do. The idea of going and asking a young lady to be married to me when I already had a wife!" (Joseph told Taylor that if polygamy is "not entered into right away, the keys will be turned," meaning Mormons will be denied entry to heaven.) "The subject was very repugnant to my feelings," Eliza Snow wrote upon learning the doctrine. Don Carlos died without experiencing the Saints' full embrace of polygamy. Snow and Young accommodated themselves to the new teaching. By 1846, John Taylor had married thirteen wives.

In the early 1840s, Joseph encouraged the apostles to take additional wives, and the inner circle sometimes engaged in dynastic polygamy, or sealed marriages that seemed primarily political in nature. Joseph married Willard Richards's fifty-eight-year old sister Rhoda,

A rare 1845 daguerreotype of Willard Richards, his first wife
Jennetta, and their son, Heber. Richards married two teenage girls
in 1843, and Jennetta died at age 27, two years later and three months
after this picture was taken. Heber "always maintained that his mother
died of a broken heart," according to biographer Clair Noall.
Credit: Daughters of Utah Pioneers

and soon afterward married Brigham Young's fifty-six-year old sister Fanny. He urged Richards to marry two teenage girls in 1843. Richards's first wife, Jennetta, died just two years later, "of a broken heart," according to her son Heber.

Most polygamous marriages were for "time and eternity," signifying that the man and the woman might have sexual relations on earth ("time") but also be joined in a larger family at the end of time ("eternity"). The larger the family that gathered to greet the Second Coming, Joseph taught, the greater the heavenly exaltation for all concerned. It is probable that Joseph married Rhoda Richards and Fanny Young for dynastic reasons, for "eternity" only. After Joseph's death, Brigham Young married many of the Prophet's widows, including Brigham's first cousin Rhoda Richards, partly to ensure that the two massive clans would be together for all time.

Smith eventually married dozens of wives, including five pairs of sisters and two pairs of mothers and daughters, of whom fourteen were already married.* He introduced thirty-three of his followers to plural marriage. By the time of his death, there were 124 plural wives living in Nauvoo. At times, his invocation of the new rite seemed quite casual. One day Joseph was chatting about celestial marriage with Brigham and the unmarried Fanny Young. Fanny ventured the opinion that she planned to be alone in heaven. "I shall request the privilege of being a ministering angel," she told the men. "That is the labor that I wish to perform. I don't want any companion in that world."

"Sister, you talk very foolishly," Joseph upbraided her. "You do not know what you will want." He turned to Brigham. "Here, Brother Brigham, you seal this lady to me."

They were married on the spot.

The Prophet's relation with the Sessions family illustrates the claustrophobic nature of Nauvoo polygamy. In 1838, Joseph officiated at the wedding of nineteen-year-old Sylvia Sessions to Windsor Lyon. Four

---

*Scholars disagree on the number of wives Joseph had. Todd Compton estimates thirty-three; George D. Smith says thirty-eight; Fawn Brodie lists forty-eight; D. Michael Quinn counts forty-six.

years later, Joseph married Sylvia himself. A few weeks after that, he married Sylvia's mother, Patty Bartlett Sessions.

Smith didn't limit himself to asking his closest friends if he could marry their sisters. He also wooed their own wives and daughters. One day in 1841, after Apostle Heber Kimball had returned from a proselytizing mission to England, Joseph approached him and said God had commanded him to marry Heber's wife, Vilate. "He was dumbfounded," his grandson Orson Whitney said. Kimball didn't eat, drink, or sleep for three days, and prayed continually.

Finally, Heber and Vilate walked over to meet Joseph in a private room at the Nauvoo Mansion. "Brother Joseph, here is Vilate," Kimball said.

Smith "wept like a child" and proceeded to seal, or marry, Heber and Vilate to each other "for time and all eternity." "Brother Heber, take her and the Lord will give you a hundredfold."

It was a test of love and faith, Joseph explained. He had never wanted to marry Vilate after all. Smith called this the "Abrahamic test." He acted out almost the same scenario with his friend, the Apostle John Taylor.

But he did want to marry the Kimballs' fourteen-year-old daughter.

By 1843, Joseph had won both Vilate and Heber over to the doctrine of plural marriage. At the Prophet's urging, Heber had married a young woman named Sarah Noon, whose husband had deserted her. After considerable praying, Vilate grudgingly accommodated herself to the union. "Her heartstrings were already stretched until they were ready to snap asunder," her daughter Helen later wrote. Then Joseph asked the couple for their only daughter's hand in marriage.

Speaking with his daughter in their home, Kimball, a pillar of the church, broached the subject of polygamy delicately. Would you believe me, he said, if I told you it was right for married men to take other wives?

I would not! exclaimed Helen, who had never shown anger to her father before.

Heber stunned his daughter by telling her that her close friend, Sarah Ann Whitney, had already joined Joseph in celestial marriage. Helen was close to the Whitneys; in fact, she was infatuated with Sarah's brother, Horace, and hoped to marry him. Heber insisted that she bow to Joseph's will. "If you will take this step, it will ensure you eternal salvation and exaltation and that of your father's household and all your kindred," Heber explained to her.

In her autobiography, Helen hinted that she contemplated fleeing, or something worse; "I will pass over the temptations which I had during the twenty four hours after my father introduced me to the principle."

The family again presented themselves to the Prophet. "None but God and the angels could see my mother's bleeding heart," Helen wrote, when Joseph asked if Vilate would agree to the union.

"If Helen is willing I have nothing more to say," Vilate replied. "In her mind, she saw the misery which was so sure to come," Helen recalled. "But it was all hidden from me." Joseph married her in the upper room of his redbrick store, on a cold rainy Sunday, May 28, 1843.

Helen Mar Kimball was a devoutly religious, unworldly young girl raised in the insular Mormon culture. Apparently no one had prepared her for what Joseph would do to her when they were alone. She was three months shy of fifteen years old; young, but of marriageable age. (Nauvoo required a girl to be fourteen years old to marry. Statewide, the age of consent was ten.) "I would never have been sealed to Joseph, had I known it was anything more than a ceremony," Helen later told her mother. "I was young and they deceived me, by saying the salvation of our whole family depended on it."

People change. Forty years later, with the US government waging a full-scale war against Mormon polygamy in Utah, Helen Mar Kimball Whitney—she did marry her childhood sweetheart, though "for time only"—published an eighty-page brochure-apologia, "Why We Practice Plural Marriage," refuting "those who make our religious faith a pretext for stirring up the public mind against us."

An adventure not unlike the Kimballs' befell Apostle Orson Pratt. After her husband returned from a mission trip to England, Sarah Pratt complained that Joseph Smith had tried to seduce her. Sarah said she rebuffed Smith. As he often did when confronted by female accusers, Joseph smeared her, publicly accusing her of adultery with another man. He went so far as to suggest that Pratt "marry a virtuous woman—and sire a new family." Orson Pratt fled his home and temporarily lost his mind. Brigham Young spent several days with his disturbed colleague, "whose mind became so darkened by the influence and statements of his wife, that he came out in rebellion against Joseph, refusing to believe his testimony or obey his council."

The Quorum of the Twelve excommunicated both Pratts, although within a few weeks they reconciled with Joseph and rejoined the Saints. Orson "repented in dust and ashes." Sarah's return proved to be temporary. She later divorced Orson and helped found Salt Lake City's Anti-Polygamy Society. She evinced nothing but contempt for her "gray headed" husband, "taking to his bed young girls in mockery of marriage. Of course there could be no joy for him in such an intercourse except for the indulgence of his fanaticism and of something else, perhaps, which I hesitate to mention."

Then Joseph tried to seduce the wife of his second counselor, William Law.

Ɪ Ɪ Ɪ

WILLIAM LAW WAS A DISTINCT AND POWERFUL PRESENCE IN Nauvoo. Unlike most of the faithful, he had not suffered persecution in Missouri with Joseph, nor had he freshly arrived from England. Neither was he poor, and dependent on the charity of Joseph or the Saints' tithings to bankroll his arrival in Illinois.

Law was a tall, blue-eyed, charismatic Irishman who had made a considerable fortune operating a lumber mill in Ontario, Canada. At age twenty-four, he married the nineteen-year-old Jane Silverthorn, who inherited a substantial estate from her father. Law was the president of the Mormon stake in Churchville, Ontario, and migrated south at Joseph Smith's suggestion. During a missionary visit to nearby Toronto, Joseph worried that political unrest might affect his flock and suggested that Canada's Saints gather south of the border. (Apparently, Joseph was unaware that Law was a MacKenzieite, a follower of William Lyon MacKenzie, the leader of an ineffectual armed rising against Canada's British sovereigns.) By coincidence, Joseph happened upon William Law's small caravan of seven wagons while they were emigrating from Ontario to Nauvoo in 1839. Smith, accompanied by Porter Rockwell and Dr. Robert Foster, was heading to Washington, DC, to demand reparations for the Saints' Missouri expropriations from President Martin Van Buren.

Law, who had trained as a doctor, arrived in Nauvoo with $30,000, which Joseph urged him to invest in the city. "You must not be a doctor here, let some Gentiles come and do that," Smith counseled him. "Buy lands, build mills, and keep a store to keep you running."

William and his brother Wilson did just that. They opened a steam-powered flour mill and a lumber mill on Sydney Street, where the Mississippi lapped against the southern edge of the new town. They bankrolled a general store, which competed with Joseph's red-brick store right across Water Street, and they purchased a dozen full-sized building lots on the slopes of the hill where the Nauvoo Temple was slowly taking form. They also operated a brickyard, and owned 580 acres of farmland on the prairie east of the city. The Laws were devout and energetic members of the Nauvoo community. "No man could be better fitted to his station," a newspaper reported, calling Law "wise, discreet, just, prudent—a man of great suavity of manner and amiability of character." The paper likewise praised Law's "correct business habits" and "great devotion to God." When Joseph's father died in 1841, Smith appointed his brother Hyrum to the vacant office of church patriarch, and by revelation assigned Hyrum's job as counselor in the First Presidency to William Law. According to a special revelation, Law had been granted the power to heal the sick and cast out devils.

Wilson Law also became a member of Nauvoo's ruling inner circle. Wilson was commissioned a brigadier general in the Nauvoo Legion and served as president of the City Council. When the Missouri sheriffs kidnapped Joseph in Dixon's Ferry, the Law brothers led a flying squad of sixty mounted Nauvoo Legionnaires that galloped northward to rescue the Prophet. When Joseph first caught sight of his rescuers, "I walked out several rods to meet the company," he said. "William and Wilson Law jumped from their horses, and unitedly hugged and kissed me, when many tears of joy were shed." Two streets in Nauvoo were named after the brothers: Wilson Street and Law Street.

Writing to a faith-challenged Mormon friend who refused to follow Joseph Smith to Nauvoo, William Law called the Prophet "a honest upright man . . . I have carefully watched his movements since I have been here,"

> And I assure you I have found him honest and honourable in all our transactions which have been very considerable . . . as to his follies let who ever is guiltless throw the first stone at him, I shan't do it.

When a court in the state capital of Springfield, Illinois, allowed Joseph to elude yet another arrest warrant from Missouri, Wilson Law hailed the event with a devotional poem in Nauvoo's official *Times and Seasons* newspaper:

> All hail to our Chief! Who has come back with honor—
> With glory's bright halo encircling around;
> From the highest tribunal in this great republic,
> Where falsehood and slander caused him to be bound.

William Law first caught wind of the plural marriage doctrine in early 1843. He reacted strongly: "If an angel from heaven was to reveal to me that a man should have more than one wife, if it were in my power I would kill him." In Joseph's inner circle, only two men refused to accept the new teaching, Law and William Marks, the stake president, or nominal religious leader of Nauvoo. Joseph recognized Law's power, and sent his brother Hyrum to the Laws' home with a copy of the polygamy revelation. It "paralizes the nerves, chills the currents of the heart, and drives the brain almost to madness," Law confided to his diary.

Law told his wife, Jane, that he would take the matter up with the Prophet, who would surely renounce this adulterous blasphemy. Don't count on it, Jane predicted, as she had every reason to know. Joseph had already attempted to seduce her, and when her accusation later became public, he denounced her as a whore.

Why would Joseph try to seduce the wife of the powerful, independent-minded Law? Most likely, he lusted after the beautiful Jane Law, and intended to exercise his droit du seigneur. Smith's loyal secretary William Clayton offered a different explanation. Clayton reported that a restive Emma was agitating for a plural *husband* in 1843, in exchange for her continued silence on polygamy. Supposedly, Emma desired William Law as her consecrated lover, thus Joseph Smith was in effect proposing a wife swap. Another dubious story that circulated in official church circles held that Joseph refused to seal William and Jane Law for eternity because William was an adulterer. Thus it was *Jane* who seduced Joseph on her own behalf, seeking a companion to greet the Second Coming. William Law's son Thomas later opined that Joseph wouldn't have had the gumption to make advances to his mother. "In such a case, my father would not have started a paper against him," Thomas told an interviewer. "He would have shot his head off."

In his dairy, Law noted that Joseph "had lately endeavored to seduce my wife, and had found her a virtuous woman."

When William Law confronted Joseph with a copy of the polygamy revelation, it turned out that Jane had guessed right. Joseph stood by the new doctrine.

"Yes, that is a genuine revelation," the Prophet said, at what was to be the two men's final encounter in January 1844.

"But in the Book of Doctrine and Covenants there is a revelation just the contrary of this," Law replied.

"Oh, that was given when the church was in its infancy," Joseph explained. "Then it was all right to feed the people on milk, but now it is necessary to give them strong meat."

Law's son Richard claims that his father threw his arms around Joseph's neck, begging him to recant the new theology. "My father

pleaded for this with Joseph with tears streaming from his eyes. The Prophet was also in tears, but he informed [William] that he could not withdraw the doctrine, for God had commanded him to teach it, and condemnation would come upon him if he was not obedient to the commandment.

When Law returned home to describe this encounter to Jane, she said: "That was what I fully expected." She then suggested that her husband sell his substantial property and business holdings and flee Nauvoo. But Law had decided that he wanted to stay and fight. "I wanted to tread upon the viper," he said.

He was not alone.

॒ ॒ ॒

POLYGAMY WAS RAPIDLY BECOMING THE WORST-KEPT SECRET IN Nauvoo.* The young Gentile Charlotte Haven reported on a mission-

---

* For decades, some Mormon apologists denied polygamy's existence, arguing: why were there no children born of plural marriage? In 1880, Elder Ebenezer Robinson quoted Hyrum Smith as saying that if a plural wife "should have an offspring, give out word that she had a husband who had gone on a foreign mission." Robinson further recollected that "there was a place, a few miles out of Nauvoo, in Illinois, where females were sent" to bear children away from the scrutiny of their friends and neighbors. In 1905, Mary Rollins told a Salt Lake City audience that three of Joseph's children reached adulthood, their identities concealed by "different names."

ary who returned from England with a wife and child, "and I am told that his first wife is reconciled to this certainly at first unwelcome guest to her home, for her husband and some others have reasoned with her that plurality of wives is taught in the Bible." "Poor, weak woman!" Haven concluded; "I cannot believe that Joseph will ever sanction such a doctrine, and should the Mormons in any way engraft such an article on the religion, the sect would surely fall to pieces, for what community or State could harbor such outrageous immorality?"

Opponents of polygamy began to seek each other out. Like William Law, Dr. Robert Foster was also developing real estate in Nauvoo. Foster was a licensed physician from Northampton County, England. Also like Law, he was a longtime Joseph Smith loyalist who held positions of authority in Nauvoo. He was the surgeon general of the Nauvoo Legion, and regent designate of the factitious University of Nauvoo. Joseph had chosen Foster to be toastmaster for the dedication of the Prophet's seventeen-room Nauvoo Mansion in the fall of 1843. "Whether we view Joseph as a prophet, a general, a mayor, or chairman of the City Council," Foster proclaimed, "if he has equals, he has no superiors."

Foster and Law were buying lumber shipped down the Mississippi from Mormon-controlled woodlots in Wisconsin and building homes for sale. Joseph objected to the lumber being used to enrich Law and Foster. He felt the building materials should properly go to the Temple construction project, and to his contemplated Nauvoo House, a hotel-headquarters to replace the Nauvoo Mansion. In 1841, Joseph received a revelation that chastised Law and Foster by name and urged them to become stockholders in the Nauvoo House, "a delightful habitation for man, and a resting-place for the weary traveler." It especially galled Smith that Foster had constructed the new Mammoth Hotel on the high ground, stealing a march on the contemplated Nauvoo House. At an 1843 gathering, he lashed out at "Dr. Foster's mammoth skeleton, monuments of Dr. Foster rising all over town . . .

Does that coat fit you, Dr. Foster? Pretty well! Put it on then. This is the way people swell like the ox or the toad.

Siting the hotel on the plateau behind the future temple site was a jab at Joseph. The Law brothers owned vast tracts of farmland near the temple, and many building lots on the high ground. On behalf of the church, Joseph owned many unsold lots on the "flat," which had only recently been drained, and was still hot and insect infested. Joseph needed to sell his downtown lots to stay current on payments to the men who sold him the city back in 1839. "The upper part of the two has no right to rival those on the river," Smith said. "We have been the making of the upper part of the town; we began here first." But Foster and Law pursued their business ventures, and they had no problem wooing workers to their projects. They paid wages in gold, silver, or convertible cash. Joseph liked to settle all his debts in scrip—often coupons redeemable at his general store—or in IOUs that had become a de facto, albeit devalued, currency in Nauvoo.

Smith was competing with the Law brothers and with Robert Foster. But their differences were not limited to the marketplace. While Law was struggling with Joseph over polygamy, Foster arrived home one evening to find the Prophet dining, à deux, with Foster's wife, Sarah. After Smith left, the hot-tempered doctor drew a pistol and threatened to shoot Sarah if she didn't explain Smith's visit. She held her peace, so Foster grabbed a second pistol, thrust it into her hand, and yelled, "If you don't tell me, either you or I will shoot!" Sarah fainted.

When the vapors parted, Sarah admitted that Smith had been explaining his "spiritual wife" doctrine to her and had tried to seduce her. Around the same time, according to Smith's diary, Foster confronted Willard Richards with a similar accusation:

> "You," shaking his fists in his face, "are another Damned black hearted villain. You tried to seduce my wife on the boat when she was going to New York and I can prove it. And the oath is out against you."

Smith ordered Foster to stand trial, then thought better of it when he learned that the doctor planned to call forty witnesses and mount an aggressive defense. Nonetheless, Smith waged a vigorous smear campaign against Foster in the church newspaper, the *Times and Seasons*. "I have seen him steal a number of times," Joseph said in an affidavit reprinted in the paper. "When riding in the stage, I have seen him put his hand in a woman's bosom, and he also lifted up her clothes. I know that [the Foster brothers] are wicked, malicious, adulterous, bad characters; I say it under oath; I can tell all the particulars from first to last."

Indeed, Foster's brother Charles was also on Smith's blacklist. The Prophet publicly accused him of writing a letter to the *New York Tribune*, alleging impropriety in the temple's finances. Not long after, Robert Foster pulled a pistol on Smith, saying he "would be God damned if he didn't shoot the Mayor."

The Fosters and the Laws found plenty of allies in their opposition to Joseph. Attorney Francis Higbee had sued Smith, unsuccessfully, for his attempted seduction of Nancy Rigdon. Higbee himself had been courting the young woman. Smith held nothing back when it came to smearing Francis Higbee's reputation. Characteristically, Smith also hurled mud at Rigdon, whom he indeed had tried to seduce. One of his apostles called Sidney Rigdon's young daughter "notorious in this city . . . regarded, generally, little, if any better, than a public prostitute." The *Times and Seasons* newspaper censored part of Joseph's testimony about the Higbee brothers, "which is too indelicate for the public eye or ear . . . so revolting, corrupt, and disgusting has been the conduct of most of this clique, that we feel to dread having any thing to do with the publication of their trials." Having washed its hands, so to speak, the newspaper did report—twice— that Francis Higbee "had got a bad disorder with the French Girl," an itinerant, unnamed prostitute.

Higbee's brother Chauncey had been severed from the church for conduct remarkably akin to Joseph Smith's. When three women told the High Council that Chauncey had seduced them, he invoked the

101

polygamy defense. "It was right to have free intercourse with women if it was kept secret," Higbee said. "Joseph Smith authorized him to practice these things." The campaign against the Higbees mesmerized the Saints, because their father, Elias Higbee, had been a High Council member and a close friend of Joseph Smith. That didn't prevent the Mormon hierarchy from launching an extraordinary tirade against Chauncey Higbee, accusing him of the "unspeakable crime" of sodomy. William Smith, Hyrum Smith, and Brigham Young at different times charged Chauncey with "leading young men into difficulty," at the behest of John C. Bennett, a former first counselor of the church, turned rabid apostate.

Two years after taking his first plural wife, Joseph was actively prosecuting polygamists in the Nauvoo courts. In the ecclesiastical High Council, Joseph accused Harrison Sagers of seducing his sister-in-law, Phoebe Madison, and of "using my name in a blasphemous manner, by saying that I tolerated such things." This was merely a show trial, as the pseudonymous reporter for the Warsaw *Signal* correctly reported. "Had the accused been dealt with according to his crime," wrote "The Traveler," "he would have been divested of his office and cut off from the church. . . . Instead the said Sagers was *discharged* by the Prophet." A month later, Joseph allowed Sagers to marry Phoebe, and three other wives besides.

Smith's hypocrisy concerning polygamy was breathtaking. Immediately before marrying Fanny Young, he wrote in his journal that he had "walked up and down the streets with my scribe.

> Gave instructions to try those persons who were preaching, teaching, or practicing the doctrine of plurality of wives. . . . I have constantly said no man shall have but one wife at a time, unless the Lord directs otherwise.

Just a few months later, the *Times and Seasons* announced that yet another rank-and-file Saint had been tried for polygamy:

NOTICE.

As we have lately been credibly informed, that an Elder of the Church of Jesus Christ, of Latter-day Saints, by the name of Hyram Brown, has been preaching polygamy, and other false and corrupt doctrines, in the county of Lapeer, state of Michigan.

This is to notify him and the Church in general, that he has been cut off from the church, for his iniquity; and he is further notified to appear at the Special Conference, on the 6th of April next, to make answer to these charges.

JOSEPH SMITH.

HYRUM SMITH.

In April 1844, Smith arranged for Robert Foster, William and Wilson Law, and Jane Law to be excommunicated from the church, with the Higbees soon to follow. Law told Joseph that he couldn't be excommunicated in absentia, according to church law, because he had been appointed to the First Presidency by divine revelation. His plea fell on deaf ears. But Joseph's enemies—"one or two disaffected individuals," Smith called them—were more powerful than he realized. Just a few days after his excommunication, William Law organized the True Church of Latter-day Saints, which began meeting at his house. By early May, their meetings were attracting three hundred worshippers and had to be held outdoors. Law insisted that he remained faithful to original Mormon teachings and refused to call himself a prophet. Joseph had once had the ear of the Lord, Law proclaimed, but now he had fallen.

Nauvoo was a company town, and Joseph had little trouble infiltrating the dissidents' ranks. He inserted two young men, Robert Scott and Dennison Harris, into the meetings of the True Church. Before the third meeting, held at William Law's newly built brick house a block away from the riverbank, Joseph warned the pair that they might be in jeopardy. "Be sure that you make no covenant, nor enter into any obligations whatever with them," he said. This proved to be timely advice.

At this gathering, attended by two hundred men and three mysterious, veiled women who claimed that Joseph and Hyrum Smith had tried to seduce them, Francis Higbee decided to administer a loyalty oath to would-be opponents of Joseph's church: "Do you solemnly swear, before God and all holy angels, that you will give your life, liberty, your influence, your all, for the destruction of Joseph Smith and his party, so help you God?"

The two boys "resolutely and manfully refused" to take the oath, Harris later recounted to a friend, "stating that Joseph Smith had done them no harm and they were too young to understand these things." The dissenters, "these fiends of the bottomless pit," supposedly threatened to kill the boys, then reconsidered when they realized the ensuing investigation would inevitably expose the plotters. Joseph received a full account; "To the Prophet these two boys told their harrowing story."

Law had his own undercover agents. "I kept a detective or two among those who were in the confidence of the Smiths," he told an interviewer. Law's detectives apparently told him of Joseph's occasional plans to "put him aside," or "use him up"—that is, kill him—using poison or violence.

Joseph's emboldened detractors were suddenly attacking on all fronts. Wilson Law and Francis Higbee collaborated on two vitriolic poetic satires, "Buckeye's Lamentation for Want of More Wives," and "The Buckeye's First Epistle to Jo," the latter gleefully published in Thomas Sharp's Warsaw *Signal* on April 25, 1844. (Higbee was born in Ohio, hence "Buckeye.") The "Lamentation" announced the less-than-shocking news that Joseph and the apostles had been taking plural wives, in a style indebted to Alexander Pope:

> But Joe at snaring beats them all,
> And at the rest does laugh;
> For widows poor, and orphan girls,
> He can ensnare with chaff,
> He sets his snares around for all,

—And very seldom fails
To catch some thoughtless *Partridges*,
Snow-birds or *Knight*-ingales!

The poem none-too-subtly referred to Joseph's wives Emily and Eliza Partridge, Eliza Snow, and to Martha Knight, the Prophet's seventeenth wife.

Attacks of a very different kind quickly followed. In late May 1844, William and Wilson Law charged Joseph with adultery in the Hancock County court at Carthage. They accused the Prophet of living "in an open state of adultery" with Maria Lawrence, between October 1843 and May 1844. William Law not only accused Joseph of fornicating with the young girl, but he also suspected the Prophet had misappropriated the young girl's substantial, $7,750 inheritance, for which Law was a co-guarantor.

The Laws filed their claim in Carthage to sidestep Nauvoo's hermetic judicial system. At the same time, William Law sent $2,000 to a publisher in Quincy, Illinois, to purchase a "5 d press with a 25" x 38" platen," and printing supplies. The Laws and their confederates were going into the newspaper business.

Nauvoo Temple

PART TWO

"Oh! Illinois! thy soil has drank the blood /
Of Prophets martyr'd for the truth of God."

6

"THE PERVERSION
OF SACRED THINGS"

This day the Nauvoo Expositor goes forth to the world,
rich with facts, such expositions as make the guilty
tremble and rage. . . .

—*William Law's diary, Friday, June 7, 1844*

I N THIS HIGH-STAKES POKER GAME, NONE OF THE PLAYERS WERE
bothering to hide their hands. Not only had the Fosters and Laws
filed separate complaints, one for adultery and the other for "false
swearing," against Joseph in state court at Carthage, they also announced their plans to publish a new, independent newspaper outside
the ambit of Smith's benevolent dictatorship. The city's two existing
newspapers, the *Nauvoo Neighbor* and the *Times and Seasons*, were
organs of the ruling theocracy, both edited by Apostle John Taylor.
The new entrant would be something else entirely. "The paper I think
we will call the Nauvoo Expositor," dissident Francis Higbee explained
to the newspaper editor, Thomas Gregg,

for it will be fraught with Joe's peculiar and particular mode of Legislation; and a dissertation upon his *delectable* plan of Government; and above all, it shall be the organ through which we will herald his *Mormon* ribaldry. It shall also contain a full and complete exposé of his *Mormon seraglio*, or *Nauvoo Harem*, and his unparalleled and unheard of attempts of seduction.

The editorial team assembling the *Expositor* inside the Laws' printing office on Mulholland Street, just a few hundred feet from the Nauvoo Temple site, was a motley crew. William Law supplied the capital. He, the Higbees, and the Fosters supplied the vitriol. The nominal editor, the Gentile lawyer Sylvester Emmons, later admitted that "none of us knew anything about journalism. I had written a few letters that were published in the New York *Herald*, so in organizing the forces, I was elected as editor." Emmons claimed to be a member of a Nauvoo clique, "a Gentile club, smarting under grievances unendurable, [that] sympathized with the seceders." Publishing the *Expositor* was "a hazardous enterprise," he judiciously noted, "and the result might have been seen, if the seceders had exercised a fair share of caution."

But theirs was not a cautious enterprise. A couple of weeks before their first issue, the *Expositor*'s owners distributed a flyer detailing what exactly they intended to expose. Nominally devoted to "the general diffusion of useful knowledge," the newspaper's prospectus struck directly at the heart of Nauvoo's one-man rule. The Laws and their colleagues demanded the repeal of the Nauvoo Charter, which arrogated so many powers to the man they now regarded as a fallen prophet. They vowed to print the "FACTS AS THEY REALLY EXIST IN THE CITY OF NAUVOO *fearless of whose particular case the facts may apply*." The dissidents also advocated "unmitigated DISOBEDIENCE TO POLITICAL REVELATION" made by the city's "SELF-CONSTITUTED MONARCH."

Smith had faced worse, much worse, in the pages of far more august newspapers than a putative journal edited by a tiny claque of disaffected Saints. The paper's prospectus didn't overtly mention polygamy, although its promise to censure "gross moral imperfections" hinted at things to come. Joseph could still allow himself to hope that the prurient details of his inner circle's plural marriages would remain secret. But the allusion to a "self-constituted monarch" gave pause. Was it possible that the Laws and Fosters planned to expose the Council of Fifty, whose members had been sworn to strictest secrecy? How would the world react to discovering that a presidential candidate had appointed himself "King of the Kingdom of God and His Laws with the Keys and powers thereof"?

Even without seeing the paper, Joseph sued for peace. He sent his trusted aide Dimick Huntington to treat with Robert Foster. But the refractory doctor sent Huntington packing, with a fiery response to Smith: "You have trampled upon everything we held dear and sacred . . . we set hell at defiance, and all her agents." Uncowed, Joseph then dispatched his first counselor, Sidney Rigdon, to William Law's house, offering terms: If the Laws and the Fosters would stand down, the Council of Fifty would reinstate them into the church and restore their ecclesiastical status. William Law would be second counselor, number three in the hierarchy again, and his wife could also rejoin the Saints. Law offered a counterproposal. We won't publish our paper, he said, if Joseph would publicly apologize for teaching and practicing "the doctrine of the plurality of wives." Law also wanted Joseph to acknowledge that the whole polygamy scheme was "from Hell."

That was not a deal Rigdon could make. Soon afterward, the first thousand copies of the *Expositor* rolled off the printing press.

Editor Emmons was away from Nauvoo on publication day, June 6, 1844; he had business in Springfield. He later claimed that "I had prepared some manuscript—a salutatory and some other articles—in which the case was drawn rather mild." The paper that hit the streets in his absence contained considerably more ginger. "During my absence," Emmons said, "Charley Foster and some others took the privilege of inserting articles that reflected rather severely upon the character and Christian conduct of the prophet. . . . Charges of a heinous nature were

NAUVOO EXPOSITOR.

—THE TRUTH, THE WHOLE TRUTH, AND NOTHING BUT THE TRUTH.—

VOL. I.]   NAUVOO, ILLINOIS, FRIDAY, JUNE 7, 1844.   [NO. 1.

But here his musings were interrupted by the clatter of horses' hoofs, approaching at a swift pace behind him, and the next moment a horseman, muffled in a large cloak, reined up his steed, with a powerful jerk, at his side. They rode on for some distance in silence, until Henry, for that was our hero's name, addressed him with—

"A fine evening, sir!"

ing into the bower, clasped her to his breast. The blush which overspread her face at being thus caught, was dispelled by the joy of beholding him in whom her earthly happiness was centred.

"Now, I declare," said Adeline, playfully tapping his shoulder, "that you have become quite a truant! I have not seen you for more than a

ses to her; so I up un told um that as how I b'lieved so, and that there was a weddin up there this morning. Lord love you, sir, he look'd the colour o' old white Peggy there, till I thought the mon war gone crazy; but he starts off all at once towards yer honer's house; so I thought, maybe, he was an old friend, and war in order 'cause ye——— didn't ax him to the wed-

—we forget! and when at last we rise with exhausted strength from th sick-bed, our souls often awake as ou of a long night into a new morning.— So many things, during the illness the body, conspire to soften the feel ings; the still room; the mild twiligh through the window curtains; the lo voices; and then, more than kind words of those who surround us

The front page masthead of the first and only issue of the *Nauvoo Expositor*

preferred against him, and to have such charges published was a fearful ordeal for him."

The four-page, six-column broadsheet bore the trappings of any midcentury, small-town American newspaper. The front page featured a simple poem ("The Last Man"), and a short, sentimental story. The *Expositor* had a wedding announcement, a few humorous snippets, and ads—one for a penmanship course, another placed by the Law brothers themselves, offering to mill grain "toll free" for Saints too poor to pay their fees. (This was quite politic of them, given that Joseph had publicly denounced their real estate profiteering.) The paper reprinted brief overseas dispatches from Russia and the "papal dominions," as well as an account of Philadelphia's anti-Catholic riots.

A woman named Lucinda Sagers placed this notice:

WHEREAS my husband, the Rt. Rev. W. H. Harrison Sagers, Esq., has left my bed and board without cause or provocation, this is to notify the public not to harbor or trust him on my account, as I will pay no debts of his contracting. More anon.

This questionable character was the aforementioned Harrison Sagers, whom Joseph had allowed to secretly marry his young sister-in-law, Phoebe Madison.

But no one bought the *Expositor* for its account of Jewish persecutions in Saint Petersburg, or its article about nativist riots back East. The Laws and the Fosters appreciated the ferocious power of a well-edited newspaper, and they devoted most of the column space to attacking Joseph Smith and his comrades.

To do that, they needed to lay a little groundwork. First and foremost, the editors insisted that they were faithful Mormons: "We all verily believe, and many of us know of a surety, that the religion of the Latter Day Saints, as original taught by Joseph Smith . . . is verily true, and that the pure principles set forth in those books, are the immutable and eternal principles of Heaven." One hears an echo of the Declaration of Independence in their claim to be "striking this blow at tyranny and oppression . . . though our lives be the forfeiture."

The editors' first concern was polygamy, "the perversion of sacred things." By way of condemning "the vicious principles of Joseph Smith, and those who practice the same abominations and whoredoms," the dissidents printed a long, baroque, fictionalized account of the attempted seduction of an unnamed young immigrant girl from England. The innocent girl arrives in Nauvoo, where Joseph's panders promptly pounce on her. They inform her that "God has great mysteries in store for those who love the lord, and cling to brother Joseph." Next, the girl is

> requested to meet brother Joseph, or some of the Twelve, at some insulated point . . . or at some room, which bears upon its front—Positively NO Admittance. The harmless, inoffensive and unsuspecting creatures are so devoted to the Prophet and the cause of Jesus Christ that they do not dream of the deep laid and fatal scheme which prostrates happiness, and renders death itself desirable.

What follows is predetermined; the girl learns that "she should be his (Joseph's) Spiritual wife; for it was right anciently, and God will tolerate it again." There is the hint that Joseph has impregnated the girl,

113

who is "sent away for a time, until all is well." She returns, "as from a long visit." Her spirit has broken, "but no one knows the cause, except the foul fiend who perpetrated the diabolical deed."

Many of the paper's readers would have recognized the actual story of Martha Brotherton, an English girl who said she had been targeted for seduction by the Prophets' outriders. The real-life Brotherton was an eighteen-year-old from Manchester, England, who arrived in Nauvoo with her parents and siblings. In a letter widely reprinted during the summer of 1842, she described her attempted seduction almost exactly as the *Expositor* had it: Two apostles, Brigham Young and Heber Kimball, began making cryptic comments to her, for example, "Sister Martha, are you willing to do all that the Prophet requires you to do?" Would she like to learn "the mysteries of the kingdom"? And so on. They then led her to the second floor of Joseph's famous red-brick store, to a locked room marked "Positively no admittance." Soon the Prophet entered the room. Suddenly, Smith and Kimball walked out, leaving her alone with Young. According to Brotherton's account, Young stood up, locked the door, slid the second-story window shut and drew the curtain across it. Swearing her to secrecy, Young made his pass. "Have not you an affection for me," he inquired, "that, were it lawful and right, you could accept of me for your husband and companion?" Brotherton resisted, and Young explained the new order of marriage: "Brother Joseph has had a revelation from God that it is lawful and right for a man to have two wives; for as it was in the days of Abraham, so it shall be in these last days."

Martha was still unconvinced, so Young kissed her and left the room. He pocketed the key, and promised to return with Joseph, who would explain the new doctrine. A few minutes later Joseph came in, and assured Brotherton, as he assured so many other young women, that Young's proposal was "lawful and right before God." Brotherton continued to resist. She pleaded for time to think, which the men granted her, provided "you will never mention it to anyone." "I do promise it," she replied, although that is a promise that she did not keep. Her story, gleefully exploited by anti-Mormons in Illinois and Missouri, appeared in at least four regional newspapers, including the St. Louis *Bulletin*. She and her parents fled Nauvoo. Her brother and two sisters, who remained faithful to the church, swore an affidavit denouncing Martha as "a willful inventor of lies."

Brigham Young finally had his way with the attractive young girl from Manchester. Six years after her death, Young sealed himself to her for eternity in a proxy marriage in 1870. Martha's sister Elizabeth, a plural wife of the apostle Parley Pratt, stood in for the deceased.

Another life story, this one without the thin veil of fiction, also appeared in the maiden issue of the *Expositor*. The Laws' fellow dissident and former church first counselor Austin Cowles signed an affidavit declaring the doctrine of plural wifery to be heretical. Cowles explained that Hyrum Smith read the polygamy revelation to the Nauvoo High Council in 1843, and that Cowles resigned immediately afterward. Cowles didn't explain that Joseph had taken his daughter Elvira as a plural wife while the girl was living in the Smith household. In the Byzantine kinship calculus of Joseph Smith's Nauvoo, Cowles was rebelling against his own son-in-law.

The *Expositor* editors also assailed Joseph's temporal ambitions, citing his "attempt at Political power and influence, which we verily believe to be preposterous and absurd . . . WE do not believe that God ever raised up a prophet to christianize a world by political schemes and intrigue." They especially mocked his ongoing presidential campaign as a "flourish of Quixotial chivalry, to take, by storm, the presidential chair." They also spread rumors of Smith's financial skullduggery, which had been reported as far away as New York. They accused him of selling "property at most exorbitant prices" and of "humbug practiced upon the saints by Joseph and others . . . to gull the saints the better on their arrival at Nauvoo, by buying the lands in the vicinity and selling again to them at tenfold advance." The astute reader knew that the Law brothers were in the property business themselves, competing with Smith and the church.

Finally, they accused Smith of blasphemy and "false doctrine." How could the Prophet blaspheme? By contending "that there are innumerable gods as much above the God that presides over this universe, as he is above us;

> And if he varies from the law unto which he is subjected, he, with all his creatures, will be cast down as was Lucifer: thus holding forth a doctrine which is effectually calculated to sap the very foundation of our faith. . . .

Here the dissidents were calling out Joseph's startling new theology unveiled in the King Follett sermon, his contention that God was once a man who lived on earth, and advanced spiritually under the tutelage of a preceding god. This was indeed blasphemy against the established Christian church, but could a prophet guided by heavenly revelation blaspheme his own theology? Joseph had already rewritten both the Old and New Testaments and created holy rituals, all of them inspired by his direct communications with God.

Copies of the *Expositor* flew out the doors of the Laws' print shop. "Every one who could raise five cents bought a copy," said one local resident. The editors optimistically announced that the *Expositor*, "worthy of the patronage of a discerning and an enlightened public," would appear on every succeeding Friday, inviting readers to spend $2 for an annual subscription. William Law expressed confidence that future issues "will set forth deeds of the most dark, cruel and damning ever perpetrated by any people under the name of religion since the world began."

Ι Ι Ι

THERE WOULD BE NO SECOND ISSUE THE NEXT FRIDAY, NOR ANY Friday after that. Joseph Smith quickly decided that Nauvoo didn't need an independent newspaper. By 10:00 a.m. the next day, Saturday, Mayor

Joseph Smith had convened the Nauvoo City Council and was rail-ing against the whole *Expositor* crowd—editor Emmons, the Laws, the Higbees, the Fosters, and Cowles.

The City Council, established by Nauvoo's generous City Charter, was little more than a cat's paw for the Prophet-mayor. The council kept an eye on public safety, monitored off-leash dogs, and repeatedly tried to regulate grog shops, which sprang up like wildflowers in the sometimes boisterous riverside town. In 1843, the eager-to-please council awarded the town's liquor monopoly to . . . Joseph's Nauvoo Mansion. "A hotel that is a temperance house cannot support itself," was Joseph's rationale, speaking as an innkeeper and not as the revealer of the Word of Wis-dom, "and if anybody needs those profits, I do." On a more serious note, the council passed several special ordinances strengthening Nauvoo's power of habeas corpus, meaning that the local court could free virtually any Mormon indicted by an out-of-town sheriff or marshal. The council even enacted a "Special Ordinance in the Prophet's Case vs. Missouri" stipulating that anyone crossing the Mississippi to arrest Joseph Smith for alleged crimes in Missouri could be arrested and committed to "the city prison for life."

The council didn't pretend to be an independent deliberative body, and it certainly didn't act like one when Joseph and Hyrum Smith started inveighing against their enemies. In its first session after the *Expositor*'s publication, the council promptly stripped Emmons of his duties as a city councillor. ("Who was Judge Emmons?" Hyrum asked. "When he came here he had scarce 2 shirts!") Curiously, the council took no sim-ilar action against City Councillor William Law, nor against his brother Wilson, the president of the City Council—although both men were vigorously tarred, in absentia. The Laws were denounced as rapacious capitalists, enriching themselves at the expense of the poor. Joseph complained that William hounded him for a $40 debt when Smith was imprisoned in Missouri, adding that Law was an adulterer and a de-spoiler of virgins to boot. Joseph called Jane Law, the woman who re-buffed his sexual advances, "a whore from Canada." A witness named

Peter Haws spun a particularly lurid tale about Wilson Law, who purportedly seduced a teenage English orphan entrusted to Haws's care. Joseph chimed in that "certain women came to complain to his wife [Emma] that they had caught Wilson Law on the floor at Mr. Haws in the night."

Brother Hyrum raged against the Fosters and the Higbees ("What good have they ever done?") and accused their shadowy accomplice Joseph Jackson—the same Joseph Jackson who served as an aide-de-camp to the Prophet, and claimed to "make bogus" in the Smith homestead— of lusting after Hyrum's seventeen-year-old daughter, Lovina. Hyrum casually asserted that Jackson's main line of work was counterfeiting, and he let slip that Francis Higbee had "the pox," that is, syphilis. While much of the fulminating had only a tenuous basis in fact, many of the charges leveled at Jackson seemed to be true. He was an itinerant free-booter with a powerful sense of personal intrigue; he once called at the Nauvoo Mansion when Joseph was absent. "You tell the Prophet that the wickedest man on earth called to see him," Jackson said to Emma. Acting as an agent for Missouri sheriffs hoping to kidnap Smith, Jackson had attempted to ingratiate himself with the Prophet. In a raucously unreliable memoir, Jackson claimed he had sought favor with the young Lovina to learn more about Joseph's personal life. For good measure, Jackson accused Smith of attempting to seduce his own sister, a sister-in-law, and a niece—the young Lovina.

Joseph waxed purple on the subject of Austin Cowles's affidavit concerning the secret revelation on polygamy. Plural wifery had "nothing to do with the present time," Joseph insisted. "The Mayor said he had never preached the revelation in private as he had in public—had not taught it to the anointed in the Church, in private, which many confirmed." The members of the High Council would have known this was poppycock, as several of them had already taken plural wives, with Joseph's secret blessing.

What was to be done? Noxious printing presses were nothing new on the frontier, and tradition dictated: destroy them. The Mormons had experienced the furor of an aggrieved readership back in 1833 when the church-owned newspaper in Independence, Missouri, the *Evening and Morning Star,* published an ill-advised opinion on slavery. The opinion was ill-advised because the *Star* did not wholeheartedly endorse Negro bondage. The paper's editor, William Phelps, wanted to extend an olive branch to some free blacks who had converted to Mormonism. In an article titled "Free People of Color," the paper casually celebrated the fact that "much is being done toward abolishing slavery."

In Independence, where Joseph believed Adam and Eve had disported themselves in the Garden of Eden, those were fighting words. The "old settlers," mainly transplants from Southern states, already disapproved of Mormon missions to the Indians, whom Smith had declared to be the original inhabitants of Eden. Now the whiff of abolitionism seared their nostrils. Although Phelps immediately published a mendacious climbdown in an extra edition, recanting any warm feeling about blacks ("Our intention was not only to stop free people of color from emigrating to this state, but to prevent them from being admitted as members of the Church"), it was too late. A mob destroyed the press, razed its office building, and tarred and feathered two editors imprudent enough not to flee.

In more recent memory, down the river in Alton, Illinois, an angry mob killed the abolitionist editor Reverend Elijah Lovejoy and drowned his *Alton Observer* printing press in the Mississippi. Lovejoy had been warned. Mobs had tossed his two previous presses into the river. When the citizens arrived to burn his premises on the night of November 7, 1837, the Presbyterian minister managed to push one of their ladders off his roof and brandished his gun. He quickly perished in a hail of gunfire.

Joseph was no pro-slavery firebrand. Quite the opposite; his presidential platform encouraged the gradual freeing of America's African population. But he did take a page from the anti-abolitionist playbook when dealing with the *Expositor.* In a second, daylong City Council meeting, he asked out loud how the town could rid itself of the paper, "a greater nuisance than a dead carcass. . . . What the opposition party wanted was to rise a mob on us and take the spoil of us as they did in Missouri. . . . The Mayor said the Constitution did not authorize the press to publish Libels—and proposed the council make some provision for putting down the Nauvoo *Expositor*."

Joseph Smith had created a vast and arcane theology, replete with theories governing salvation, the end of times, and the stratification of everlasting life. He was an accomplished and creative intellectual freelancer, so it came as no surprise that he cobbled together a legal rationale for closing down the *Expositor*. His first instinct, invoking the US Constitution, to which he often professed fealty, was a nonstarter. The words "libel" and "nuisance" appear nowhere in that document. There are ten words in the Constitution's First Amendment governing freedom of speech and the press, the most important one being "freedom." So with the help of Nauvoo's city attorney, George P. Styles, Joseph started rummaging around the law books, looking for a pretext to destroy the noisome newspaper.

The Illinois constitution was no help. "The printing presses shall be free to every person," the statute read, "and no law shall ever be made to restrain the right thereof." The field of common law torts held out hope, specifically William Blackstone's famous four-volume *Commentaries on the Laws of England*, published in 1826. Joseph Smith, who occasionally made sport of the legal profession, loved Blackstone, and believed the *Commentaries* had a totemic effect on the lawless frontier. When Elder Erastus Snow was hoping to avoid imprisonment by a Missouri judge, Joseph advised him to "plead for justice as hard as you can, and quote Blackstone and other authors now and then, and they will take it all for law." It worked. Blackstone was commonly cited in courtrooms across the young United States, and the renowned jurist directly addressed the question of abating nuisances:

> Whatsoever unlawfully annoys or does damage to another is a nuisance; and such nuisance may be abated, that is, taken away or

removed, by the party aggrieved thereby, so as he commits no riot in the doing of it. . . .

In a footnote, Blackstone conveniently explained that a newspaper could constitute a "private nuisance": "So it seems that a libelous print or paper, affecting a private individual, may be destroyed, or, which is the safer course, taken and delivered to a magistrate." Immediately after invoking Blackstone, Hyrum Smith opined that best way to deal with the *Expositor* would be "to smash the presses all to pieces and pie [scatter] the type." Soon afterward, the council adopted the fateful resolution:

> To the marshal: "You are hereby commanded to destroy the printing press from whence issues the Nauvoo Expositor, and pi the type of said printing establishment in the street, and burn all the Expositors and libelous handbills found in said establishment; and if resistance be offered to your execution of this order by the owner or others, demolish the house: and if anyone threatens you or the Mayor or the officers of the city, arrest those who threaten you, and fail not to execute this order without delay, and make due return thereon."

By order of the City Council,

JOSEPH SMITH, MAYOR

Even before the council disbanded at 6:00 p.m., Chief of Police Jonathan Dunham and City Marshal John Greene, leading a force of over one hundred men armed with muskets, knives, and pistols, converged on the Laws' two-story brick office on Mulholland Street. Chauncey Higbee and Charles Foster were present, and they put up no resistance as the mayor's men methodically trashed the interior of the newly constructed brick building. "All was done in perfect order," a Dr. Wakefield testified at a subsequent inquest that cleared everyone of any misdoing, "as peaceably as people move on a Sunday."

While two companies of the Nauvoo Legion kept watch, the police posse began applying sledgehammers to the printing press. Foster recorded the "work of destruction and desperation":

> They tumbled the press and materials into the street, and set fire to them, and demolished the machinery with sledge hammer, and injured the building very materially. We made no resistance; but looked on and felt revenge, but leave it for the public to avenge this climax of insult and injury.

After destroying William Law's $2,000 letterpress, the whooping Mormon mob tossed every combustible they could find—office furniture, type drawers, spare copies of the *Expositor*—into the street, and lit a bonfire. Nauvoo's prospects for an independent political voice went up in smoke.

After sundown, the bumptious crowd headed through the center of town for the Nauvoo Mansion, to be congratulated by Joseph. "I gave them a short address [and] told them they had done right," the Prophet noted. "They had executed my order required of me by the city council that I would never submit to have another libelous publication established in this city." His speech "was loudly greeted by 3 cheers 3 times," he recalled. Then "the posse dispersed all in good order."

Meanwhile, Robert Foster and William Law had spent the day in Carthage, discussing the situation in Nauvoo. The locals urged Law to move his independent newspaper to Carthage, as it was sure to be destroyed in Nauvoo. "I did not believe it," he wrote in his diary. He believed it when he rode back into Nauvoo, and his horse's hooves passed over the fragments of lead type lying in the muddy street. "We rode over our type, and over our broken office furniture," he recalled.

> The work of Joseph's agents had been very complete; it had been done by a mob of about 200. The building, a new, pretty brick structure, had been perfectly gutted, not a bit had been left of anything.

JOSEPH HAD OVERSTEPPED. THE ATTACK ON THE NEWSPAPER, coupled with his other startling démarches in early 1844, were costing him loyalty. Missionary Isaac Scott wrote a long letter to his wife's parents in Sutton, Massachusetts, detailing the outlandish happenings in Nauvoo:

> A plurality of gods. A plurality of *living* wives. . . . These with many other things are taught by Joseph, which we consider are *odious* and doctrines of the devil.

"Joseph had a revelation last summer," Scott continued, "purporting to be from the Lord, allowing the Saints to have ten living wives at one time.

> I mean certain conspicuous characters among them. They do not content themselves with young women, but have seduced married women. I believe hundreds have been deceived. Now should I yield up your daughter to such wretches?

Scott related how Joseph had excommunicated the Law brothers and Austin Cowles and "delivered [them] over to the buffetings of Satan" without any due process whatsoever. Then,

> Joseph called his Sanhedrin together, . . . tried the press and ordered the city marshal to take three hundred armed men and go burn the press, and if any offered resistance, to rip them from the guts to the gizzard. These are his own words.

The reaction outside Nauvoo was far more intense. Joseph had told the City Council that destroying the *Expositor* would "excite our enemies abroad." He was right. Joseph had handed his enemies a mortal weapon to wield against him, and they did.

Thomas Sharp sprang into action. He threw an "extra" edition of the Warsaw *Signal* onto his presses, trumpeting Charles Foster's on-the-scene account of the trashing of the *Expositor*:

> Mr. Sharp:—I hasten to inform you of the UNPARALLELED OUTRAGE, perpetrated upon our rights and interests, by the ruthless, lawless, ruffian band of MORMON MOBOCRATS, a the dictum of that UNPRINCIPLED wretch Joe Smith.

Foster provided a gripping account of the attack, and Sharp immediately unleashed his ire:

> War and extermination is inevitable! Citizens ARISE, ONE and ALL!!!— Can you stand by, and suffer such INFERNAL DEVILS!! to ROB men of their property and RIGHTS, without avenging them. We have no time for comment, every man will make his own. LET IT BE MADE WITH POWDER AND BALL!!!

This was the trespass that Sharp and the Hancock County Mormon-haters had been waiting for. Inflamed citizens swarmed mass meetings in Carthage, Warsaw, and the surrounding towns. Then news arrived that Joseph Smith had yet again escaped arrest for a crime. When Francis Higbee swore out a complaint accusing Joseph of inciting a riot to destroy the *Expositor*, the Carthage court sent Constable David Bettisworth to Nauvoo to arrest Smith. Similar gambits had failed in the past, and this one did, too. A local justice of the peace simply vacated Higbee's motion. "Court decided that Joseph Smith had acted under proper authority in destroying the establishment of the Nauvoo Expositor on the 10th inst.," the order read; "that this was a malicious prosecution on the part of Francis M. Higbee; and that said Higbee pay the costs of suit, and that Joseph Smith be honorably discharged from the accusations and of the writ, and go hence without delay."

The next day, Joseph himself, ruling as chief of the Nauvoo Municipal Court, acquitted the other seventeen men accused of attacking the newspaper.

When Bettisworth returned to Carthage empty-handed, the city was dumbfounded. "Joseph has tried the game too often," one citizen grumbled. The hapless constable journeyed to Nauvoo a second time, again butted heads with Mormon justice, and lost again. Local magistrate Daniel Wells, a Jack-Mormon, or Mormon sympathizer, who owned a farm next door to Joseph's, tossed out a second riot charge.

The Mormons continued to manufacture their own justice, and it enraged the old settlers. In Carthage, Captain Samuel Williams of the Carthage Greys said the old citizens were apoplectic with rage: "Such an excitement have never witnessed in my life." Seven hundred irate citizens jammed the town green for an anti-Mormon rally, railing against "the mad Prophet and his demoniac coadjutors." The word "extermination" was again ringing from the rafters.

The three hundred anti-Mormons who assembled in nearby Warsaw resolved that Smith had "violated the highest privilege in government; and to seek redress in the ordinary mode would be utterly ineffectual." The time had come to "exterminate the wicked and abominable Mormon leaders, the authors of our troubles . . . a war of extermination should be waged to the entire destruction, if necessary for our protection, of his adherents."

Documents adopted in both Carthage and Warsaw demanded that the Mormons of Hancock County be herded into the Nauvoo city limits and forced to turn over "the Prophet and his miscreant adherents. . . . If not surrendered, a war of extermination should be conducted." Every man in the county should "each one arm and equip ourselves forthwith." The second Mormon War had begun.

7

"CRUCIFY HIM! CRUCIFY HIM!"

I have got all the truth which the Christian world possessed, and an independent revelation in the bargain, and
God will bear me off triumphant.

—*Joseph Smith's final sermon, June 16, 1844*

ON SATURDAY, JUNE 15, JOSEPH SMITH DISCERNED THE FIRST
stirrings of the popular revolt set off by the burning of the
Expositor offices. "Two brethren come from Lima," he recorded in his
diary. "Said Colonel Levi Williams had demanded the Mormons' arms.
Father Morley wanted to know what to do."

Isaac Morley was a veteran of the Missouri troubles and Joseph's
stake president in Lima, an exposed Mormon settlement thirty miles
south of Nauvoo. Levi Williams was a prosperous farmer and bellig-
erent Mormon-hater who owned a 113-acre farm south of Warsaw.
Williams had legitimate military credentials. A veteran of the War of
1812, he served as a ranger in Illinois's Black Hawk War against the
local Indian tribes. He had risen to command the Fifty-ninth Regiment
of the Illinois militia, headquartered in Warsaw. Williams despised
the Saints, whom he viewed as unwanted interlopers in an otherwise

peaceful corner of the world. In 1843, Williams led a mob that kidnapped an accused Mormon horse thief and dragged him into Missouri for trial. Joseph in turn ordered his police force to kidnap the kidnappers, an idea that foundered two miles short of Williams's farm, which proved to be too well defended for the Saints to attack. The excitable Williams once tarred and feathered a militiaman who refused to join a vigilante raid against the Saints.

According to Morley's letter, Williams's outriders presented the Lima Saints with three options: "We, the Mormon people, must take up arms and proceed with them for your arrest, or take our effects and proceed immediately to Nauvoo, otherwise give up our arms, and remain quiet until the fuss is over."

Joseph counseled Morley to "Instruct the companies to keep cool, and let all things be done decently and in order."

> If the mob shall fall upon the Saints by force of arms, defend them at every hazard unless prudence dictate the retreat of the troops to Nauvoo, in which case the mob will not disturb your women and children; and if the mob move towards Nauvoo, either come before them or in their rear and be ready to co-operate with the main body of the Legion.

Separately, Joseph learned of "considerable excitement" in Warsaw, which had just received a shipment of arms from Quincy. Joseph confided to his diary that the real excitement would probably begin next week.

Joseph then took a moment to indulge in an un-Joseph-like pursuit. He spent some time alone in his second-floor office examining Benjamin West's famous painting "Death on the Pale Horse," which was touring the United States. "A Gentleman is now in our city who has for exhibition West's painting of *Death on the Pale Horse*," the *Nauvoo Neighbor* reported. "Judging from the known celebrity of the artist, and from the number of testimonies we have seen, it must be worthy of attention." It would be hard to explain how the masterpiece

Benjamin West's 1796 painting "Death on
the Pale Horse." *Credit: Detroit Institute of Arts*

found its way to Nauvoo, *if* it found its way to Nauvoo. The painting
did tour outside of Philadelphia and New York, but Joseph may have
been staring at a copy.

West was a Pennsylvania-born artist who had achieved phenom-
enal success in Europe. Twice elected president of London's Royal
Academy of Arts, he was also a court painter for King George III.
The king had commissioned "Death," but then rejected the painting as
"a Bedlamite scene." The tableau disturbed other audiences as well.
Skeletal Death, mounted on the pale charger, has arrived on earth to
slaughter its inhabitants. To his right and left ride the biblical killers
of the Book of Revelation, one mounted on a white horse ("Its rider
held a bow, and he was given a crown"), the other on a red mount
("Its rider was given power to take peace from the earth"), together
wreaking havoc among the mortals. Black, menacing storm clouds
hover in the background.

Contemplating Benjamin West's painting alone in his upstairs study,
Joseph, who could recite long portions of the Bible from memory, could
easily call to mind the famous verse from Revelation 6 that West had

chosen to illustrate: "And I looked, and behold, a Pale Horse, and his name that sat on him was Death."

Was Joseph experiencing a premonition of his own fate? It's possible. The *Expositor* had violated the sanctity of his interlocking directorate of secret committees. The Laws and their confederates had betrayed him, exposing his secret Kingdom of God and multiple marriages for all the world to see. If Smith was despondent, he showed little hint of it, and his characteristic energy and optimism would resurface again and again during the final days of his life.

⚊ ⚊ ⚊

THE PREVIOUS THURSDAY NIGHT, JOSEPH HAD SHARED A CURIOUS dream with the Saints:

> I thought I was riding out in my carriage, and my guardian angel was along with me. We went past the Temple and had not gone much further before we espied two large snakes so fast locked together that neither of them had any power. I inquired of my guide what I was to understand by that. He answered, "Those snakes represent Dr. Foster and Chauncey L. Higbee. They are your enemies and desire to destroy you; but you see they are so fast locked together that they have no power of themselves to hurt you."

In the dream, the Laws capture Joseph, bind him, and throw him into a "deep, dry pit," not unlike Joseph the dreamer in Genesis, whose brothers heave him into a dry pit, expecting that animals will devour him.

Suddenly, in the dream, the tables are turned and the Laws need Joseph's help:

> I looked out of the pit and saw Wilson Law at a little distance attacked by ferocious wild beasts, and heard him cry out, "Oh! Brother Joseph,

come and save me!" I replied, "I cannot, for you have put me into this deep pit."

On looking out another way, I saw William Law with outstretched tongue, blue in the face, and the green poison forced out of his mouth, caused by the coiling of a large snake around his body. It had also grabbed him by the arm, a little above the elbow, ready to devour him. He cried out in the intensity of his agony, "Oh, Brother Joseph, Brother Joseph, come and save me, or I die!" I also replied to him, "I cannot, William; I would willingly, but you have tied me and put me in this pit, and I am powerless to help you or liberate myself."

In a short time after my guide came and said aloud, "Joseph, Joseph, what are you doing there?" I replied, "My enemies fell upon me, bound me and threw me in." He then took me by the hand, drew me out of the pit, set me free, and we went away rejoicing.

Ӿ Ӿ Ӿ

RAIN WAS THREATENING THE NEXT DAY WHEN JOSEPH APPEARED before several thousand Saints assembled in the Temple-side "grove," sometimes called the Bowery. Weather be damned. "If it does rain, I'll preach this doctrine, for the truth shall be preached," Joseph insisted to the audience arrayed in the gently sloping glen in front of him, many of them perched on the stumps of harvested jack oaks. Bishop Newel Whitney offered a prayer, and the choir sang a Baptist hymn, "Mortals Awake!" which had been collected into the Mormon hymnal.

Joseph returned to the Book of Revelation as the inspiration for what would prove to be his fiery, final sermon to the faithful Saints. He began by reading Revelation 3, in which Christ, speaking through John of Patmos, chides three churches that have fallen away from orthodox Christianity. One of the retrograde churches "has a name of being alive, but you are dead . . . If you do not wake up, I will come like a thief" and "blot your name out of the book of life." Another church is rich, prosperous, arrogant, and smug. "You do not realize that you are wretched, pitiable, poor, blind and naked," Christ tells the church, hurling his famous imprecation: "I wish that you were either cold or hot. So, because you are lukewarm, and neither cold nor hot, I am about to spit you out of my mouth."

The message was clear: Nauvoo, Joseph's latter-day Zion, had strayed from Christ's message, just like the wayward churches of John's time. The *Expositor* had hammered away at his doctrine of the plurality of gods, accusing Joseph of "holding forth a doctrine which is effectually calculated to sap the very foundation of our faith." The arrow had struck home. "You know that of late some malicious and corrupt men have sprung up and apostatized from the Church of Jesus Christ of Latter-day Saints," Joseph proclaimed, "and they declare that the Prophet believes in a plurality of Gods, and, lo and behold! we have discovered a very great secret, they cry—'The Prophet says there are many Gods, and this proves that he has fallen.'"

Joseph was recapitulating the famous argument of the King Follett sermon, that just as God was the father of Jesus Christ, "you may suppose that He had a Father also."

> Where was there ever a son without a father? And where was there ever a father without first being a son? Whenever did a tree or anything spring into existence without a progenitor? And everything comes in this way. . . . I despise the idea of being scared to death at such a doctrine, for the Bible is full of it.

He then cited biblical examples of the plurality of gods, claiming, for instance, that "Paul says there are Gods many and Lords many."* Smith also applied his modest knowledge of Hebrew, pointing out that "Elohim," the Old Testament word for "god," is a plural form, and is almost

---

* In 1 Corinthians 8:5, Paul seems to be saying the opposite: "For though there be that are called gods . . . to us there is but one God, the Father."

always used plurally when God, or Elohim, creates the world. It was a stretch to argue that the Old Testament Israelites were polytheists, although Joseph did just that. "In the very beginning the Bible shows there is a plurality of Gods beyond the power of refutation," he declared. "The word Elohim ought to be in the plural all the way through—Gods. The heads of the Gods appointed one God for us; and when you take [that] view of the subject, it sets one free to see all the beauty, holiness and perfection of the Gods." Biblical scholars have called *Elohim* an example of the "plural of excellence," akin to the "plural of majesty," better known as the "royal we."

The biblical precedents allowed Joseph to both sermonize and indulge in some self-pity. "Paul, if Joseph Smith is a blasphemer, you are. I say there are Gods many and Lords many. . . . But if Joseph Smith says there are Gods many and Lords many, they cry, 'Away with him! Crucify him! Crucify him!'"

"They found fault with Jesus Christ because He said He was the Son of God, and made Himself equal with God," Joseph continued. "They say of me, like they did of the Apostles of old, that I must be put down."

The rain started to fall. "I wish I could speak for three or four hours; but it is not expedient on account of the rain," Joseph told his audience. The mature Joseph Smith was not a man to turn the other cheek, and he concluded his remarks with a ritual thrashing of his enemies. "Oh, poor, blind apostates!" he thundered. "They swear that they believe the Bible, the Book of Mormon and the Doctrine and Covenants and then you will get from them filth, slander, and bogus-makers plenty."

"God never will acknowledge any traitors or apostates," he continued. "All men are liars who say they are of the true Church without the revelations of Jesus Christ and the Priesthood of Melchizedek, which is after the order of the Son of God." His opponents, he argued, "have apostatized from the truth and lost the priesthood" and "build upon other men's foundations . . . without authority from God."

"Did I build on any other man's foundation?" Joseph asked, and then answered his own question. "I have got all the truth which the

Christian world possessed, and an independent revelation in the bargain, and God will bear me off triumphant." What of the Law brothers, the Fosters, and their followers in the Reformed Church? "When the floods come and the winds blow, their foundations will be found to be sand, and their whole fabric will crumble to dust."

The rainfall became "severe," Joseph reported, and the Saints scattered to their homes.

⚹ ⚹ ⚹

LATER THAT DAY, JOSEPH REACHED OUT, FOR THE SECOND TIME during the crisis, to Governor Thomas Ford. The previous week, Smith had orchestrated a letter-writing campaign by prominent Saints, regaling the former judge with legal arguments ("See Chitty's Blackstone Bk. iii:v, and n., &c., &c") to justify the assault on the *Expositor*. Ford never responded. Now Smith dispatched another letter, by courier, alerting Ford that "an energetic attempt is being made by some of the citizens of this and the surrounding counties to drive and exterminate 'the Saints' by force of arms." Smith implored Ford "to come down in person with your staff and investigate the whole matter without delay, and cause peace to be restored to the country." Fancifully, Joseph offered to place the Nauvoo Legion under Ford's command, "to quell all insurrection and support the dignity of the common weal."

The letter ended, "I remain, sir, the friend of peace, and your Excellency's humble servant, JOSEPH SMITH."

8

ENTER PONTIUS PILATE

The Mormons, however, were becoming unpopular,
nay odious, to the great body of the people.

—*Governor Thomas Ford*, History of Illinois

THOMAS FORD WAS THE ACCIDENTAL GOVERNOR OF ILLINOIS. A short man with a high forehead and a sallow complexion, he was a modestly distinguished jurist who had twice been elected as a state judge. Ford was sitting on the state supreme court when the Democrats nominated him for the governorship in 1841. Adam Snyder, the party's first choice, had died unexpectedly. Ford claimed he never aspired to higher office, and he may have been telling the truth.

Illinois divided its votes between the Democrats, the party of the popular former president Andrew Jackson, and the insurgent, modernizing Whigs. The Mormons, who voted en bloc for the party that best suited their needs at the time, had been leaning Democratic, partly because Smith had become infatuated with the ambitious young legislator Stephen Douglas. As a young state supreme court justice, Douglas had helped Joseph out of a jam, voiding a warrant for his arrest issued by a Missouri court. Joseph didn't forget his friends, and Douglas didn't forget that Mormons accounted for several thousand votes in Hancock County. Douglas took the time to visit Nauvoo, praising the Mormons for their energy and enterprise in transforming the swamp into one of Illinois's largest cities. Smith pretended to remain neutral in Illinois factional feuds, but he clearly had a soft spot for the feisty, five-foot-four "Little Giant" who would soon vie for the presidency against his fellow Illinois legislator, Abraham Lincoln. "DOUGLAS is a *master spirit*, and *his friends are our friends*," Smith proclaimed.

Thomas Ford was no Stephen Douglas. He was a tortured soul. Though only forty-one years old when elected governor, "he appeared like a man weary of human nature and of life," one contemporary reported. The Illinois governorship, Ford thought, "was feeble and clothed with but little authority." In his posthumously published *History of Illinois,* Ford derided the state's successful pols, said to carry "a gourd of possum fat" with which to grease colleagues and constituents. Ford ridiculed 1830 gubernatorial candidate William Kinney, who "went forth electioneering with a Bible in one pocket and a bottle of whiskey in the other; and thus armed with 'the sword of the Lord and the spirit' he could preach to one set of men and drink with another, and thus make himself agreeable to all." Kinney's glad hand did not meet Thomas Ford's approval. "Thank God such scenes are no more to be witnessed in Illinois," he wrote, disdainfully. (Kinney lost the election.)

By contrast, Ford saw himself in the company of John Tyler and James Polk, two other politicians catapulted into office by happenstance. President Tyler, he noted, "was accidentally made vice-president by the Whigs, and accidentally became president, by the death of Gen. Harrison." Tyler, derided by contemporaries as "his accidency," exerted "no moral force," Ford wrote, doubtless thinking of the many accusations of pusillanimity hurled at him. Ford, like Tyler, was a Democrat-turned-Whig, and somewhat indifferent to party politics. "Neither Tyler nor Polk had much distinguished themselves in their respective parties," Ford said, and "so it was with the humble person who was now to be elected governor of Illinois."

This was not exactly a ringing self-endorsement.

Ford's many detractors suggested that he had the short man's inferiority complex. He stood only five feet, five inches tall, making him the butt of the unflattering Mormon rhyme: "Governor Ford he was so small / He had no room for a Soul at all." (In a dream, Brigham Young once saw "Tom Ford about 2 1/2 feet high.") Worse yet, he spoke in a squeaky voice, and his sharp nose canted slightly to one side. Ford was "so wholly wanting in self-confidence and practical business sense that he was an utter failure as a lawyer," memoirist John F. Snyder reported. Ford experienced a near-breakdown at his own inauguration ceremony, in front of the Illinois General Assembly: "He read but a small way when his voice failed, and he sunk down on the seat or table on which he was standing." Another man picked up his notes and finished the speech. This and other embarrassing shortfalls were ascribed to his fondness for drink. Snyder said Ford consumed "artificial courage to fortify his feeble animation. . . . He had recourse to stimulants, which grew to a confirmed and ruinous habit."

A competent writer who hoped to enrich his family with his prolix *History*, Ford occasionally demonstrated sound judgment. When the Prairie Pirates, the notorious Illinois banditti of the 1820s threatened his Ogle County home, Ford supported the vigilante "regulators" who brought the outlaws to justice, usually at the end of a rope. Ford presided over the mass trial of the hundred vigilantes who executed John Driscoll and his son in cold blood. The good citizens, many of them Ford's prosperous neighbors, were acquitted, with nary an objection from the bench.

Before and after the murders of Joseph and Hyrum Smith, Ford correctly perceived that there would be no peace in southwestern Illinois until the Mormons departed. Yet he could be maddeningly obtuse. He wrote that Joseph Smith had been accused of "sanctioning a polygamy by some kind of spiritual wife system, which I never could well understand." With hundreds of rowdy militiamen crowding the streets of Carthage and Warsaw, Ford often chose to believe the old settlers' protestations of innocent intentions vis-à-vis the Mormons—bristling muskets notwithstanding.

In fairness, Ford assumed a heavy burden when he defeated the fire-breathing Mormon-hater Joseph Duncan for the governorship. (Joseph Smith named his horse "Joe Duncan," and took great pleasure in whipping it.) The state was $313,000 in debt. Its warrants were selling at a 50 percent discount, "and there was no money in the treasury whatever; not even to pay postage on letters." There was worse news, Ford wrote:

> The treasury was bankrupt; the revenues were insufficient; the people were unwilling and unable to pay high taxes; and the State had borrowed itself out of all credit. A debt of near fourteen millions of dollars had been contracted for the canal, railroads and other purposes. The currency of the state had been annihilated.

In June 1844, Ford was facing what looked like a civil war in Hancock County, with hourly reports of old settlers forming militias bent on marching into Nauvoo. Like everyone, he knew that the well-outfitted Nauvoo Legion drilled constantly and seemed ready and eager to meet any threat with powder and cannon fire. Ford decided to insert himself into the festering chaos. For seven days in June, he moved the governor's office to Carthage, at the epicenter of Hancock County's anti-Mormon fervor.

Ford fancied himself to be an honest broker to the warring factions. He did have a tenuous claim to objectivity; in the governor's race, Ford hadn't courted Mormon votes. He once suggested that Joseph Smith was "a water witch," referring to the old dowsing days in upstate New York, and on the campaign trail he urged revision or repeal of Nauvoo's overgenerous charter. The Saints voted for him anyway, Duncan's anti-Mormon theatrics being more than they could bear. Ford won the governorship by a comfortable margin, and, unlike the Stephen Douglases of the world, felt no need to kowtow to the Saints.

At the same time, the Pecksniffian Ford had disdained the Hancock natives, whom he well remembered from his days of judicial circuit-riding, trying cases downstate. "The early settlers," he wrote, "were, in popular language, 'hard cases.'" Ford was a snob who had no use for the crude, bigoted, violence-prone "mobocrats" who persecuted the Saints, it sometimes seemed, just because they were there.

For the Mormons, however, Ford proved to be the wrong man in the wrong place at the wrong time. Trying to avert a civil war, he displayed an unerring instinct for doing the wrong thing, and for misreading evidence right under his nose. He wasn't particularly decisive, and almost every decision he made in June 1844 proved to be the wrong one.

Ɨ Ɨ Ɨ

CARTHAGE, ILLINOIS, WAS THE SEAT OF HANCOCK COUNTY. ITS founders hailed from Carthage, Tennessee, and named the nascent village for their hometown. Carthage had been surveyed just a year or two before Nauvoo, but was tiny by comparison. The immigrating Saints had swollen Nauvoo's population to about 10,000. In the summer of 1844, it was the same size as the infant Chicago, which would quickly become one of the largest cities in the country. Carthage, located smack in the center of the county, had fewer than a thousand residents and not much to show for itself: a few stores, a handful of saloons, and the clapboarded, two-story-tall Hamilton House hotel, operated by Artois Hamilton and his family. The scalawag Isaac Galland, who sold the Mormons their dubiously titled Nauvoo real estate, briefly published the *Carthagenian* newspaper, which failed within a year. An 1837 gazetteer reported that Carthage had small congregations of Baptists, Congregationalists, and Methodists: "What is perhaps worthy of remark, they all hold meetings in the same house."

Since 1839, Carthage had one feature to boast about—its new court-house, erected in the middle of the village green. The circuit court met for one week in May and one week in October, and the circuit-riding attorneys, their clients, and hangers-on guaranteed full occupancy at Hamilton's hotel. The courthouse had seen one trial of note: *People v. William Fraim*. Fraim, a twenty-one-year-old Irish deckhand, had killed a man in a drunken brawl in neighboring Schuyler County. In 1839, the thirty-year-old novice lawyer Abraham Lincoln was prospecting for work outside his base in the state capital, Springfield, when he happened upon Fraim's case. The one-day trial ended badly for Lincoln, and for Fraim. A judge sentenced the young Irishman to hang, ignoring Lincoln's subsequent motion to set aside the verdict.

Fraim's execution was a huge event in tiny Carthage. The citizens erected a gallows in a field about a mile outside of town, so the maximum number of spectators could attend. Schools let out for the day, and families gathered at the hanging with food and picnic blankets. In the three weeks since his trial, Fraim had become a local celebrity. Because Carthage had no jail, he was imprisoned in the second-floor jury room of the town's new courthouse. His windows faced the schoolyard, and Fraim made many friends among the young children frolicking during recess. By all accounts, they were sorry to lose him.

Although no murders had come to trial in the intervening years, Carthage did remedy its lack of a jail. By June 1844, the town had built a compact, two-story prison, with split-level quarters for a jailer and his family, as well as locked dungeon cells.

After the destruction of the *Expositor*, Carthage was rapidly becoming an armed camp. Joseph Smith's prediction that anti-Mormon "excitement" would come to Hancock County was borne out by his journal: "2 Brothers arrived from Carthage this eve and said about 300 mobbers were collected in Carthage to come upon Nauvoo"; "Brother from Bear Creek come and made affidavit before Recorder that 150 Missourians were to cross to Warsaw next morning on way to Carthage"; "It was reported the Mob was still gathering at Carthage and that William and Wilson Law had laid a plan to burn the printing office of Nauvoo *Neighbor* this night and strong police were on duty."

In neighboring Warsaw, Joseph's fiery enemy Thomas Sharp was filling his newspaper with equally disturbing reports. Sharp insisted that Hyrum Smith had threatened his life and that he planned to march on Warsaw and sack the *Signal* the way the Saints had trashed the *Expositor*. "A rumor is afloat that the Mormons have melted the type of the Expositor office and converted them into bullets"; "We have just learned that Joe has ordered all his followers into Nauvoo. The settlements around are with all despatch obeying the order."

> To our friends at a distance we say come! We are too weak in the county without aid to effect our object. Come! You will be doing your God and your country service, in aiding us to rid earth of a most Heaven daring wretch.

Just as he had spies inside William Law's insurgent group, Joseph also had a spy in Carthage. He sent a young Mormon named Gilbert Belnap to attend an anti-Mormon rally, probably because Belnap had just arrived in Nauvoo and was a stranger in Hancock County. But the Carthaginians were watching the Nauvoo road like hawks, and three men interrogated Belnap on the outskirts of town, asking him his business. The young man claimed he needed to visit the recorder's office, and the thugs followed him there. Inside, a "low-bred backwoodsman from Missouri" started boasting about the Mormon men he had killed and women whom he had forced into prostitution. A knife emerged, a scuffle ensued. Eventually, Belnap was allowed to attend the anti-Mormon rally, revealing his true mission when he galloped out of town just moments after it ended. A small mob of pursuers failed to catch him, and Belnap rode hell for leather until his horse collapsed in the mud near the Nauvoo Temple. Breathless and filthy, he ran to the Nauvoo Mansion to report directly to Joseph.

In his newspaper, Sharp gleefully related that soldiers from Illinois, Missouri, and Iowa were answering his call, all of them bent on finishing off the Mormons. "Captain [William] Grover last week obtained from Quincy 59 muskets," according to the June 19 edition of the *Signal*. "D.W. Mathews, who was sent last Saturday to St. Louis, has just returned by the Die Vernon [steamboat]," the paper added. "He has succeeded in procuring cannon, and has brought up a good supply of ammunition. . . . We expect a six pounder tomorrow night from Quincy." Warsaw, just twenty miles southwest of Carthage, had mobilized its three-hundred-man militia, under Colonel Levi Williams.

In a series of letters sent to his father in Ridgefield, Connecticut, George Rockwell, a dedicated and erudite anti-Mormon, explained how he left his business in the hands of his clerks to campaign full time against the Hancock County Saints. "I can assure that I take much pleasure in lending my humble aid to expel a band of citizens from the state," Rockwell said, "the leaders of whom are deserving a thousand deaths." Rockwell lived in Warsaw and wrote stirringly of the old citizens' travails at the hands of Joe Smith and his followers. "The Mormons were increasing fast in the County," he explained, "their political influence had been so guided by revelation that it bid fair to sap the very foundations of our government." Like many self-appointed spokespeople for the old settlers—Sharp and Colonel Levi Williams would be two others—Rockwell had arrived in Illinois only a few years before.

Writing from Alton, about seventy-five miles south of Carthage, Rockwell told his father that he had spent several sleepless nights riding into adjoining counties to recruit anti-Mormon militia brigades. Rockwell was carrying a requisition order signed by Governor Ford, instructing the Alton arsenal to send all of its state-owned muskets and cannon to Warsaw, where several hundred men were intending to march north and invade Nauvoo. With forces assembling in Carthage and Warsaw, Rockwell predicted that "the Mormons will be routed" within the next few weeks.

> Unless they should alter their minds and submit to the laws, and lay down their arms, in which event their lives will be spared, (excepting Joe Smith and a few of his advisers) but the City of Nauvoo will be destroyed.

They number 3 or 4000 men well armed and will probably make a desperate resistance. Joe is trying to ape Mahomet, indulges in all kinds of licentiousness and has become a formidable foe to the State.

ʃ ʃ ʃ

UPRIVER, JOSEPH WAS PREPARING NAUVOO FOR WAR. THE LEGION drilled every morning at 8:00 a.m. and remained on alert until the late afternoon. "Every man almost slept on his arms and walked armed by day," recalled Legionnaire Oliver B. Huntington, "ready at a moment's warning to lose their lives, or lay them in jeopardy in defense of our rights." Joseph issued instructions to the city police and to Jonathan Dunham, the major general commanding the Nauvoo Legion: guard the waterfront and station pickets along the roads leading into the city. Nauvoo's forty-man police force was on high alert, on the lookout for spies, importuning strangers, checking bona fides. The *Expositor*-inspired dissidents numbered just a few hundred at most, in a population of over 10,000 Saints. Nonetheless, Joseph and Nauvoo's leaders fretted about fifth columnists who might be helping the restive Hancock County militias. "At Nauvoo, a bayonet bristles at every assailable point!" a St. Louis newspaper reported. "Boats are not permitted to tarry, nor strangers permitted to land."

On the following day, June 18, Joseph donned his gold-braided, buff-and-blue brigadier general's uniform and summoned the Nauvoo Legion to a full-dress review in front of his home. Apostle William Phelps read a brief, inflammatory dispatch from the Warsaw *Signal*, detailing the anti-Mormons' preparations for war. Standing atop the wooden frame of the unfinished barbershop and inn being built for Porter Rockwell, under a bright sun and a radiant blue sky, Joseph delivered one of his most magnificent orations, a ninety-minute-long self-vindication and stirring call to arms.

A stylized lithograph of Joseph's final address to the
Nauvoo Legion, with the Nauvoo Mansion in the
background; by Mormon artist John Hafen in 1888
Credit: Utah State Historical Society

"We have never violated the laws of our country," he began.

We are American citizens. We live upon a soil for the liberties of which
our fathers periled their lives and spilt their blood upon the battlefield.
Those rights so dearly purchased, shall not be disgracefully trodden under foot by lawless marauders without at least a noble effort on our part
to sustain our liberties.

"Will you all stand by me to the death," he shouted, "and sustain
at the peril of your lives, the laws of our country, and the liberties and

privileges which our fathers have transmitted unto us, sealed with their sacred blood? "AYE!" the serried soldiers, and hundreds of citizens surrounding them, shouted in reply.

"Good!" Smith thundered. "If you had not done it, I would have gone out there"—Smith pointed west, across the Mississippi river—"and would have raised up a mightier people."

Smith pulled his four-foot-long, tempered-steel cavalry saber from its sheath and brandished the blade above his head.

"Come, all ye lovers of liberty, break the oppressor's rod, loose the iron grasp of mobocracy, and bring to condign punishment all those who trample under foot the glorious Constitution and the people's rights!" he shouted. "I call God and angels to witness that I have unsheathed my sword with a firm and unalterable determination that this people shall have their legal rights, and be protected from mob violence, or my blood shall be spilt upon the ground like water, and my body consigned to the silent tomb."

Joseph again introduced the theme of mortal sacrifice. "I do not regard my own life," he told the thousands of assembled Saints. "I am ready to be offered a sacrifice for this people; for what can our enemies do? Only kill the body, and their power is then at an end."

The sword that Joseph unsheathed would never be sullied with a drop of blood. And he would never address the Saints again.

☥ ☥ ☥

AMID THE RISING TENSIONS, A CARTHAGE "CITIZENS COMMITTEE" traveled to Springfield to ask Governor Ford to call out the state militia to keep the peace in Hancock County. Ford had a different idea. He would journey to Carthage and guarantee the peace himself. He established his headquarters at Artois Hamilton's hotel, down the street from the county courthouse. The hotel had become the de facto headquarters for the men bent on forcing Joseph to face justice, not only for destroying the *Expositor* but also for evading the Laws' complaints of adultery and "false swearing" filed in May. Wilson Law, Robert Foster, and the Higbees had taken refuge there, and several of Joseph's lesser-known enemies hovered nearby. Apostle John Taylor, whom Joseph sent to negotiate with Ford, reported that Carthage "was filled with a perfect set of rabble and rowdies, who, under the influence of Bacchus, seemed to be holding a grand saturnalia, whooping, yelling and vociferation as if Bedlam had broken loose."

Carthage was a teeming epicenter of anti-Mormon agitation. Attending a mass meeting with several hundred old citizens, Samuel O. Williams, an officer in the Carthage Greys militia, told a friend "that we all felt that the time had come when either the Mormons or the old citizens had to leave." The wife of Thomas Gregg, an editor and occasional anti-Mormon pamphleteer, wrote to her husband from Carthage: "You have no idea what is passing here now, to see men preparing for battle to fight with blood hounds; but I hope there will be so large an army as to intimidate that 'bandit horde' in Nauvoo." Within just a few days, about 1,300 militiamen and would-be regulators would gather in Carthage. "Strike, then!" Sharp urged his readers. "For the time has fully come."

The town center had become a vast military bivouac. The three hundred elite Carthage Greys had pitched their tents on the main square and were drilling four hours a day. Militia regiments from neighboring McDonough, Brown, Adams, and Schuyler Counties soon joined them. Journalist B. W. Richmond reported that "about six acres of ground, in the open space in the centre of town, was covered with ordinary camp-meeting tents, and into these the soldiers were crammed pell-mell without order or discipline.

Some were playing cards, and others drinking, or boiling potatoes in small iron pots or roasting bits of bacon impaled on sharp sticks, or baking corn-cakes. Many were pretty drunk, and let out without reserve what was going on in the camp. "Death to the prophet!" was the watchword.

146

In later life, Eudocia Baldwin, who was fifteen in 1844, had rosier memories of the Carthage town square. She remembered that her hometown had become "the scene of great bustle and excitement":

We children went sometimes to see the drilling and parading—delighted with the tumult and commotion, the music of fife and drum, the waving and fluttering of the stars and stripes in the warm June breezes. The galloping hither and thither of Colonels and Aides de Camp with very rich silk sashes, and very bright swords, shouting *very* peremptory orders—were sights and sounds never to be forgotten by children unaccustomed to any warlike demonstrations. . . .

High above all could be heard the droning and shrieking of the bagpipes, for the ubiquitous Scotchman was there to furnish this to us novel and animating music.

Shortly after arriving, Ford addressed the restive militias, who alternately feared a Mormon attack or wanted to march on Nauvoo posthaste. Ford told the men that he intended to follow the law. The Mormons would answer for the destruction of the *Expositor*, but his audience would have to agree to support the governor's "strictly legal measures." In his own account of his speech, Ford reported that "the assembled troops seemed much pleased with the address." When he finished, "the officers and men unanimously voted with acclamation, to sustain me in a strictly legal course, and that the prisoners should be protected from violence."

Ford was talking about hypothetical prisoners. Conjuring up the Mormon leadership to stand trial for the destruction of the *Expositor* was easier said than done. Ford picked up on Smith's earlier letter and initiated a back-and-forth exchange, entreating the Prophet to give his side of the story. Fearing violence, Smith sent two advisers, Taylor and John Bernhisel, to Carthage to meet with Governor Ford. Simultaneously, he fired off a letter to President John Tyler in Washington, asking for "that protection which the Constitution guarantees in case

147

of 'insurrection and rebellion,' [to] save the innocent and oppressed from such horrid persecution." Smith never had much luck with US presidents, and the Mormons' official history makes no note of a reply.

The governor listened to Smith's emissaries and immediately summoned Joseph and other members of the City Council to Carthage to stand trial. "Your conduct in the destruction of the press was a very gross outrage upon the laws and the liberties of the people," Ford wrote. "It may have been full of libels, but this did not authorize you to destroy it." He plaintively added that "there are many newspapers in the state which have been wrongfully abusing me for more than a year," but Ford insisted he would "shed the last drop of my blood to protect those presses from any illegal violence."

"The whole country is now up in arms," Ford wrote, "and a vast number of people are ready to take the matter into their own hands." If Smith refused to surrender voluntarily, Ford wrote, he would authorize the militias and proto-militias gathered in Carthage to go get him. A war against the Mormons, Ford warned, "may assume a revolutionary character, and the men may disregard the authority of their officers." In other words, it could turn into a bloodbath.

Smith answered immediately, writing at midnight on June 22. "We dare not come," he insisted—three times. "Your Excellency promises protection. Yet, at the same time, you have expressed fears that you could not control the mob." In a curious aside, Smith said, "We have been advised by legal and high-minded gentlemen from abroad, who came on the boat this evening to lay our grievances before the Federal Government."

The "high-minded gentlemen" were two sons of the famous South Carolina statesman John C. Calhoun, who was running for president. Smith had many dealings, none of them very fruitful, with Calhoun, one of the prominent politicians he petitioned for reparations following the Mormons' expulsion from Missouri. Indeed, Calhoun had yet again stiffed Joseph when the Prophet asked him to support the Saints' interests in his presidential campaign. On a whim, Calhoun's two young sons, "who spent money freely," had convinced their riverboat captain to stop at Nauvoo for two hours, while they bearded the famous Mormon prophet. Patrick, the older brother, was an army officer en route to an assignment in the West. John Jr. suffered from consumption and was touring the Mississippi for his health.

Wending their way through the darkness to Joseph's mansion, they found the sprawling structure guarded by three hundred armed men. Two trusted lieutenants, Alpheus Cutler and Reynolds Cahoon, stood at the door, ordered to admit no one. After some palaver, the men found themselves in the presence of Joseph, who interrupted a tense meeting with his closest advisers to entertain the young travelers. "At first he thought we were spies sent by the governor," John C. Calhoun Jr. reported. Then Joseph invited the boys into his ground-floor drawing room.

"He gave us a full description of his difficulties, and also an exposition of his faith, frequently calling himself the Prophet," Calhoun wrote. Moments after the men left him to return to their steamboat, Joseph fired off his letter to Ford and resumed his interrupted meeting.

Repairing to his upstairs study, Smith huddled with his brother Hyrum, Willard Richards, and several other church leaders. He handed Ford's "the whole country is up in arms" letter around, for all to read.

"There is no mercy here," he remarked.

"No," Hyrum replied. "Just as sure as we fall into their hands, we are dead men."

"What shall we do, Brother Hyrum?"

"I don't know."

Suddenly, Joseph had an idea. He said that all Ford and the Carthage mobbers wanted was to get hold of him and Hyrum. So they should disband the Legion and restore Nauvoo to its peaceable self. He was certain they would come to search for them, but: "Let them search. We will cross the river tonight, and go away to the West."

149

Barely an hour before, Joseph had told Hyrum that he was determined to go to Washington, DC, and lay his case before President Tyler. He instructed Cahoon to put Emma and Hyrum's family on a steamboat heading east, to Portsmouth, Ohio. Whatever the destination, Joseph was determined to leave Nauvoo. He told Porter Rockwell to ready a boat for a nighttime crossing to Iowa. Before he left, he instructed William Clayton to hide or destroy the records of the Council of Fifty. Clayton buried them, then dug them up a few weeks later.

The decision taken, Hyrum emerged from the mansion and shook Cahoon's hand. "A company of men are seeking to kill my brother Joseph, and the Lord has warned him to flee to the Rocky Mountains to save his life," Hyrum said. "Goodbye, Brother Cahoon, we shall see you again."

Right behind him strode a silent, sobbing Joseph, with a handkerchief clapped to his face and tears streaming down his cheeks. His final journey had begun.

9

SURRENDER

BANK OF THE RIVER MISSISSIPPI, SUNDAY, 2 P.M.

TO: His Excellency Governor Ford:

SIR: I now offer to come to you at Carthage on the morrow, as early as shall be convenient for your posse to escort us into headquarters, provided we can have a fair trial, not be abused. . . .

—Excerpt from Joseph Smith's letter
to Thomas Ford, June 23, 1844

JOSEPH AND HYRUM'S DRAMATIC FLIGHT ACROSS THE MISSISSIPPI did not take them to the Rockies, as they had speculated to some friends, nor to Washington, DC, as Joseph had confided to Emma. The hegira took them nowhere. When the exhausted pair washed up near Montrose, in the Iowa Territory, at daybreak, there was no one home at the house where they intended to stay. Joseph sent Porter Rockwell back to Nauvoo to fetch horses, telling him to prepare for a trip to the Great Basin in the Rocky Mountains the next day. He handed Rockwell a letter for Emma, urging her not to despair. "I do not know where I shall go, or what I shall do," he wrote, "but shall endeavor to get to the city of Washington . . . may God Almighty bless you and the children and mother. My heart bleeds."

While the four men were battling the currents and the flotsam of the wild Mississippi, word of Joseph's flight flashed through Nauvoo. Even a benign dictatorship, lacking a dictator, grinds to a halt. With rumors swirling of an imminent invasion from Carthage, the leaderless Saints panicked. "Some were tried almost to death to think Joseph should leave them in the hour of danger," Vilate Kimball wrote to her husband Heber. "[Joseph and Hyrum's] giving themselves up is all that will save our city from destruction." A fierce debate sprang up among Joseph's intimates. In the early morning, Stephen Markham, the brigadier general whom Joseph had instructed to disband the Legion, encountered businessman Hiram Kimball and several other prominent Saints loudly discussing Joseph's fate in the middle of the city.

"It is a bailable case and there is no danger," Kimball assured the group, arguing that Smith could face a magistrate in Carthage without fear. Joseph's disappearance would "lessen the value of property—also ruin a number of men," he added, presumably including himself.

Kimball asked Markham to join a committee that would summon Joseph back to Nauvoo. "Mind your own business, brethren, and let Joseph alone," Markham replied. "I have my orders from him."

As Kimball and Reynolds Cahoon strode toward the Nauvoo Mansion, another Saint, Wandle Mace, overheard the two men fretting about the economic consequences of Joseph's disappearance. He heard the pair insisting that Governor Ford was the Mormons' friend, and he would protect Joseph if he returned to stand trial in Carthage. Mace couldn't believe his ears. "I believed the governor to be in perfect harmony with the mob," Mace said, "and if Joseph recrossed the river, he would be murdered. Should we, for the sake of a little property, be so selfish as to push him into the very jaws of death!"

Kimball and Cahoon entered the mansion to confer with the distraught Emma. That morning she had already received two messages from Ford. As usual, he was a fountain of contradictory pronunciamentos. First, he threatened to invade Nauvoo with his many militias, reimpose martial law, and search for Hyrum and Joseph, "if it took three years to do it." Second, Joseph's private attorney told her that Ford had guaranteed safe passage for Joseph, and a fair trial, if he surrendered himself in Carthage. Emma hashed out the dilemma with Kimball and Cahoon, then handed a letter to her nephew Lorenzo Wasson to carry to Joseph across the river.

Wasson, Kimball, Cahoon, and Rockwell were back on the Iowa shoreline by 1:00 p.m. The foursome found Joseph and Hyrum at the home of Mormon William Jordan, with their food and belongings strewn around the floor, waiting to be packed onto horses.

Wasson handed Emma's letter to Joseph. Ford will protect you, she wrote. Please come back.

Cahoon started up again, reaffirming the points made in Emma's letter. "You always said if the church would stick to you, you would stick to the church, now trouble comes and you are the first to run," he charged. "When the shepherd deserts his flock, who is to keep the wolves from devouring them?" Kimball and Wasson accused Joseph of cowardice, complaining that their property would be destroyed as a result.

"If my life is of no value to my friends it is of none to myself," Joseph said. He turned to his childhood friend Rockwell, possibly his most loyal follower, and surely his most ferocious. "What shall I do?"

"You are the oldest and ought to know best," Rockwell answered. "As you make your bed, I will lie with you."

Joseph then turned to Hyrum, and asked, "Brother Hyrum, you are the oldest, what shall we do?"

Apparently swayed by Emma's letter and by the pleadings of the terrified Saints, Hyrum suggested returning to Nauvoo. "Let us go back and give ourselves up, and see the thing out. Let us go back and put our trust in God, and we shall not be harmed. The Lord is in it. If we live or have to die, we will be reconciled to our fate."

Joseph thought for a moment, then answered. "If you go back I will go with you. But we shall be butchered."*

I I I

FROM THE IOWA SHORE, JOSEPH DASHED OFF A LETTER TO FORD: My co-defendants and I are coming to Carthage, as you asked. Joseph proposed to meet Ford's posse the following day, Monday, June 24, at the Mound, a promontory six miles east of Nauvoo. Joseph likewise alerted his lawyers that he would be facing charges in Carthage the next day. Ambling back to the river, he commented to Rockwell, "It is of no use to hurry, for we are going back to be slaughtered." He commented that he would like to address the Saints one last time, that evening.

"We can send out word, and have them hear you by starlight," Rockwell said.

Events quickly overtook this idea.

Instead, Joseph spent the night at the mansion, with Emma and his four children: the thirteen-year-old adopted Julia; Frederick, the blond eight-year-old; six-year-old Alexander; and his oldest son, Joseph Smith III, age eleven. As a grownup, young Joseph recalled that his father called him into one of the mansion's large reception rooms, then blessed him in front of the family: "If anything should happen to me, you will know who is to be my successor. This, my son, has been blessed and set apart, and will in time succeed me."

The next morning, Joseph told his family, "I go as a lamb to the slaughter, but if my death will atone for any faults I have committed during my lifetime I am willing to die." At 6:30, he exited the mansion and kissed each of his children good-bye. Several hundred Saints, in-

---

* The story of Joseph's return from Montrose has different shadings, depending on who is telling it. After the widowed Emma refused to join Brigham Young and the Latter-day Saints in Utah, the official church history blamed her for Joseph's death: "It was the strong persuasions of Reynolds Cahoon, Lorenzo D. Wasson and Hiram Kimball, who were carrying out Emma's instructions, that induced Joseph and Hyrum to start back to Nauvoo."

cluding his weeping, aged mother, Lucy, had gathered outside the mansion to see him off.

With his infant children hanging off his frame, Joseph asked: "Emma, can you train my sons to walk in their father's footsteps?"

"Oh, Joseph, you're coming back!" his wife cried. Smith posed the question twice more, and each time Emma gave the same answer, with tears filling her eyes. "Oh, Joseph, you are coming back."*

Thus Joseph began his journey along his Via Dolorosa. As promised, he and all his seventeen co-defendants in the *Expositor* affair mounted their horses and started the half-day's journey to Carthage. The assemblage was a Who's Who of the Latter-day Saints: patriarch Hyrum; Rockwell; Dunham, the brigadier general of the Legion; John Greene, the police chief; Nauvoo's constable and coroner, Dimick Huntington; the former newspaper editor and Joseph's chief ghostwriter, William Phelps. Friends who hadn't been named in the indictment, such as Willard Richards, the *Maid of Iowa* riverboat captain, Dan Jones, and Joseph's lawyer, James Woods, rode out with them. As the riders moved up the high ground leading to the unfinished Temple, Joseph gazed backward at the neatly platted city nestled alongside the mammoth, glistening Mississippi. "This is the loveliest place and the best people under the heavens," he remarked. "Little do they know the trials that await them."

Riding eastward, the group encountered a mounted company of sixty well-disciplined McDonough county Union Dragoons on their way to Nauvoo. Their commander, Captain James Dunn, halted Joseph, and explained that Governor Ford had ordered him to reclaim the state-owned weapons in the hands of the Nauvoo Legion: three cannon and about

---

* Mormon lore maintains that Joseph left his home without the protection of his sacred priesthood garment, worn by all Saints who receive their temple endowment. Contradictory accounts say that Emma had him remove the garment, or that Joseph hadn't been wearing the muslin underclothing because of the summer heat. Many years later, Brigham Young claimed that Joseph told Willard Richards: "Willard, you will stand where the balls will fly around you like hail and men will fall dead by your side, and if you will never part with this garment there never shall a ball injure you." Richards survived the assault on the Carthage jail.

two hundred and fifty muskets. The newly minted apostate Wilson Law, former Legion major general, had told Ford exactly how many guns to ask for. He probably knew that the Saints had many more weapons of their own, but those weren't subject to government seizure. Joseph acquiesced, and he and Dunn agreed that the handover might go more smoothly if the Prophet himself were present. Smith sent James Woods and a friend, Abram Hodge, ahead to Carthage to explain his change of plans, and to garner intelligence.

Back in Nauvoo, Joseph bade farewell to his family a second time, repeatedly comparing himself to "a lamb going to the slaughter." Joseph told friends that he didn't expect to see them again. "I am calm as a summer's morning," he said to his friend Henry Sherwood. "I have a conscience void of offense toward God and toward all men. If they take my life I shall die an innocent man, and my blood shall cry from the ground for vengeance, and it shall be said of me 'He was murdered in cold blood!'"*

Chicago journalist B. W. Richmond had traveled to Nauvoo to interview Lucinda Morgan, the famous widow of anti-Freemason author Captain William Morgan. Instead, he found himself reporting a much larger story. A non-Mormon, Richmond's dispatches were unclouded by church affiliation, so he saw a very different, characteristically relaxed Joseph Smith lounging in the mansion prior to his second departure for Carthage. "I saw a large, well dressed individual seated on a trunk at the further end of the hall, quietly smoking a cigar, who was pointed out to me as Joseph Smith." Richmond wrote. "He was easy in his manners and seemed sure of an acquittal if he could get a fair hearing."

Richmond and Smith rode on horseback to Nauvoo's Masonic Hall, where the Saints were loading their muskets and cannon onto wagons for Major Dunn.

---

* Some of the more dramatic, or quotable, episodes of Joseph's martyrdom may have been interpolated into the official church history. In 1844, Isaac Scott wrote to his in-laws in Massachusetts: "You will likely hear a great deal about Joseph's innocence, such as 'I go as a lamb to the slaughter' . . . All these statements, I believe, are false and got up for the purpose of reconciling the minds of the Church. I believe they had not the least idea that they were going to be murdered."

Emma asked Joseph for a blessing before his departure, but he claimed not to have time to compose one. Instead, he suggested that "she write out the best blessing she could think of," and he would sign it when he returned. Emma wrote out a prayer, hoping that she would lead a righteous life and find favor with God. In the final paragraph of the blessing, she wrote:

> I desire with all my heart to honor and respect my husband as my head, ever to live in his confidence and by acting in unison with him retain the place which God has given me by his side.

For almost her entire life, Emma viewed herself as married to one man, who was solely married to her. Within just a few years, her idée fixe became a grand delusion. She would convince herself and at least one of her sons that polygamy had never existed, and that Joseph had remained true to his original marriage vows.

Around sundown, Smith and his military escort rode out a second time toward Carthage. This time they encountered Hodge on the wooded outskirts of Nauvoo, riding back from the county seat. In Carthage, the innkeeper Artois Hamilton had pointed to the Carthage Grey militiamen camped on the town square and remarked, "Hodge, there are the boys that will settle you Mormons."

"We can take as many men as there are there out of the Nauvoo Legion, and they would not be missed," Hodge replied.

In his hasty horseback conversation with the Smiths on the Nauvoo-Carthage road, Hodge offered nothing but foreboding. "If it was my duty to counsel you," he said to Hyrum, "I would say, do not go another foot, for they say they will kill you, if you go to Carthage."

Smith and his friends continued their journey.

If Dunn and the Mormons thought they could sneak into Carthage at midnight, they were mistaken. The Carthage Greys caught sight of the mounted entourage and immediately started whooping and jeering.

"Where is the damned prophet?"

"Stand away, you McDonough boys," they yelled at Dunn's dragoons, "and let us shoot the damned Mormons."

"God damn you, old Joe, we've got you now."

"Clear the way and let us have a view of Joe Smith, the prophet of God, He has seen the last of Nauvoo. We'll use him up now, and kill all the damned Mormons."

If anyone doubted that they meant business, many of the Greys launched their muskets into the air and watched them parabola back to earth, their bayonets impaled into the soft ground.

The hullabaloo interrupted Governor Ford's slumber inside the Hamilton House. The woozy governor stuck his head out of his bedroom window. "I know your great anxiety to see Mr. Smith, which is natural enough, but it is quite too late tonight for you to have the opportunity," he said. "I assure you, gentlemen, you shall have that privilege tomorrow morning, as I will cause him to pass before the troops upon the square, and I now wish you, with this assurance, quietly and peaceably to return to your quarters."

This would prove to be yet another of Thomas Ford's bad ideas.

⅄ ⅄ ⅄

CARTHAGE WAS ON EDGE. OVER 1,000 CITIZEN SOLDIERS WERE milling around town with nothing to do. They were either spoiling for a fight or eager to go home and tend their farms. Inactivity was itself frightening; suppose the Nauvoo Legion attacked *them*? Trigger fingers were tense, noted Alton, Illinois, newspaper editor George T. M. Davis, who had come to cover the big story. "No one could close his ears against the murmurs that ran throughout the entire community," Davis wrote.

> Little squads could be seen at the taverns, at the tents of the soldiers, and in every part of the town . . . expressions falling from the lips [of the men] could leave no other impression upon any sane mind,

than that they were determined that the Smiths should not escape summary punishment.

To complicate matters, the motley militias milling around Carthage answered to no overall commander. According to the Illinois Constitution, Ford was their commander in chief. But he commanded no one on the ground. In theory, Brigadier General Minor Deming of the Southwestern Illinois Militia's Fourth Division oversaw the "many" county militias. But Deming, a well-educated, liberally inclined Yankee who tended a rural farm far from the anti-Mormon hotbeds of Carthage and Warsaw, was deemed to be an unreliable Jack-Mormon with secret, pro-Saint leanings. A decade earlier, when Illinoisans tried to fight the Black Hawk War, military discipline had been chaotic, wracked by company mutinies and mass desertions. It hadn't improved. The militia men answered to their colonels and captains, usually prominent merchants or farmers who shared their men's concerns—and their loathing of the Hancock County Mormons.

Keeping his promise of the previous evening, Ford summoned the Carthage Greys and the McDonough county militia to gather in front of the Carthage courthouse the next morning to "meet" Joseph and Hyrum Smith. It's doubtful that the troops had any curiosity about meeting the Prophet and his brother. More likely, they hoped to see their faces so they could pick them out of a crowd, if a battle, melee, or mob lynching ensued. Ford led the Smith brothers out of the Hamilton House, introducing them as "generals," the titles they claimed as leaders of the Nauvoo Legion. This didn't sit well with the militias, who considered the titles fraudulent. Joseph had walked on a game leg since his harrowing childhood operation and could never serve in a regular army or militia unit. Even if he were completely healthy, his religious status would have exempted him from service. His appearance triggered a near-mutiny among the excitable Greys. The militia surrounded Joseph and his tiny entourage, tossing their hats and brandishing their swords. They cursed "the damned Mormons" again and again.

"The Greys commenced hissing and smarming and making all kinds of *hellish* sounds," lieutenant Samuel Williams reported. "I tried to stop it but I couldn't. I had no more command over them than I would have had over a pack of wild Indians."

"There were at least a hundred men loaded to shoot Joe Smith," his lawyer Woods recalled, "but I was on his right and he was on Captain Dunn's right. I was between Smith and the militia."

"At this demonstration of feeling on the part of the Greys, Jo *actually fainted,*" Williams recalled. Perhaps Smith's knees buckled, or he felt faint; this account is Williams's alone.

Woods had been lawyering and circuit-riding in the area for six years. "I knew almost every man in the crowd," he said. "They told me afterwards that but for me, Joe would have never passed through the lines alive; they did not want to hurt me."

Deming, the nominal military commander, threatened to place several of the most aggressive Greys under arrest. Suddenly, their commander, Robert F. Smith, leaped up on a wagon and asked his men if they would submit to Deming's order.

"No!" they cried.

"Then load with ball cartridges!"

The Greys were so "wrought up . . . that the least notion to execute the order would in all probability have closed the career of the two prisoners," the Warsaw *Signal* reported.

Deming quickly countermanded his own order of arrest. On the first day of the Smiths' arrival in Carthage, he had lost control of his troops. Ford's personal guarantee of the Mormons' safety was moot.

Having sampled the hostility of the mobbing militias, Joseph and Hyrum would now get a taste of Carthage justice. In the afternoon, the Smiths and their seventeen co-defendants charged with destroying the Nauvoo *Expositor* met the man who would decide their fate: Robert F. Smith, justice of the peace and captain of the restive Greys—the same man who had led the Greys' mutiny on the town green! Smith was a bona fide Mormon-hater and a founding member of a "correspondence committee" formed the previous year to rid Hancock County of Mormons, by force if necessary. This was the same Robert Smith who had signed a bank note guaranteeing a portion of Joseph's ill-fated steamboat purchase, which landed them both in bankruptcy court.

Not surprisingly, Justice Smith started playing fast and loose with the law. He agreed to free all the defendants on bail, which he set at an extremely high $500 apiece. John Fullmer, an officer with the Nauvoo Legion who had followed the Smiths into Carthage, noted that the bail was more than twice the fine for the offense, had the defendants been convicted. "It was evident that the magistrate intended to outreach the pile of the brethren, so as to imprison those on trial for want of bail," he noted. But Fullmer and many of the other Mormons present offered their property as surety, and all the defendants were released.

With two exceptions. Earlier in the day, two of Smith's enemies, the Mormon apostates Augustine Spencer and Henry Norton, had filed pleas accusing Joseph and Hyrum of treason for placing Nauvoo under martial law. The captain of the Greys said it was too late in the day to argue the charges. Joseph's lawyer, Woods, insisted that Smith needed a mittimus warrant, signed by a justice of the peace, to send his clients to jail. I just happen to have one, replied Smith, who was also a justice of the peace. He pulled the document from his pocket.

Joseph objected to "such bare-faced, illegal, and tyrannical proceedings," to no avail.

Back at the Hamilton House, Woods and Justice Robert Smith both appealed to Governor Ford, a former Illinois supreme court justice, for guidance. To the Mormons, Ford argued that the governor had no judicial authority in Carthage or anywhere else in Illinois and could not prevent the Prophet from going to jail. To Justice Smith, he said, You have the Greys at your disposal. Enforce your order.

The judicial and extrajudicial maneuverings consumed several hours, during which Joseph Smith entertained visitors and curiosity seekers at the bustling hotel. His friend Cyrus Wheelock recalled that Smith even greeted some of the Greys inside his room:

General Smith asked them if there was anything in his appearance that indicated he was the desperate character his enemies represented him to be; and he asked them to give him their honest opinion on the subject.

The reply was, "No, sir, your appearance would indicate the very contrary, General Smith; but we cannot see what is in your heart, neither can we tell what are your intentions."

According to Wheelock, Joseph answered:

Very true, gentlemen, you cannot see what is in my heart, and you are therefore unable to judge me or my intentions; but I can see what is in your hearts, and will tell you what I see. I can see that you thirst for blood, and nothing but my blood will satisfy you.

For the second time in just two days, the visiting journalist B. W. Richmond happened upon Joseph Smith, this time in the Hamilton House while the Prophet was waiting on his fate. Richmond had taken the pulse of the Carthage militias and was certain that Smith was facing mortal danger. In a half-hour conversation in a foyer on the hotel's second floor, Richmond "told him plainly his danger, which seemed in no way to disturb him. He appeared straightforward in the expression of his feelings and opinions," Richmond reported,

and evinced much acquaintance with the world; together with a complete knowledge of the fickleness of human nature. As I parted with him he presented his hand and said, "Stranger, if I fall by the hands of assassins, tell the truth about my boys"—a name by which he called his friends.

As this conversation ended, Joseph Smith ceased to be a free man. Constable David Bettisworth, who had been trying to arrest Joseph for almost two weeks, showed up at Joseph's room to escort him to jail. Now Smith was no longer visiting Carthage on his own recognizance, sojourning at Hamilton's hotel. Now he and his brother were in jail for treason.

Unlike the previous charges laid against Smith, treason was not a bailable offense. Thus the two brothers had to walk the two and half blocks to the Carthage jail, through the drunken, armed mob, and amid the ranks of the jumped-up Greys. Justice Smith assigned Captain Dunn and his McDonough militia to escort Joseph and his entourage to the jail. Eight comrades, including Lorenzo Wasson, John Greene, Willard Richards, and John Taylor, formed a cordon around Joseph and accompanied him to the two-story brick jailhouse. Stephen Markham carried a large hickory cane he called a "rascal beater" and flailed it more than once, as drunken Mormon-haters penetrated the shield of guards and threw themselves through the darkness at Joseph.

Some time after 9:00 p.m., the Mormons met George Stigall, the Carthage jailer. Their stay would prove to be a most unusual one. The Mormons, and Stigall's wife and children, were the sole occupants of the two-story, four-room building. (The Stigalls' housekeeper was Lucy Clayton, daughter of William Clayton, one of Joseph's personal scribes.) Jailhouse security was sporadic. Occasionally, Stigall would demand that visitors produce passes, but sometimes not. Some visitors were frisked for contraband, some not. When the group first arrived, Stigall placed them in an iron-barred, second-floor criminal cell. Within a few hours, he moved them downstairs to the more spacious, but less secure, debtors' quarters.

As Joseph and the Saints settled in to their first night as prisoners, Emma Smith received a brief letter from her husband:

DEAR EMMA.—I have had an interview with Governor Ford, and he treats us honorably. Myself and Hyrum have been again arrested for treason because we called out the Nauvoo Legion but when the truth comes out we have nothing to fear. We all feel calm and composed.

Joseph mentioned that Ford planned to send some militia to Nauvoo, "to protect the citizens," and doubtless to keep an eye on the Nauvoo Legion as well. Smith expressed the wish that the Illinois troops "be kindly treated. . . . I do hope the people of Nauvoo will continue pacific and prayerful."

One of Joseph's voluntary cell mates was Dan Jones, a short, wiry Welsh riverboat captain who was a recent convert to Mormonism. In April 1843, Jones agreed to ferry two hundred British Saints from New Orleans on a perilous trip up to Nauvoo, where chunks of ice still clogged the Mississippi. Greeting his people on the pier, Joseph broke into tears when he learned how bad weather repeatedly threatened Jones's pocket-sized steamer. "Bless this little man!" Joseph exclaimed upon meeting the doughty captain, who quickly agreed to be baptized, and to allow Smith to buy half ownership of the *Maid of Iowa*. Now Jones had chosen to face death with his Prophet and his colleagues, whom Jones found remarkably composed. The Mormons spent "the first night of our imprisonment in pleasant conversation about 'the secret of godliness,'" he remembered. "I had never seen them so cheerful and so heavenly minded, nor had I before thought that Carthage jail was the gate of paradise."

⚜ ⚜ ⚜

THE NEXT DAY, WEDNESDAY, BEGAN UNEVENTFULLY. AT 7:00 A.M., Stigall moved his family and relocated his guests to his own upstairs bedroom, which had a bed, mattresses for Stigall's children, a writing desk and chairs, and curtained windows. John Taylor remembered that Stigall "and his wife, manifested a disposition to make us as comfortable as they could." The Stigalls shared their ample meals with their Mormon guests, eating at the same table, and charging them for board.

Joseph regaled his cell mates with two of his dreams. The first one, in which he was trapped in a pit by the perfidious Laws, he had shared with the Saints the previous week. In the second dream, he saved a foundering ship "by wadeing through the foaming surf and leading her out into the open sea," his cell mate Jones recalled. "The interpretation he gave, I believe was the stranding of the great ship 'Uncle Sam' owing to rejecting a safe Pilot." Separately, Jones recalled, Joseph "gave frequent intimations that he would soon gain his liberty, and soar on high beyond the 'rage of mobs and angry strife.'"

Jones decided to work on the bedroom door, which had no lock. Wielding a pen knife—Stigall's searches were cursory indeed—Jones was trying to fashion a crude latch for the upstairs door, without much luck. Leaning out of the windows, Joseph, Hyrum, and several other Mormons preached scripture to the guards. The official church history, compiled many years later, reports that several Greys left their posts, convinced of the prisoners' innocence. There were no independent reports of such converts.

Just before 10:00 a.m., Governor Ford and militia colonel Thomas Geddes arrived at the jailhouse for a forty-five-minute interview with Joseph. The governor and the Prophet restated their set positions at some length. Ford outlined the cases against Joseph, his spurious use of the Nauvoo courts to escape prosecution, and again condemned his ill-advised attack on the newspaper, "the great bulwark of American freedom." Joseph invoked Blackstone, "one of the most eminent English barristers," to justify his actions against the "foul, noisome, filthy sheet." He offered to make restitution to the Law brothers for their lost investment, which drew no response from Ford.

The governor repeated that he couldn't interfere with the administration of justice and mentioned his plans to travel to Nauvoo the next day, to assure himself that the town was safe. He promised to take Joseph with him if he did.

With Ford preparing to leave the cell, Joseph said, "Governor Ford, I shall look to you for protection."

"And you shall have protection, General Smith," Ford answered. "I do not, however, apprehend danger. I think you are perfectly safe either here or anywhere else."

Geddes later said that Ford vented his frustration with the Prophet after the two men left the jail and ambled back to the center of town. "It's all nonsense!" Ford exclaimed. "You will have to drive these Mormons out yet!"

"If we undertake that, governor, when the proper time comes, will you interfere?"

"No, I will not," Ford said, and added after a pause: "Until you are through."

After lunch, Captain Robert Smith summoned Joseph and Hyrum to the courthouse. The call subjected the Mormons to yet another harrowing trip through the armed mob gathered around the jail.

Leaving his cell, Joseph "walked boldly into the midst of a hollow square of the Carthage Greys. . . . Evidently expecting to be massacred in the streets before arriving at the Court House, [he] politely locked arms with the worst mobocrat he could see." His brother and Willard Richards followed suit, and the three of them stumbled across the town square together, clinging to their tormentors for dear life. The taunts came fast and furious:

"Now Old Joe, if you are a prophet, how did you come to the jail like this?"

"Oh, if Joe were a prophet, he would soon call for a legion of angels and we would all be killed, and he would escape."

Years later, Dan Jones saw echoes of Christ's Passion story in Joseph's torments: "One was forcibly reminded of the taunting and jeering of the Jews to our holy and meek Redeemer, so similar did their words and actions prove their spirits to be."

The scene at the courthouse was brief. Joseph's lawyers argued for a continuance, hoping to free their client in the interim. His attorney, Woods, noted that his client had been "committed to jail without any examination whatsoever." Ominously, two of Joseph's enemies, Chauncey Higbee and the lawyer-editor Thomas Sharp, appeared for the prosecution, arguing for a speedy trial. When Joseph left the courthouse, he thought he would return for a hearing the next day. But that night Robert Smith changed the date on what would prove to be the fateful warrant, from Thursday, June 27, to Saturday, June 29. A small detail, but one that ensured that Joseph and Hyrum Smith would remain imprisoned without a hearing for three days, instead of just one.

Just before supper, Joseph's uncle John Smith came to visit the brothers in jail, having traveled over 150 miles from Macedonia, Illinois. The Greys guarding the jailhouse said they didn't care who the old man was, he wasn't coming in. Joseph argued on behalf of "so old and infirm a man," and—after a thorough search—the Greys let him enter. When John Fullmer returned to the jail to spend the night with his friends, the surly guards rifled through the pockets of his overcoat. But they didn't search his boots. Fullmer smuggled in a small, single-barreled pistol, which he gave to Hyrum.

That night, the five jailed men—the two Smiths, Fullmer, Richards, and Jones—went to bed late. When Joseph and Hyrum tumbled into the one bed, Richards, the official church historian, was still writing at the desk by candlelight. The men could hear disturbances from the street outside during the night: swearing, yelling, and eventually, a gunshot. The report woke Joseph up. He got out of bed and lay down on the floor between Jones and Fullmer. The three men started whispering, like campers trying not to wake others sleeping next to a campfire.

"I would like to see my family again," Joseph said. "And I would to God that I could preach to the Saints in Nauvoo once more." Fullmer assured him that all of them would make it home safely, and that Joseph would preach again, many times.

Richards finally joined Hyrum in the bed, and when everyone seemed to be asleep, Joseph turned his head to whisper to Jones.

"Are you afraid to die?" Joseph asked.

"Is it that time?" Jones replied. "Engaged in such a cause I do not think that death would have many terrors."

Joseph answered, "You will yet see Wales, and fulfill the mission appointed you before you die."

Within a year, Jones was back in Wales, preaching the Book of Mormon to potential converts. Five years later, he would escort a band of 250 Welsh men and women across the Atlantic, and then across the Great Plains to found the "Welsh settlement" in the Salt Lake Valley.

10

"THE PEOPLE ARE NOT
THAT CRUEL"

Your friends shall be protected, and have a fair trial by
the law. In this pledge I am not alone; I have obtained
the pledge of the whole of the army to sustain me.

—*Governor Thomas Ford to Dan Jones*

THURSDAY, JUNE 27, 1844, IN CARTHAGE, ILLINOIS, DAWNED
rainy, humid, hot, and glum. Again, Joseph shared a dream with
his cell mates. He dreamed that he was back in Kirtland, Ohio, where
the Saints had gathered in 1831. He walked out to his old farm, "which
I found grown up with weeds and brambles." He ventured inside his
dilapidated barn, when he was suddenly set upon by "a company of
furious men [whose leader] ordered me to leave the barn and farm,
stating it was none of mine, and that I must give up all hope of ever
possessing it." No, Joseph objected that the church had given him this
farm. But his opponent refused to yield. "He then grew furious and
began to rail upon me, and threaten me, and said it never did belong
to me nor to the Church.

While he was thus engaged, pouring out his bitter words upon me, a rabble rushed in and nearly filled the barn, drew out their knives, and began to quarrel among themselves for the premises, and for a moment forgot me, at which time I took the opportunity to walk out of the barn about up to my ankles in mud.

When I was a little distance from the barn, I heard them screeching and screaming in a very distressed manner, as it appeared they had engaged in a general fight with their knives. While they were thus engaged, the dream or vision ended.

After relating his dream, Joseph asked Dan Jones to speak with the guards outside the jail, to find out what had woken him during the night. Franklin Worrell, a tall, strapping, twenty-five-year-old shopkeeper and assistant postmaster from Carthage, was commanding the six-man detachment of Greys. Worrell was gregarious and popular. Like Joseph, he had made many friends by extending credit to his customers. He was also an active anti-Mormon agitator, who, like his commander, Robert Smith, headed up a local correspondence committee that spread news of Mormon depredations, real and imagined. Worrell advised Jones not to worry about random noises in the night. "We have had too much trouble to bring Old Joe here to let him ever escape out alive," Worrell continued, "and unless you want to die with him you better leave before sundown, and you are not a damned bit better than him for taking his part."

Jones said that he didn't expect to hear that from the man charged with guarding Smith's life.

"You'll see that I can prophesy better than old Joe," Worrell spat back. "Neither he nor his brother nor anyone who will remain with them will see the sun set today." A Grey leveled his musket at Jones, cocked it, and said he "would love to bore a hole through old Joe."

Overhearing this exchange from inside the jail, Joseph and Hyrum urged Jones to report the conversation to Governor Ford. The riverboat captain scurried over to the Hamilton hotel, where he found

Ford simultaneously handing out orders and packing his things. Ford was leaving for Nauvoo, as announced, although he had decided to go without Joseph.

Ford insisted that he had taken measures both to guarantee Joseph's safety in Carthage and to defuse tensions generally. He planned to send all his troops home, save for three companies. As he later explained it, the numbers were against him. Even with four separate militias under his command—Carthage, Warsaw, and the visitors from McDonough and Schuyler Counties—Ford believed he had at most 1,700 men, 1,200 muskets, three cannons, and provisions for only two days. Many of the men wanted to go home. Furthermore, the state treasury had no money to pay for their rations. The Nauvoo Legion had at least 2,000 soldiers and could probably swell its ranks to over 3,000 if necessary. If full-scale civil war broke out, Ford thought the Legion could probably muster a superior force on short notice and overwhelm the old settlers. He openly worried that his "regulators" might march on Nauvoo, stage a bloody provocation, and proceed to massacre "women, inoffensive young persons, and innocent children." "To think of beginning a war under such circumstances was a plain absurdity," he later wrote.

In his hotel chamber, Ford explained his thinking to Brigadier General Minor Deming and the assembled militia captains. "The governor seemed plagued by the foul fiend Flibbertigibbet," John Hay commented. "He changed his mind every hour." One of the three remaining companies would accompany him to Nauvoo that morning, on a combination reconnaissance–peacekeeping mission–show of force. There had been talk of rousting a Mormon counterfeiting cabal, which Ford suspected was just a pretext for vigilante action. Ford assigned two companies of the Carthage Greys, under Robert Smith's command, to stay in the center of Carthage and protect the jail. The six-man guard would remain posted outside the jailhouse doors, and the rest of the Greys were to stay in their tents on the public square, about one-quarter mile away.

He chose the Greys, he explained, because "they were the elite of the militias," and their leader, Robert Smith, "a most respectable citizen, and honorable man." Yes, he had witnessed their mutiny just two days previously, and yes, Ford recognized that "they and their officers were the deadly enemies of the prisoners." But in June 1844, in southwestern Illinois, Ford concluded, "It would have been difficult to find friends of the prisoners."

Jones burst in on Ford just as he was concluding his war council and preparing to ride off to Nauvoo. He told Ford that he had proof that the prisoners' lives were in grave danger.

"You are unnecessarily alarmed for your friends' safety," the governor replied. "The people are not that cruel."

Astonished by Ford's naïveté, Jones reminded the governor that he had guaranteed the Mormons' safety. "They are also master Masons," Jones added, "and as such I demand of you the protection of their lives."

An onlooker reported that Ford, a fellow Mason, briefly turned pale.

"If you do not do this, I have one more desire," Jones said.

"What is that, sir?"

"It is that is the Almighty will preserve my life to a proper time and place, that I may testify that you have been timely warned of their danger."

As Joseph predicted, Jones would survive his stay in Carthage, and he later wrote a valuable first-person account of the Prophet's final days.

Elder Cyrus Wheelock also found his way to Ford's suite to importune the governor with his own warning: the Mormons "are safe as regards the law, but they are not safe from the hands of traitors, and midnight assassins who thirst for their blood and have determined to spill it."

"Your friends shall be protected, and have a fair trial by the law," Ford assured him. "In this pledge I am not alone; I have obtained the pledge of the whole of the army to sustain me."

Ford busied himself to leave, and Jones tried to return to the jail. But the guards refused him entry. Chauncey Higbee emerged from

the swarming crowd of ill-wishers to tell Jones that they "were determined to kill Joe and Hyrum and that I had better go away to save
myself." Willard Richards appeared at the jailhouse door and handed
Jones a letter from Joseph to the renowned lawyer Orville Browning,
in Quincy. In the letter, Joseph pleaded with Browning to come north
and rescue him. Jones galloped out of Carthage with the letter, which
the mob milling around the jail assumed was a summons from Joseph
to the Nauvoo Legion. Jones reported that he fled Carthage "in the
midst of a cloud of dust with bullets whistling through the air."

Cyrus Wheelock did gain entrance to Joseph's quarters, and the
guards forgot to check his bulky raincoat when he entered. Like Fullmer the night before, he was carrying a gun, this one a small, six-
shooter revolver known as a pepperbox. Unobtrusively, he slipped the
gun into Joseph's pocket. Joseph knew Wheelock planned to return to
Nauvoo that evening. The county was on a war footing, and anti-Mormon militia were guarding the roads into and out of town.

Joseph said that Wheelock himself might need the gun, but Wheelock insisted that Joseph keep it.

Joseph took out Fullmer's revolver and handed it to his brother
Hyrum.

"You may have use for this."

"I hate to use such things or to see them used," Hyrum replied.

"So do I," said Joseph, "but we may have to, to defend ourselves."

Hyrum took the pistol.

ℸ ℸ ℸ

THAT SAME MORNING, JOSEPH WROTE HIS LAST LETTER TO EMMA,
and to the Saints in Nauvoo:

DEAR EMMA.—

The Governor continues his courtesies, and permits us to see our
friends. We hear this morning that the Governor will not go down

173

with his troops today to Nauvoo, as we anticipated last evening; but if he does come down with his troops you will be protected. . . .

There is no danger of any extermination order. Should there be a mutiny among the troops (which we do not anticipate, excitement is abating) a part will remain loyal and stand for the defense of the state and our rights. . . .

JOSEPH SMITH.

P. S. Dear Emma, I am very much resigned to my lot, knowing I am justified, and have done the best that could be done. Give my love to the children and all my friends, Mr. Brewer, and all who inquire after me; and as for treason, I know that I have not committed any, and they cannot prove anything of the kind, so you need not have any fears that anything can happen to us on that account. May God bless you all. Amen.

P.S. 20 min to 10—I just learn that the Governor is about to disband his troops, all but a guard to protect us and the peace,—and come himself to Nauvoo and deliver a speech to the people. This is right as I suppose.

While Wheelock was carrying Joseph's letter to Nauvoo, Governor Ford and a detachment of Captain Dunn's McDonough County Dragoons were on the road to Warsaw, where they had agreed to meet the local militia at a crossroads outside of town. The previous day, Ford and Deming had instructed the Warsaw commander to prepare his troops to march to Nauvoo, with two cannons. The men of the Warsaw militia, three hundred strong, thought they would be accompanying Ford into Nauvoo, and they had plunder on their mind. Thomas Sharp had issued his call for a Mormon extermination campaign only a few days before.

In Warsaw on this muggy Thursday, John Hay watched his father, a surgeon, ride out with the militia to the crossroads near some railroad shanties. The dilapidated shacks had been built to supply a contemplated Carthage-to-Warsaw railway that foundered in the Panic of 1837. "They went out in high glee, fully expecting to march to the city of the Saints," reported Hay, who was a teenager at the time. "Every man clearly understood that Nauvoo was to be destroyed before they returned."

When Colonel Levi Williams and his Warsaw regiment met Ford at the crossroads, they learned that their marching orders had been rescinded. Ford had gotten wind of their intentions and did not want them to march on Nauvoo after all. He pointedly confiscated their cannons, which he suspected they would put to ill use. "They were annoyed . . . at losing the fun of sacking Nauvoo," Hay wrote.

Most of the men returned to Warsaw. But Thomas Sharp was on the scene, and both Colonel Williams and his son were Mormon-haters of some renown. Just a few days earlier, Joseph had learned of Williams père harassing Isaac Morley and the Saints in Lima, Illinois, and the father-son team had continued terrorizing Saints and Jack-Mormons in Hancock County all week. Levi Williams had just threatened to confiscate the weapons of any militia unwilling to participate in the anti-Mormon crusade and ordered the tarring and feathering of a militiaman deemed insufficiently suffused with hatred for Joseph Smith.

Two of Williams's Warsaw captains—lawyer William Grover and businessman Mark Aldrich—also despised Mormons and tried to rally their troops to march on Carthage. Grover's men ignored the speechifying and headed home. The majority of Williams's men headed home as well, but about a hundred of them agreed to ignore Ford's wishes and march back to Carthage. As if by prearrangement, a rider arrived from Carthage, announcing that the coast was clear. Ford and Dunn's McDonough County Dragoons had left Carthage and were headed to Nauvoo.

Now only the Carthage Greys—the same men who had just staged a riot, calling for Joseph's blood—stood between the Warsaw men and the imprisoned Smiths. But the dispatcher reported that the Greys would not oppose an assault on the jail. Williams, Grover, Aldrich, and about a hundred of their men began the fifteen-mile march to Carthage, where Joseph and his friends sat waiting in the jail.

⚜ ⚜ ⚜

INSIDE THE CARTHAGE JAIL, THE PRISONERS ATE THEIR LUNCHES. Joseph, Hyrum, and Willard Richards ate upstairs in Stigall's family room, while John Taylor and Stephen Markham dined on the ground floor. After eating, Richards felt queasy, and Joseph asked Markham to fetch a pipe and some tobacco to settle his friend's stomach. Markham left the jail, borrowed a pipe from yet another Jack-Mormon, the local sheriff, Jacob Backenstos, and bought some tobacco in a nearby store. Ominously, the store's proprietor, John Eagle, "threw out considerable threats against the Mormons and in particular against me," Markham later wrote.

As he strode back to the jail, another local accosted Markham.

"Old man, you have got to leave the town in five minutes!"

"I shall not do it," Markham answered, "Neither can you drive me. You can kill me but you cannot drive me."

But they could. A dozen Greys quickly surrounded him and started poking at him with their bayonets, urged on by Eagle. The innkeeper Artois Hamilton emerged from his hotel and told Markham he had better leave town, "as I would only get killed if I remained. 'You can't do the prisoners any good,' he said."

Hamilton offered to fetch Markham's horse. Markham objected, but minutes later, he was in the saddle, his boots filled with blood from the constant bayonet pricks. The Greys "formed a hollow square around me," Markham said, and accompanied him to the forest on the edge of town.

Apprised that Markham had been run out of town, the jailer Stigall sensed danger. He suggested the Mormons might be safer if he locked them into the secure prison cell on the second floor. The barred cell had two-and-one-half-foot-thick walls with thin, arrow-slit windows. "After supper we will go in," Joseph said.

The four Mormon prisoners were alone now, "our spirits dull and heavy," John Taylor wrote. The stone jail was oppressively hot in the late afternoon. Even with all the bedroom windows open, and stripped to their shirts and breeches, the Mormons were sweltering. The four men gave one of the guards a dollar and sent out for a bottle of wine, "to revive us." The man quickly returned with the wine, some tobacco, and a few pipes. The four prisoners drank from the bottle and shared the remaining wine with their jailers.

The wine had the opposite of the desired effect; "We all of us felt unusually dull and languid, with a remarkable depression of spirits," Taylor remembered. In a desperate attempt to buoy their mood, Hyrum suggested that Taylor, who had a beautiful voice, sing the popular folk hymn, "A Poor Wayfaring Man of Grief."

In the song, the narrator generously offers food, clothing and solace to a destitute wayfarer. Ultimately, the singer finds the wayfarer locked in prison,

condemned to meet a traitor's doom at morn

The stranger asks if his benefactor was willing to die for him;

The flesh was weak, my blood ran chill,
But the free spirit cried, "I will!"

The imprisoned stranger is Jesus Christ. Through his generosity to his savior, the singer has attained salvation.

Joseph chose this moment to ask Willard Richards if he was willing to die with him, and with Hyrum.

"Brother Joseph, you did not ask me to cross the river with you," Richards answered. "You did not ask me to come to Carthage. You did not ask me to come to jail with you. Do you think I would forsake you now? But I will tell you what I will do; if you are condemned to be hung for treason, I will be hung in your stead, and you shall go free."

"You can't do that," Joseph replied.

Repeating the affirmation from the song, Richards insisted, "I will!"

Taylor, sitting at the open, west-facing window, said he saw something: a band of men, their faces smudged, emerging from the woods and charging toward the jail. Then the Smiths and Richards heard a clamor at the bottom of the staircase.

꙳ ꙳ ꙳

FOURTEEN-YEAR-OLD WILLIAM HAMILTON OF THE CARTHAGE Greys, son of the innkeeper, was the first to spot the irregulars approaching the woods along the Warsaw road. Hamilton's captain had stationed him atop the Carthage courthouse, telling him to watch for activity on the Nauvoo road, to the north. For obvious reasons, the Greys worried that Joseph's storied Legionnaires might be invading Carthage from the northwest. By chance, Hamilton trained his field glasses in a different direction and spotted an armed force, on horseback and on foot, trailed by wagons, entering the woods on the outskirts of town, about two miles away. Thirty minutes later, around 4:30 p.m., he saw about 125 men emerging from the woods in single file, stealing alongside an old rail fence, less than a mile from the jail. The men had smeared their faces with mud and with gunpowder, and some wore their jerseys or coats turned inside out. Still, Hamilton recognized them as Warsaw militia. The boy tried to alert the Greys, but Captain Smith was nowhere to be found.

Eudocia Baldwin, whose brothers were serving in the Greys—one had just joined the six-man guard posted at the jail—reported that the Greys were either asleep, in disarray, or both. Baldwin and other Carthage residents panicked, assuming that a Mormon force of marauding "Danites" had invaded Carthage to free Joseph and exact retribution on his persecutors. Robert Smith and his lieutenant Samuel Williams finally mobilized their men in a storm of shouting and swearing. "Come on, you cowards—damn you come on!" Baldwin heard them cry. "Those boys will all be killed."

In hindsight, William Hamilton noted that, "for one of the best drilled and equipped companies in the state at that time," the Greys were forming ranks like a bunch of stumblebums. "I have always thought the officers and some privates were working for delay," he wrote.

While the Greys fussed with their muskets and cartridge belts a few hundred yards away on the town common, the irregulars had already reached the jail. The jailer Stigall and Worrell's guard offered no resistance. Someone fired shots at the jailhouse entrance, which were later determined to be either blanks or harmless warning shots aimed over the heads of Worrell's men, who quickly fled. A bullet whistled into Mrs. Stigall's kitchen, where she was baking bread in a Dutch oven.

The inflamed Warsaw militia—one eyewitness saw a keg of whiskey in their baggage train—stormed up the staircase to the room where the Mormons had gathered, firing their weapons as they climbed.

Dan Jones's effort to fashion a crude latch for the second-floor door had failed. It couldn't be locked. Richards and Hyrum Smith threw themselves against the door to keep out the angry mob, but bullets started popping through the flimsy wood. The second shot fired entered Hyrum's skull on the left side of his nose. Simultaneously, a musket ball shot from the ground through one of the open windows hit Hyrum in the back. He fell backward, crying, "I am a dead man." His lifeless body lay in the middle of the floor, blood pouring from his wounds.

Joseph and John Taylor rushed past Hyrum's body to the door. Willard Richards had stationed himself behind the hinges, trying to push the door closed. But Joseph pulled out his six-shooter and started firing though the narrow opening between the door and the frame. Three of the chambers fired, and Joseph made his shots count. He wounded three assailants on the staircase, one in the arm, one in the shoulder, and another in the face. When Smith wasn't shooting, Taylor was swinging Markham's massive, gnarled "rascal beater" walking stick to knock down the bayonets and musket barrels poking through the cracked-open doorway.

But soon Joseph ran out of bullets. He hadn't managed to grab Hyrum's pistol in the melee, so now the Mormons were fighting their well-armed enemies with nothing more than muscle power, a gnarly walking stick, and a cane.

"It certainly was a terrible scene," Taylor recalled.

> Streams of fire as thick as my arm passed by me as these men fired, and, unarmed as we were, it looked like certain death. . . . It certainly was far from pleasant to be so near the muzzles of those fire-arms as they belched forth their liquid flames and deadly balls.
>
> While I was engaged in parrying the guns, Brother Joseph said, "That's right, Brother Taylor, parry them off as well as you can." Those were the last words I ever heard him speak on earth.

As mobbers from the bottom of the stairs pushed forward, more musket barrels poked through the doorway. Soon the killers invaded the room. Taylor ran from the door to an open window on the north side of the jail, hoping against hope that a militia, or even the Nauvoo Legion, had come to the Mormons' aid. He thought of jumping the fifteen feet to the ground, but he saw the jail surrounded only by blackfaced Warsaw mobbers screaming anti-Mormon curses. A bullet from the door entered his thigh and flattened itself against the bone. A second bullet flying through the window struck him in the midriff, shattering his pocket watch and propelling him back into the room. "If I had fallen out, I should assuredly have been killed," Taylor recalled, "if not by the fall, by those around and this ball intended to dispatch me was turned by an over-ruling Providence into a messenger of mercy and saved my life."

A famous 1878 painting by Danish convert C. C. Christensen depicts
Hyrum Smith slain in the Carthage jail cell; Joseph, dressed in white,
symbolizing his innocence; John Taylor batting down musket barrels
with his cane; and Willard Richards hiding behind the cell door.
Credit: Brigham Young University Art Museum

Falling to the floor, the blood-spattered Taylor rolled under the bed
for safety. The mob fired two more bullets into him, "cutting away a
piece of flesh from his left hip as large as a man's hand," Richards reported. Taylor was left for dead, his watch stopped at 5:16 p.m.

Desperately hoping for safety, Joseph Smith followed Taylor to the
window, planning to jump. A mobber named Gallagher shot him in
the back from the doorway, and shots from the ground struck Joseph
in the chest and back. Smith tumbled out the window, crying, "O Lord
my God," the first words of the Masonic cry for help, "O Lord my God, is
there no help for the widow's son?" His body fell near a raised wooden
curb surrounding a well.

There was to be no pity for the widowed Lucy Mack's son. Mobber
William Voorhis grabbed Joseph's body and propped it up against the
well. Then he exposed Joseph's bloody chest to the angry mob.

John Taylor's watch, shattered in the melee at the Carthage Jail
Credit: LDS Church History Library

"You are the damned old Chieftain," Voorhis taunted the half-dead body of Joseph Smith, "Now go see your spiritual wives in hell!" Voorhis stood aside and watched a handful of his comrades fire several more rounds into Joseph's lifeless body.*

The mob had come for Joseph, and Joseph was dead. The mission was over. Inside Stigall's chambers, Richards was still huddling behind the door. Barely wounded—he had suffered only a minor scratch on his earlobe—he heard the killers clamber back down the jailhouse stairwell. After a few moments, he ventured, tentatively, to the window. He saw a hundred men gathered around Joseph's lifeless body. Just then, he heard Taylor's voice from under the bed.

"Stop, Doctor, take me along," Taylor said.

With the two men alone in the jailhouse, Richards dragged Taylor's bullet-ridden body into the adjoining cell and pulled a filthy mattress over him.

---

* Many fabulous details attending Joseph's death were introduced into evidence at his assassins' trial. See Chapter 12.

"That may hide you, and you may yet live to tell the tale," Richards said. "I expect they will kill me in a few moments."

Having climbed down from his rooftop perch on the courthouse, the young William Hamilton rushed to the scene. From fifty yards away, he saw Joseph Smith tumble from the second-floor window. He saw someone prop Joseph's body up against the low wall surrounding the jailhouse well. "He's dead," a mobber grunted, and the attackers vanished as quickly as they came.

Hamilton entered the jail and "found Hyrum Smith lying upon the floor on his back, dead." He didn't look into the adjoining cell, where Richards and Taylor were hiding. "After I had satisfied my curiosity, seen and been among the mob, seen the prophet shot, and seen the dead men, it occurred to me I ought to go home and tell the news," Hamilton recalled. Two hundred yards from the jail, he encountered his comrades-in-arms, the Greys, finally approaching the scene. He suggested they "about face" and return to their encampment; "Their prisoners were dead and not likely to run away."

The faked confrontation with the guards, the siege up the staircase, the slaughter of the Mormons and the brief ogling of the dead Prophet's body consumed three minutes. When Richards eventually descended the staircase and reconnoitered around the jail, he saw that the mob had vanished as quickly as it had struck. At precisely this moment, Robert Smith's Carthage Greys appeared on the scene, just "in time to see the rear portion of the mob disappearing in the distance," Eudocia Baldwin recounted.

‡ ‡ ‡

THE GREYS WERE NOT THE ONLY ONES WITH AN ASTONISHING gift of timing. At almost the very moment that the Warsaw assassins swarmed up the jailhouse stairs to kill Joseph and Hyrum, Governor Ford was addressing several thousand residents of Nauvoo. Standing atop the frame of the half-built house at the corner of Water and Main Streets—the very spot where Joseph had unsheathed his cavalry sword in front of the Legion just nine days before—the governor was in a tut-tutting mood. He chastised the Mormons for not immediately surrendering Joseph Smith after the destruction of the *Nauvoo Expositor*. "Another cause of excitement is the fact of your having so many firearms," Ford said, as if he had forgotten his own disarming of the Nauvoo Legion just four days before.

> The public are afraid that you are going to use them against government. I know there is a great prejudice against you on account of your peculiar religion, but you ought to be praying Saints, not military Saints.

Then Ford threatened the Mormons in the starkest possible terms. "If you continue to 'misbehave,'" he said, "the city may be reduced to ashes, and extermination would inevitably follow."

The Mormons couldn't believe their ears. The governor of Illinois, commander in chief of the state's many militias, responsible for protecting his citizens, was blaming *them*, and them alone, for the civil war that had erupted in Hancock County. "A severe atonement must be made," for the Saints' lawless behavior in the *Expositor* affair, Ford said, blissfully unaware that blood atonement was taking place just eighteen miles away at the jailhouse. He seemed unable to repress his inner schoolmarm: "I hope you will not make any more trouble, but be a law-abiding people, for if I have to come again it will be worse for you."

At 5:30 p.m., Ford and his entourage toured the unfinished Nauvoo Temple and made caustic remarks about the twelve, life-size, carved wooden oxen that supported the massive laver, or baptismal font. At sixteen feet long and four feet deep, the immense carved pine basin was the showpiece of the Temple, now in its third year of construction. Joseph once described the oxen, painstakingly carved by "Elder Elijah Fordham, from the city of New York," as "copied after the most beautiful five-year old steer that could be found in the country . . . the horns were formed after the most perfect horn that could be procured."

The twenty-seven-year-old Thomas Bullock, a future church historian, saw Ford's men snap the horns off the oxen and pocket them for souvenirs. Bullock later wrote that Ford seemed to know that the Smith brothers had already been murdered and was in a hurry to leave Nauvoo. Ford's account differs. As he was riding back to Carthage, Ford encountered two Greys galloping furiously from Carthage to alert him about the assassination. Ford absorbed the news and ordered the riders to return home "to prevent any sudden explosion of Mormon excitement."

Ford probably had no foreknowledge of the killings, because he later complained about their timing. "I could not believe, that any person would attack the jail, whilst we were in Nauvoo, and thereby expose my life . . . to the sudden vengeance of the Mormons," he wrote in his *History of Illinois.*

In other words, the worst possible consequence of the jailhouse lynching was that he, Thomas Ford, might have been exposed to danger.

Ɏ Ɏ Ɏ

IN CARTHAGE, THE FIRST PERSON TO MINISTER TO THE MOR-MONS was Dr. Thomas Barnes, the town coroner. Like almost every Gentile in the area, Barnes disliked Mormons. He participated in anti-Mormon rallies and claimed that Governor Ford was a thinly disguised Mormon sympathizer. Barnes also captained a shadowy company of rangers who patrolled the prairies "to range as spies and ride as expresses [message carriers]," he later revealed. But in the early evening of June 27, Barnes honored his Hippocratic oath. He quickly determined that Joseph Smith, whose bullet-riddled body he found dumped in the entrance hall of the jail, was dead. Hyrum Smith's bloody carcass lay sprawled against the far wall of the second-floor room where the Mormons had tried to defend themselves. Willard

Richards was alive and virtually unscathed. The hulking, three-hundred-pound "doctor"—Richards had trained as an herbalist—escorted Barnes to where John Taylor lay in agony, suffering from four bullet wounds. Taylor objected to being treated by Barnes. "I don't know you!" he shouted, "Who am I among? I am surrounded by assassins and murderers; witness your deeds!"

Barnes and Richards swore that they meant to help. When Taylor's resistance waned, the doctor pulled out a penknife and started cutting away the flesh between the third and fourth fingers of his left hand. Barnes then brandished a carpenter's compass, using the metal point to pry into the hand to find one of the four musket balls lodged in Taylor's body. "After sawing for some time with a dull penknife, and prying and pulling with the compasses," Taylor reported, "he ultimately succeeded in extracting the ball."

Taylor had "nerves like the devil" to withstand his impromptu surgery, Barnes later said. In a letter to his daughter many years after the fact, he complained that he never collected a fee for his services.

Richards arranged to have Joseph and Hyrum's bodies moved to the ground floor of the Hamilton hotel. A local tailor named John Macomber washed Joseph's body. His lawyer, James Woods, inventoried the Prophet's effects. Joseph had been carrying $135.50 worth of gold and silver and wearing a gold ring. In Joseph's undisturbed pockets, Woods found a pen and pencil case, a penknife and case, tweezers, and two IOUs, one for $50 from John Greene, and one from Heber Kimball.

After kicking up a fuss, Taylor agreed to be moved to the hotel, too. Artois Hamilton was less than eager to shelter the Mormons. Like everyone, he was thinking of leaving town to avoid the inevitable Mormon counterattack on Carthage. But Richards argued that it might behoove him to pose as a friend of the Saints, especially if retribution came down on the county seat.

He showed Hamilton the note he was about to send back to Nauvoo, begging the Saints to refrain from revenge:

"The People Are Not That Cruel"

Joseph and Hyrum are dead. Taylor wounded, not very badly. I am well. Our guard was forced, as we believe, by a band of Missourians from 100 to 200. The job was done in an instant, and the party fled towards Nauvoo instantly. This is as I believe it. The citizens here are afraid of the "Mormons" attacking them; I promise them no.

WILLARD RICHARDS

The man carrying Richards's note was intercepted on the road to Nauvoo and turned back. A second messenger suffered the same fate. In the early hours of Friday, June 28, Porter Rockwell galloped through the streets of Nauvoo screaming the terrifying news at the top of his lungs, waking any and all who could hear him: "Joseph is killed! God-damn them! They have killed him!"

11

JOSEPH'S HOMECOMING

Oh! Illinois! thy soil has drank the blood
Of Prophets, martyr'd for the truth of God.
Once lov'd America! what can atone
For the pure blood of innocence, thou'st sown?

—*Lines on the Assassination . . . of Generals*
Joseph Smith and Hyrum Smith,
by Eliza R. Snow, Times and Seasons

AT DAWN ON JUNE 28, A FEW VISITORS ARRIVED IN CARTHAGE from Nauvoo to reclaim the corpses of the Mormon leaders.

Joseph and Hyrum's brother Samuel, who farmed in nearby Plymouth, came to the Hamilton hotel early on Friday morning. So did John Taylor's wife, Leonora, accompanied by Dr. Samuel Bennett from Nauvoo. Carthage, which was teeming with trigger-happy militia only one day earlier, was now a ghost town. Fearing retaliation from the Mormons, the men "just frankly ran away," according to Eudocia Baldwin, whose brothers were with the Greys. Newspaper editor George Davis noted sardonically that one of the fearsome militias "proceeded with all convenient haste for their homes in Schuyler

County, conceding that *distance lent enchantment to the view.*" Only military commander Minor Deming and a handful of men were available to help the Mormons prepare the Smiths' bodies to be taken back to Nauvoo.

For the second time in twelve hours, Taylor submitted to a gruesome operation, au naturel. Dr. Bennett noticed that Taylor's thigh had swollen up and determined that the musket ball buried there had to come out.

"Will you be tied during the operation, Mr. Taylor?" Bennett inquired.

"Oh, no, I shall endure the cutting all right," Taylor answered.

And he did.

"So great was the pain I endured that the cutting was rather a relief than otherwise," Taylor later wrote. The bullet-riddled Taylor would go on to live a long, healthy, and productive life.

While Bennett carved up his patient, and Samuel Smith laid his brothers in lidless oak coffins provided by Hamilton, Leonora Taylor found an empty room on the hotel's ground floor to pray. On her knees, she was approached by the elderly Mrs. Bedell, a stalwart in the local Methodist church. "There's a good lady," Bedell purred to the young Mormon whose husband had suffered four bullet wounds for his beliefs. "Pray for God to forgive your sins, pray that you may be converted, and the Lord have mercy on your soul."

By 8:00 a.m., the arrangements in Carthage were complete. John Taylor was to remain a guest of Artois Hamilton, and of the local citizenry. Taylor later recalled seeing some of the same men that had mobbed the jail pop into his hotel room to offer condolences or to chat. One too-candid visitor told Taylor that "I ought to be killed, but it was too damned cowardly to shoot a wounded man. Thus by the chivalry of murderers I was prevented from being a second time mutilated or killed."

Taylor, who was attended by his wife, mother, and several Mormon friends, kept two loaded pistols on his bedside table. His hosts viewed him as a hostage to fortune and feared that his removal—he ultimately stayed four days—"would be the signal for rising of the Mormons."

Hotelkeeper Hamilton agreed to furnish two wagons to transport Joseph and Hyrum's coffins back to Nauvoo. The day threatened to be hot. An Indian blanket covered one of the coffins, and straw and prairie brush was heaped over the second, to prevent decomposition and to ward off flies. Willard Richards rode ahead of the wagons and Samuel Smith drove one of the teams. Eight hours later, the cortege, now accompanied by a Legionnaire riding at each of the wagon's wheels, reached the outskirts of Nauvoo, about one mile east of the still-unfinished Temple. Soon a brass band joined the procession, playing funeral dirges.

As the wagons approached Joseph's mansion in the town center, huge crowds lined the streets. As many as 8,000 people may have witnessed Joseph and Hyrum's mournful homecoming. "The inhabitants were all out in the streets, on the housetops and everywhere to see if they could get just a glimpse of him," fifteen-year-old Mary Ann Rich reported. "As they drove around to the Mansion, the people were almost frantic to get one little glimpse of him, but they were driven back by the marshal." Recent immigrants from Ireland and Wales moaned in unison, filling the air with a funereal keening rarely heard along the banks of the Mississippi. "The weeping was communicated to the crowd, and spread along the vast waves of humanity extending from the Temple to the residence of the Prophet," journalist B. W. Richmond reported. "The groans and sobs and shrieks grew deeper and louder till the sound resembled the roar of a mighty tempest, or the slow, deep, roar of the distant tornado."

Porter Rockwell's alarum had woken the Smiths' families the night before. In the Nauvoo Mansion, Joseph's four children had been crying and screaming for hours. In a downstairs room, Richmond happened upon Joseph's mother, the sixty-eight-year-old Lucy Mack Smith, stone-faced and tearless, staring out a window. When Sarah Kimball approached the Smith family matriarch, "she extended her trembling hand towards me which I clasped in silence," Kimball recalled,

> biting her lips she motioned me to be seated by her side. I think for three minutes the silence was only broken by smothered sobs from various parts of the room during which time the pressure of her trembling hand & the heaving of her swollen bosom spoke as it were volumes to my heart. . . .

Finally, Joseph and Hyrum's mother erupted. "How could they kill my boys?" Lucy burst out. "How could they kill them when they were so *precious*! I am sure they would not harm anybody in the world. There was poor Hyrum—what could they kill him for? He was always *mild*."

Six months later, Lucy Smith began work on a lengthy memoir about her son Joseph Jr. She remembered the evening of June 28, "when I entered the room, and saw my murdered sons extended both at once before my eyes,

> and heard the sobs and groans of my family, and the cries of "Father! Husband! Brothers!" from the lips of their wives, children, brother and sisters. It was too much. I sank back, crying to the Lord, in the agony of my soul, "My God, my God, why hast thou forsaken this family!"

The two coffins were borne into the mansion's dining room, and the residence's doors were locked. From the front stoop, Willard Richards delivered a short eulogy and begged the Saints to remain peaceful. The official church history records that "the people with one united voice resolved to trust to the law for a remedy of such a high-handed assassination, and when that failed, to call upon God to avenge them of their wrongs." Richards invited the faithful to return the following morning for a public viewing of their slain leaders.

In the locked dining room, Nauvoo's coroner, Dimick Huntington, his father, and stake president William Marks prepared the bodies to be shown. The three men washed the corpses thoroughly and filled the open wounds with cotton soaked in camphor. The official inventory of Joseph's wounds was particularly grisly: He had been "shot in the right breast, under the heart, in the lower part of his bowels and the right side, and on the back part of the right hip." In addition, there was an exit wound at his right shoulder blade.

The cosmetic work completed, the Huntingtons dressed the bodies in plain trousers, linen shirts, clean shorts, white neckerchiefs, and white cotton socks. The two coffins lay on a table pushed up against the dining room's western windows, looking out over the Mississippi River.

Dimick Huntington then invited the families to enter the room.

Emma Smith, pregnant for the seventh time, staggered into the dining room, supported by two friends. The moment she saw Hyrum's body, she fainted. Her friends forced a glass of water down her throat, but she fainted again and had to leave the room. Emma entered the dining room six times, each time unable to traverse the short stretch of floor to where her dead husband lay. Eventually, she gave up and sat down outside.

Hyrum's widow, Mary Fielding Smith, then entered the room with her four children. "She trembled at every step," Richmond reported,

and nearly fell, but reached her husband's body, kneeling down by him, clasped her arms around his head, turned his pale face upon her heaving bosom, and then a gushing, plaintive wail burst forth from her lips: "Oh! Hyrum, Hyrum! Have they shot you, my dear Hyrum— are you dead, my dear Hyrum!"

Her grief seemed to consume her, and she lost all power of utterance. Her two daughters and two young children clung, some around her neck and some to her body, falling prostrate upon the corpse, and shrieking in the wildness of their wordless grief.

Aided now by Dimick Huntington, Emma walked into the dining room again. She placed her hand on Hyrum's cold brow and said, "Now I can see him; I am strong now." She knelt down next to Joseph's coffin and clasped her hands around his face. Groaning, sighing, and sobbing, she cried out, "Joseph, Joseph, are you dead? Have the assassins shot you?"

Later in life, Joseph's oldest son Joseph III recalled that "no other woman bowed beside the bodies of these brothers . . . as wives to mourn and exhibit their grief . . . save my mother at my father's side and Aunt Mary at the side of my uncle Hyrum." But the eleven-year-old boy who devoted his adult life to proving that his father had never practiced polygamy, apparently failed to see Lucinda Morgan Harris standing at the head of Joseph's coffin. Three years older than Emma, the fair-haired, blue-eyed Harris was also sobbing and grief-stricken. Harris had been sealed to Joseph a few years before, while she was wed to George Harris, who chaired the City Council session that ordered the destruction of the *Nauvoo Expositor*. Lucinda had lost two husbands to mob violence. She had previously married the notorious anti-Masonic agitator William Morgan, whose body was found in Lake Ontario shortly after he published a lurid exposé of the ancient fraternal order. Lucinda Harris ended her life as a nun in the Catholic nursing order, the Sisters of Charity.

The next day found Nauvoo in mourning. Stores were closed and "every business forgotten," according to Dan Jones. On the clear, hot and sunny Saturday, starting at 8:00 a.m., 10,000 Saints found their ways to the mansion and filed past the open coffins. White cambric lined the open boxes, which were covered with black velvet, fastened by brass nails. A square of glass, hinged at the head of each coffin, allowed mourners to see the faces of Joseph and Hyrum.

The scene was not for the faint of heart. "Joseph looks very natural except being pale through loss of blood," William Clayton wrote in his diary. "Hyrum does not look so natural." Richmond reported that by noon, Hyrum's body had swollen so much that he couldn't be recognized, "the neck and face forming one bloated mass," and

blood continued to pour out of his wounds, which had been filled with cotton; the muscles relaxed and the . . . fluid trickled down on the floor and formed in puddles across the room.

Dan Jones, too, remembered seeing "the blood of the two godly martyrs mingling in one pool in the middle of the floor." Many of the mourners left the room with the Smiths' blood sticking to the soles of their shoes and boots.

To allay the stink of death, Huntington set a mixture of tar, vinegar, and sugar to boil on the mansion stove. It wasn't particularly effective. The wounds were suppurating, and the bodies rotting in the summer heat.

The dining room resounded with weeping and moaning. Joseph was the Saints' living, breathing, wrestling, drinking, sermonizing, truth-revealing champion. No one in Nauvoo didn't know him. Almost every resident had bought something—a pinch of tobacco, a plot of land—at his redbrick store. Joseph had greeted thousands of Saints at the riverside landing slips, many of the believers at the end of harrowing trans-Atlantic or transcontinental journeys. Every Mormon man, woman, and child had stood or sat on a bench or tree stump for hours at a time in the grove, listening to Joseph's speeches and sermons. Every Nauvoo resident had uprooted himself or herself, and their families, either because of Joseph Smith's preaching or because they had read the sacred Book of Mormon he composed as a young man. As he instructed, they gathered to Zion to worship in the city of their Prophet. And now, inexplicably, in the prime of his vigorous life, at thirty-nine years old, he was dead.

Commingled with feelings of sadness and despair was an understandable lust for vengeance. When Porter Rockwell burst into William Clayton's home in the early hours of June 28 to report the murders, Clayton quickly scribbled out a prayer of vengeance "upon the murderers of thy servants that they may be rid from off the earth." At virtually the same moment, Wilford Woodruff, a future church president, uttered a prayer calling down vengeance on "the American gentile nation, upon all the heads of the Nation and the State that have aided, abetted, or perpetrated the horrid deed."

Ten-year-old Mosiah Hancock later remembered how his father, Levi, led him into the room where Joseph and Hyrum were lying in state. Levi "told me to place one hand on Joseph's breast and to raise my other arm and swear with hand uplifted that I would never make a compromise with any of the sons of hell, which vow I took with a determination to fulfill to the very letter."

The little boy then laid his left hand on Hyrum's chest and repeated the vow.

"Their dead bodies . . . gave me such feelings as I am not able to describe," Allen Stout, one of Joseph's bodyguards, wrote in his journal.

> I there and then resolved in my mind that I would never let an opportunity slip unimproved of avenging their blood upon the head of the enemies of the Church of Jesus Christ . . . when I see one of the men who persuaded them to give up to be tried, I feel like cutting their throats.
>
> And I hope to live to avenge their blood, but if I do not, I will teach my children to never cease to try to avenge their blood and then their children and children's children to the fourth generation as long as there is one descendant of the murderers upon the earth.

The next year, President Brigham Young incorporated an "oath of vengeance" into the sacred endowment ritual administered to all faithful Mormons in the Nauvoo Temple:

> You and each of you do covenant and promise that you will pray and never cease to pray to Almighty God to avenge the blood of the prophets upon this nation, and that you will teach the same to your children and to your children's children unto the third and fourth generation.

The vengeance oath was to be kept secret, under penalty of death. "If any of you betray us you are traitors of course you must expect the penalties put in force [sic]," a church leader explained inside the temple. "I should not cut your throat but pray God to intervene to cut your own throat."

The oath remained in the Mormons' endowment ritual until 1927.

‡ ‡ ‡

INDEED, THE GENTILE WORLD OUTSIDE WAS EXPECTING VENGEANCE from the Saints. Hancock County was trembling in anticipation of a counterstrike from the Nauvoo Legion. True, the Mormons had surrendered several hundred muskets earlier in the week, but subsequent events would prove that there was no shortage of firearms in the Mormon capital. Angry as they were, why didn't the Saints fight back?

In principle, the Mormons were not squeamish about violence. When Missourians started attacking their farms during the Mormon War of 1838, the Saints struck back, hard. But when faced with overwhelming force, in the form of 2,500 Missouri militiamen, Joseph Smith realized that discretion was the better part of valor. Rather than see his followers annihilated, he agreed to a "peace on any terms short of battle." The punitive cease-fire terms resulted in the seizure of most Mormons' property—ostensibly, reparations for the Missourians' costs in making war on the Saints—expulsion, and, for Joseph and five other Mormon leaders, six months in a nineteen-foot-square, earthen-floored jail cell.

That was the second time in his short career as a commander in chief that Joseph had prudently backed away from a fight. In 1834, he led a paramilitary troop of about two hundred Saints from Ohio into Missouri, on a mission he called "Zion's Camp." Joseph thought the Saints' ragtag expeditionary force could teach the Missouri marauders a lesson, but he backed away from a battle, facing overwhelming odds. A cholera epidemic turned Zion's Camp into an epochal disaster, but Joseph showed that he placed a high value on the lives of his Saints.

In retrospect, Willard Richards and John Taylor exercised good judgment by calming the martial passions of the Saints. Governor Ford may have thought that the Nauvoo Legion outnumbered his militias, but if so, that would not last long. In the event of a war, or even skirmishes, Thomas Sharp's repeated calls for Mormon-killers from Iowa and Missouri to converge on Hancock County would fall on eager ears. Furthermore, there were suspicions that Joseph's cockaded Legion preferred pageantry, like full-dress parades and stagy war games, to actual fighting. Ford feared the numbers of the Legion more than their martial arts. "All the field officers who accompanied me," Ford commented, thought "that this legion is in no wise superior to the common militia, and that in fact they were inferior to most of the militia in the state."

The Mormons in Nauvoo were rudderless. Joseph was the church, and Joseph was dead. Hyrum, one of his possible successors, had also died. As part of his vainglorious quest for the presidency, Joseph had sent ten of the twelve apostles across the United States to electioneer for him. The apostles' de facto leader, Brigham Young, learned of Smith's death only in mid-July while visiting a Mormon family in Peterborough, New Hampshire. He hurried back to Nauvoo, arriving just in time for a leadership conference three weeks later.

The Saints were experiencing an unprecedented, collective anguish. Joseph had been in tight spots before, especially with state authorities and their musket-toting enforcers. But somehow, he had always escaped. Friendly Saints would hide him in an outbuilding for a few weeks; he would find the right lawyer, or a sympathetic local judge would grant him his rights as a free American. Two Missouri governors repeatedly tried to capture him, yet he always managed to slip the noose. But this time Joseph wasn't coming back, and many of the faithful experienced the loss as a body blow. Lucy Walker, one of Joseph's plural wives, remembered a midnight rap on the door announcing Joseph and Hyrum's deaths. "I seemed paralyzed with terror," she recalled, and

> . . . had no power to speak or to move. Agnes called out what is the
> news, receiving no answer, came rushing down to learn the awful
> truth. When at length we returned to our chamber and on our bended

knees poured out the anguish of our souls to that God who holds the destinies of his children in his own hands, for a time it seemed utterly impossible that he would allow his prophet to be slain by his foes. . . .

The dogs howled and barked, the cattle bellowed and all creation was astir.

Perhaps the Saints were simply too lost without Joseph. Perhaps the Nauvoo Legion wasn't ready to become a fighting force after all. There was barking and bellowing, but there was no Mormon reprisal for Joseph's killing.

⚡ ⚡ ⚡

WORD TRAVELED SLOWLY IN JOHN TYLER'S AMERICA. ALTHOUGH Samuel Morse demonstrated the telegraph just one month before the Smiths were killed, it would not enter common use for several more years. No train lines linked Carthage, Warsaw, or Nauvoo with the outside world. So only in July did the nation learn about Joseph Smith's death. In Salem, Massachusetts, Apostle Heber Kimball noted in his diary on July 9 that "the papers were full of News of the death of our Prophet. I was not willen to believe it, fore it was too much to bare." Three days later, Kimball recorded that "Elder White and myself went in to our closet and offered up the Singhs [signs] and praied that we might get some definite news pertaining the death of the Prophets." It came that day, in a letter from Kimball's wife, Vilate. "O Lord what feelings we had," he wrote.

On July 27, the *New York Daily Tribune*, still edited by Joseph's admirer James Gordon Bennett, expressed "our horror" at the "cold-blooded, barbarous, brutal outrage" that had taken place in Illinois. Whatever the Smiths had done,

how black soever were their crimes—they were defenceless and in the hands of the laws, under a solemn pledge of their protection as well as justice, and the people of Illinois had not the slightest excuse for taking it for granted that those laws would not be enforced.

"Thus Ends Mormonism!" blared the *New York Herald*, which opined that "the death of the modern mahomet will seal the fate of Mormonism." Editor Horace Greeley, already well into his career as one of the century's most famous newsmen, thought Smith's martyrdom might spur the Saints to further greatness: "The blood of Joe Smith, spilled by murderous hands, will be like the fabled dragon's teeth sown broadcast, that everywhere sprang up armed men."

"Alas for human greatness!" the authoritative Baltimore-based Whig newspaper *Niles' National Register* sardonically noted in its July 13 issue. "One of the nominated candidates for the next president is already a lifeless corpse. Even the sanctity of his high profession as a *prophet* and a *leader,* could not preserve him." The "Brief Remarker," writing in the July 25 *Hartford Courant,* waxed more direct, implying that the "great deceiver" and "great imposter" Joseph Smith got what was coming to him:

Should the internal history of Nauvoo ever be laid open and the practices enacted there be brought to the knowledge of the world, we believe the scenes which have been there practiced would astonish and disgust the American public.

Back in Illinois, the players continued to play the parts assigned to them. Thomas Sharp vilified the Mormons, and Joseph and Hyrum, as if they were still alive. Cloaking himself in the mantle of a freedom-loving patriot, Sharp denounced Joseph as a "tyrant." Invoking the "noble blood which promoted our forefathers to throw off the yoke of British oppression," the editor claimed that the mob he so assiduously provoked was "asserting . . . liberty," even while committing a "daring violation of law." Sharp called the lynching a "necessity," asking his readers, "Did they deserve death? There can be no doubt in the mind of any intelligent person acquainted with their history. . . ."

The cold-blooded attack on four men armed with a misfiring pepperbox revolver and two walking sticks emerged from Sharp's pen as a noble feat of arms. Noting that the mob stood accused of cowardice, Sharp rebutted that assertion. "Instead of cowardice, they exhibited foolhardy courage," he wrote,

> for they must have known or thought that they would bring down on themselves the vengeance of the Mormons.
>
> *True, the act of an armed body going to the jail and killing prisoners does appear at first sight dastardly,* but we look at it as though these men were the executioners of justice; and their act is no more cowardly than is the act of the hangman in stretching up a defenceless convict who is incapable of resistance. [Emphasis added.]

Sharp would never cease damning the Mormons until they had been driven from the state. He was not alone in inventing euphemisms for the grisly execution. "If the public understood our true situation," wrote George Rockwell, the Warsaw-based anti-Mormon businessman,

> I am sure that instead of calling it a "cold blooded murder" they would hold public meetings, and express their thanks to men who dared to execute justice upon two of the vilest men that ever lived. . . . That they were bad men, and deserved death I have not the least doubt. They taught their followers that the revelations of God through them were paramount to the laws of man.

The pusillanimous Thomas Ford likewise stayed in character. In a message to the people of Illinois promulgated from his safe harbor in Quincy, he bemoaned "the recent disgraceful affair at Carthage." Naturally, he saw no need to assign blame, at least not to himself. Yes, he had guaranteed Joseph and Hyrum's safety, and yes, the "peacably disposed" Mormons had surrendered their arms at his request. But "the pledge of security to the Smiths was not given upon my individual responsibility," he insisted. The militias assembled in Carthage had promised him they would guard the prisoners, according to Ford. If they had any hand in the murders, Ford said, they "have done all they could do to disgrace the State and sully the public honor."

Ford had played a double game, simultaneously trying to curry favor with the powerful Mormon electoral bloc while seeking to assuage the blood lust of the "old settlers." He failed on both counts. The Mormons justifiably blamed him for the bloodbath at the Carthage jail. But the anti-Mormon faction also disdained him. Warsaw resident Rockwell told his parents that more than two years after the Smith killings, Ford was persona non grata in Carthage. "He called at a grog shop for a glass of whiskey, but the keeper refused to sell him any," Rockwell wrote. "He insisted that his money was as good as anybody's but he was told again that he could not have the whiskey at any price and his money was not wanted." During that same trip, Ford visited Nauvoo, which the Mormons had begun to abandon in early 1846. "A committee of the ladies—'probably Gentile ladies'—presented him with a petticoat," Rockwell reported. "[Ford] is known as a tool of the Jacks—he is treated everywhere with contempt."

Several years later, when composing his *History of Illinois,* Thomas Ford speculated that a future Church of Latter-day Saints might swell to many times the size of the tens of thousands of members it claimed in 1844, "and make the name of the martyred Joseph ring as loud, and stir the souls of men as much, as the mighty name of Christ itself." Should that occur, Ford wrote, "the humble governor of an obscure State, who would otherwise be forgotten in a few years, stands a fair chance, like Pilate and Herod, by their official connection with the true religion, of being dragged down to posterity with an immortal name."

Ford has indeed been forgotten by the public at large. But Mormons still remember his faithful reenactment of Pontius Pilate's part in the execution of their Prophet and revile him for it.

Ꞵ Ꞵ Ꞵ

JOSEPH AND HYRUM'S BODIES WOULD HAVE THEIR OWN FATEFUL history. At 5:00 p.m. on June 29, 1844, the formal viewing of the corpses ended. Now began the strange saga of the Smiths' remains, a story that unfolded over the course of seventy years. With the public dispersed and the mansion's doors again locked, a few trusted Saints hustled the coffins into a tiny bedroom. They removed the corpses from their outer containers, filling the pine boxes with sand and rocks. Around sundown, with considerable fanfare, Dimick Huntington drove the sand-filled coffins to the Nauvoo cemetery, with several thousand mourners following him in procession.

At the graveyard, Williams Phelps, Joseph's favored ghostwriter—it was Phelps who drafted Joseph's presidential campaign platform—delivered an impassioned, incendiary speech in memory of the "Prince of Light." The "most lovely and Jesus-like" prophet had ascended to a place where he could wreak vengeance on his enemies, Phelps promised: he "is where he can use the treasury of snow and hail; he can now direct the lion from the thicket to lay the Gentile cities waste."

"Woe to the drunkards with Ephraim and great whore of Babylon!" Phelps railed.

For their destruction is sure, and their end near . . . rejoice ye Saints, for the triumph of the wicked is short; they can kill the body, as we have in this sample, but Mormonism is a celestial medicine and must be applied as the sovereign remedy for all sin.

He particularly vilified Governor Ford:

Tom Ford is supposed to be one of those beings that believes when a child is born, that some person has died—but unfortunately, we must come to the conclusion from analogy, that when Tom Ford was born, no body died.

After the service, the Mormons stationed guards at the fake grave site, to deceive would-be grave robbers. The Saints feared that marauders might exhume Smith's remains and take them to Missouri, where there may still have been a price on his head. There was an equally ghoulish fear that a bounty hunter might decapitate Joseph's corpse and present the severed head in return for a reward. Rumors had already spread that his killers had tried to cut the head from his lifeless body after it tumbled from the window of the Carthage jail.

So at midnight, Huntington led a secret corps of grave diggers who carried Hyrum and Joseph's coffins out the back door of the mansion, through the garden and across the street, to the Nauvoo House hotel, still under construction. The first-floor joists had been laid above the basement. Huntington's crew dug the graves underneath, and scattered wood chips, stones, and random litter over the dirt to hide their work. That evening a torrential rain erased any trace of the graves' location, which was known to only a few close family members.

This solution would prove to be temporary. Just weeks after Joseph's death, Emma was feuding with his successor, Brigham Young. Many issues divided them: How to deal with Joseph's debts, how to apportion Joseph's real estate, and, most significant, whether polygamy would remain part of Latter-day Saint doctrine. Emma still hated plural marriage and its attendant humiliations. Brigham continued to marry new wives, and to introduce more Saints into the ritual, despite significant opposition. Emma feared that Brigham might try to seize Joseph's corpse to legitimize his claim to be continuing Joseph's legacy. She was right.

Joseph had left plans for a large, pyramidal limestone crypt and memorial to be constructed for his family, at the southeast corner of the Temple. It remained unfinished at the time of his death, but that was where

Brigham wanted the Prophet to be buried. "We will petition Sister Emma, in the name of Israel's God, to let us deposit the remains of Joseph according as he commanded us," Brigham told the 1845 church conference.

> If she will not consent to it, our garments are clear—Then when he awakes in the morning of the resurrection, he shall talk with them, not with me; the sin shall be upon her head, not ours.

Joseph Smith and Brigham Young had enlarged their families through plural marriage, in part to increase their collective glory in the exaltation, when men and women come face-to-face with Jesus Christ. Brigham warned that Emma was jeopardizing Joseph's eternal life. These were stark words to a believing Mormon.

Again working with the Huntingtons, father and son, Emma arranged yet another midnight burial. Her son Joseph III remembered witnessing the disinterment and watching as one of the workers snipped a curl from his father's hair, which Emma wore in a locket for the rest of her life. The bodies were reburied across the street, near the Homestead, the two-story log cabin that Joseph and Emma occupied

The Smiths' first gravestones in Nauvoo, next to the Mississippi River
Credit: Community of Christ Archives

when they first settled in Nauvoo. Huntington and his men moved a small shed that was used as a spring house, buried the brothers in the exposed footprint, then put the shed back on top of the graves. Joseph's deceased children would eventually be buried alongside their father, and Emma's remains joined her husband's when she died in 1879.

But Joseph and Hyrum would not rest in peace.

In 1928, Joseph's grandson Frederick M. Smith fretted that the waters of Lake Cooper, formed by a new dam on the Mississippi, might flood his family's burial plots. Frederick was animated by more than a preservationist impulse. He was the president of a breakaway sect, the Reorganized Church of Jesus Christ of Latter Day Saints, and had heard rumors that Brigham Young had spirited the Prophet's remains away to Utah. After a week of excavating, a team of engineers and surveyors found the Smiths' corpses, exhumed them, and placed the remains in silk-lined coffins. Frederick Smith arranged for the coffins to be moved seventeen feet uphill, to their current resting place.

"The Utah cousins were not pleased," historian Samuel Brown drolly noted. That was an understatement. Joseph Fielding Smith, Hyrum's grandson and Frederick's cousin, said his relative had "debased himself in the sight of all honorable men as well as in the sight of God, in this unholy and sacrilegious act. . . . These remains should not have been disturbed, and such a despicable act could only be performed by those who are lacking in all the finer feelings." Fielding Smith, a future LDS president, briefly considered suing his Midwestern brethren.

Today, Joseph lies next to Emma and Hyrum, underneath a plain marble slab bearing the inscription:

> Joseph Smith
> Prophet
> Born Sharon, Vermont
> December 23, 1805
> Died Carthage, Illinois June 27, 1844

12

TRIAL BY JURY

It has always appeared to me that the persons who committed the deed ought to be made to answer for their crime.

—*Governor Thomas Ford,*
"Message to the People of Illinois"

WHO KILLED JOSEPH SMITH? THAT SHOULD HAVE BEEN AN easy question to answer. The murderers were undoubtedly familiar to the lackadaisical guards at the Carthage jail, whom they "overwhelmed" during their attack on the building. They rushed up the jailhouse stairway in broad daylight, in plain sight of Stigall, the nominal jailer, and quickly broke through the upstairs door to pour their mortal fire on the trapped Mormons. Richards and Taylor saw everything, and survived the attack. They were near-perfect eyewitnesses, highly literate men who wrote down summaries of the Carthage events soon after they happened. Richards and the Jack-Mormon sheriff Jacob Backenstos supplied lists of men who supposedly mobbed the jailhouse, but—like the names that William Clayton recorded in his diary on June 28—these merely named the Mormons' many enemies in Hancock County, rather than the actual participants in the massacre.

For instance, both Richards and Clayton placed William Law at the scene, but he was across the river in Iowa at the time.

When the time came to indict and try the nine men held responsible for Joseph Smith's murder, things went terribly wrong. (The defendants were charged only with Joseph's murder. Hyrum's killers were to be separately indicted and tried, after this first proceeding.) The case, *People v. Levi Williams, et al.*, was a farce, even by the slapdash legal standards of America's Western frontier. The four men who probably fired the shots that killed Joseph—John Wills, William Voras, fourteen-year-old William Gallagher, and Nathan Allen—simply vanished across the river to Missouri. The defense attorneys successfully excluded Mormons from the trial jury. That hardly mattered, though, as most Mormons were too frightened to leave Nauvoo to testify. The rank and file had had their fill of Illinois justice, and many of the leaders were lying low to avoid legal summonses related to the destruction of the *Expositor*. Neither Willard Richards nor John Taylor appeared in the courtroom. "They would have murdered us," said Taylor, who had sampled quite enough of Carthage's blood lust: "This prosecution is got up for the purpose of destroying the innocent and clearing the murderers." The state would have to prove that the remaining five defendants conspired to kill Smith, and it would have to make the case without their testimony. Illinois law forbade defendants in a criminal trial from taking the stand.*

That's not to say the prosecution didn't have a case. Three eyewitnesses came forward to provide new details of the June 27 killings at Carthage. Although their stories were colorful and richly imagined, almost every detail they offered at the trial proved to be fanciful, fictional, self-serving, a complete lie, or some combination of all four.

But, in the end, the witnesses' harum-scarum tales didn't decide the outcome of the trial. A bizarre, last-minute turn of events sealed the

---

* The *Upper Mississippian* newspaper of Rock Island, Illinois, reported that a sheriff tried to execute a Nauvoo arrest warrant in Burlington, Iowa, for the Law brothers, the Fosters, and one of the Higbees, accusing them of complicity in the Smiths' deaths. According to the report, William Law and the Foster brothers were briefly detained, challenged the validity of the warrant, and then disappeared. None of the men faced charges in Nauvoo, or elsewhere.

defendants' fate, possibly buttressing the Mormons' cynical prediction that the verdict had been reached before the judge gaveled the proceedings to order.

I I I

TO PROSECUTE THE HIGH-PROFILE CASE, GOVERNOR FORD CHOSE Josiah Lamborn, a once-brilliant and formidable former attorney general of Illinois. Lamborn was not Ford's first choice. Canny lawyers understood that convicting Joseph Smith's assassins would win one few friends downstate, except for the legions of Mormon voters. But the Mormons' future in Illinois was parlous at best. On May 24, 1845, the very day that the trial opened in Carthage, Brigham Young presided over a secret ceremony marking the completion of the Nauvoo Temple. There was talk of administering Joseph's holy endowment ritual to the many thousands of Saints, and then leaving Illinois forthwith. The Smiths' killings had settled nothing. True, there had been a brief hiatus in anti-Mormon agitation in southwestern Illinois. But the violence, the depredations, the raids on outlying farmhouses could start again at any moment. Joseph's successors had already begun to scout locations for a new Zion, west of the Mississippi in the Rocky Mountain Basin.

So the thirty-six-year-old Lamborn shouldered a thankless burden. His contemporaries described him as "one of the most able, untiring yet merciless prosecutors that ever lived" and "a terror to his legal opponents." Like many successful frontier lawyers, he was known for his oratory. In one famous case, Lamborn was prosecuting an elderly hog thief. The defense lawyer seemed to have won the jury's sympathy for the white-haired pignapper, characterizing his client as a man with one foot in the grave and the other foot teetering on the brink. Lamborn rose to reply: "Yes, gentlemen of the jury. His hair is whitening for that place that burns with liquid fire: one foot is in the grave, and the other is in his neighbor's hog pen."

But Lamborn had also inflicted terror on himself. In his very first year of practice, he was investigated by the Illinois Supreme Court for sharing confidential information with adversaries and was nearly disbarred. In one of his best-known cases, he was accused of suborning perjury. As a prosecutor, Lamborn somehow convinced a feeble-minded defendant to confess to a grisly murder, for which he and his brother faced the gallows. In a final coup de théâtre, the defense lawyers announced a surprise witness, and . . . the purported murder victim walked through the courthouse door. There was talk of lynching Lamborn on the spot.

The whiff of corruption perfumed every phase of his career, and he was known to be a heavy drinker. Lamborn had a crippled foot since childhood and often leaned on a friend or colleague when moving in and out of the courtroom. At a young age, the sun seemed to be setting on his storied legal career.

His opponent as chief counsel for the defense was a rival Illinois legal celebrity, Orville H. Browning. The thirty-nine-year-old trial attorney and legislator was deemed to be "perhaps the ablest speaker in the state," a state that was home to Stephen Douglas and Abraham Lincoln. Browning, who cultivated a proper demeanor in the often woolly circuit courtrooms, was intensely devout and avoided mechanical transportation, such as stagecoaches and steamboats, on the Sabbath. In contrast with Lamborn, he was a clotheshorse. On the first day of trial he was easily the best-dressed man in the courtroom, sporting a ruffled shirt, a Prince Albert coat, and a yellow pocket handkerchief.

Browning was one of Joseph Smith's favorite lawyers. He had defended Joseph against one of Missouri's many attempts to have him sent across the Mississippi for trial in the Lilburn Boggs shooting. Browning and Smith ended up arguing a habeas corpus motion in Monmouth, Illinois, in 1841 before Douglas, then a circuit-court judge. Browning lived downstate in Quincy, and he claimed to remember the bedraggled and tormented Mormons who threw themselves on the mercy of Quincy residents in December 1838, after the Missourians chased them from their homes to the banks of the freezing Mississippi River:

Great God! have I not seen it? Yes, my eyes have beheld the blood-stained traces of innocent women and children, in the drear winter, who had traveled hundreds of miles barefoot, through frost and snow, to seek a refuge from their savage pursuers. 'Twas a scene of horror sufficient to enlist sympathy froman adamantine heart.

"This unfortunate man," meaning Joseph, has suffered enough, Browning pled to judge Douglas. The lawyer said he would "gladly stand alone, and proudly spend my latest breath in defense of an oppressed American citizen." In her often entertaining memoir, Joseph's mother, Lucy Mack Smith, recalled that Browning's opponent "vomited at the feet of the judge" during his opening statement, "which, joined to the circumstances of his advocating the case of the Missourians, who are called pukes by their countrymen . . . was a source of much amusement to the court."

Joseph recorded in his journal that Browning's oration moved both the spectators and Judge Douglas to tears. ("Were there onions about?" editor Sharp sneered in the Warsaw *Signal*.) Douglas dismissed the arrest warrant, and yet again Joseph appreciated the worth of a good lawyer. Joseph Smith addressed the last letter of his life to Browning, sent at 12:20 p.m. from the Carthage jail on the day that he was killed. He informed Browning that he and Hyrum would be facing treason charges on Saturday morning; "We request your professional services at that time, on our defense, without fail." A few hours later he was dead.

Now Browning was defending the mobbers who killed him. Several lawyers insisted on helping Browning, including Calvin Warren, who had been embroiled with defendant Mark Aldrich and Joseph Smith in the failed Mormon settlement in Warren, south of Nauvoo. Aldrich was in the dock as the commander of the Warsaw Cadets and the Warsaw Rifle Company, two units that rallied at the railroad shanties near Golden's Point on the day of the Smiths' murder. Aldrich and about a hundred and fifty of his men had ignored Governor Ford's order to disband and stolen into Carthage to attack the jail. Three other defendants were also Warsaw militia leaders: former state senator Jacob Davis, who had unsuccessfully courted Mormon votes in a congressional election that he lost; Captain William Grover, the self-styled governor of the "Warsaw Legislature" who liked to make sport of the Mormon "Nephites" and "his most Sublime Excellency," Joseph Smith; and the ferocious Mormon-hater Levi Williams. Young William Hamilton correctly observed that the Smiths' murderers were "a respectable set of men."

Judge Richard M. Young, a former US senator, presided. Young was a veteran circuit-riding judge who had tried cases alongside the up-and-coming Thomas Ford, back when towns like Carthage held trials in taverns and schools, not in dignified, two-story courthouses. Young was an accomplished fiddler and raconteur, six feet, two inches tall and handsome, "the finest looking man in the state," according to one contemporary. No one suggested that he favored either the Mormons or their enemies. As an Illinois senator, Young had placed Smith's laundry list of grievances against Missouri before the Senate when the Prophet visited Washington in 1839, hoping to secure reparations from Congress and the Van Buren administration. Young even loaned his famous constituent some money to tide him over during his visit to the capital.

Young had much to recommend him, most of all his bravery. When the proceedings began, Carthage was mobbed by outsiders. A thousand men, almost all of them armed, camped out on the Carthage green, ostensibly on the qui vive for the always-rumored Mormon invasion of their hearths and homes. The second-floor courtroom held about two hundred spectators, who packed it to capacity during the Smiths' murder trial. Muskets and sidearms were brandished in the chamber. "Everybody . . . attending court comes armed to the teeth," a correspondent for the *Missouri Republican* reported, "as if they were attending a militia muster instead of attending a court of justice." The wild anti-Mormon onlookers routinely stamped their feet to protest any démarche perceived to favor the Saints and felt free to shout out caustic remarks about the proceedings. Young "was in duress," Governor Ford reported, and "did not consider his life secure any part of the time."

The jury, laboriously chosen after extensive pretrial shenanigans, was perhaps the best that could be hoped for. There were no Mormons, but none of the twelve men had any discernible record of anti-Mormon agitation, either.

On Saturday morning, May 24, 1845, at 7:00 a.m., Young gaveled the first day into session.

Lamborn's prosecution got off to a shaky start, as the prematurely decrepit attorney limped to the front of the courtroom. "The eyes of the whole country are upon us," Lamborn intoned at the beginning of his rambling, disjointed opening statement. The case "has not only excited a feeling of considerable interest among the people of the United States, but throughout the civilized world." He immediately struck a curious note of self-pity. "I came here under the direction of the governor, but I have to stand alone," he told the jury, whose members were probably indifferent to his plight. "I have an array of learned Counsellors against one. I was commanded to seek assistance, but it cannot be had. I therefore stand alone, in this trial and in this community, unaided by council, to vindicate the Law of Man."

It didn't matter whether Joseph Smith was innocent or guilty of the charges that imprisoned him, Lamborn said, "but he has suffered an awful atonement, for any offence he might have committed . . . a reckless mob, came here, on these peacable prairies, and took that man from Jail and murdered him." Then the prosecutor hectored his listeners, accusing them of complicity in Smith's murder: "The guilt of this crime hangs over you, as a blight, and curse, which is destroying your character, and gnawing at the root of your prosperity. It is a blood stain upon your character, and a foul blot, which cannot be erased, but with vengeance, and rigour, to deal out the law, as the law is."

One of the first witnesses he interrogated swore he had been in Westboro, Massachusetts, during June and July. Lamborn hadn't bothered to interview him before the trial, which was not uncommon on the Illinois circuit, or elsewhere. The prosecutor wanted the next two witnesses to help him prove that Sharp and the militia commanders conspired to rally their troops for an attack on the Carthage jail, after Governor Ford had formally disbanded their troops. This argument hinged on testimony from Golden's Point, from which most of the Warsaw militia had returned home as Ford had instructed, though some had proceeded to storm Carthage. But Lamborn's first two witnesses had memory freeze. Militiaman John Peyton did remember Captain Aldrich calling for volunteers to march on Carthage. Lamborn pressed Peyton:

Q: Did he say anything about Joseph Smith?

Peyton waited "some considerable time" to reply:

A: I think he said that Joe Smith was now in custody, and the Mormons would elect the officers of the county, and by that means Joe would select his own jury and get free . . .

Q: Was anything said about killing Joseph Smith?

A: No.

Q: Did [Aldrich] say what should be done with him?

A: No . . .

Q: Then it was Aldrich that was in favor of going to Carthage?

A: I don't know that it was Aldrich, or some other of them. There was something said in the crowd about going to Carthage, I think.

Q: What did the people there, upon the ground, in common with these men, say they were going to Carthage for?

A: I could not tell what their intention was. They did not say.

Unable to extract a confession, Lamborn turned to his next witness. He called Lieutenant Franklin Worrell to the stand. Worrell commanded the ineffectual corps of six guards stationed right in front of the Carthage jail. He would testify that some of the guards were lollygagging at the bottom of the jailhouse staircase when the marauders snuck up along the fence next to the jail. Worrell, the shopkeeper and assistant postmaster, was well known and well liked in Carthage.

Predictably, the witness reported that there was much confusion during the assault. "There was a great crowd," he said, "as thick as in this courtroom. Their pieces were going off all the time and [there was] so much noise and smoke that I could not hear anything what was said or done."

Lamborn never asked why Worrell and the Greys had so spectacularly failed to offer any resistance to the mob. Instead, he inquired if Worrell saw any of the defendants at the jail.

No, Worrell replied. Although he said he did recall seeing Aldrich and Williams in Carthage afterward.

Under questioning, Worrell allowed that as a successful storekeeper, he knew about one-third of the residents of Hancock County.

So did you recognize any members of the mob who assaulted the jail? Lamborn asked.

No, Worrell said.

Worrell, who had stood in the eye of the storm in front of the Carthage jailhouse, yielded absolutely nothing to Lamborn's muddled queries. With no substantial testimony to refute, Browning and the defense declined to cross-examine.

A few moments later, Lamborn shocked the courtroom by recalling Worrell to the witness stand.

Objection! Browning cried. He and Lamborn approached Judge Young.

Browning had a solid argument. Because there had been no cross-examination, there were no new facts to justify Worrell's recall. Lamborn had taken his bite at the apple, and there was no rule of procedure that guaranteed him another one. But Lamborn's powers of suasion triumphed. Young ruled that Worrell could continue testifying, as long as Lamborn agreed to open new lines of questioning.

The prosecutor had new questions, plugging the huge gaps in his earlier, slipshod inquiries.

Q: Do you know if the Carthage Greys, that evening, loaded
their guns with blank cartridges?

Objection! "You need not answer that question," Browning shouted.

A: I will not answer that question, I know nothing about the
Carthage Greys, only the six men that I had to do with.
Q: Did those six men load their guns with blank cartridge that
evening?
A: I will not answer it.

Young affirmed Worrell's right not to answer a question that might
incriminate himself, and Worrell took the hint. The next time Lamborn asked, Worrell again declined to answer. No one would ever
know whether the Greys were protecting Joseph with unloaded guns,
or not.

Writing many years later, John Hay commented that "it would be
difficult to imagine anything cooler than this quiet perjury to screen a
murder."

⚹ ⚹ ⚹

CAME NOW THE TRIAL'S MOST SENSATIONAL WITNESS, TWENTY-
four-year-old William Daniels, a cooper and recent Mormon convert
who claimed to have seen and heard every detail of the conspiracy to
kill Joseph Smith. Daniels supposedly remembered the events of the
previous June as if they happened yesterday. Daniels insisted that the
deceased Joseph Smith had appeared to him in a vision and escorted
him to a mountaintop. There, the Prophet offered the impressionable
lad a "glass of clear, cold water," blessed him, and urged him to tell all
he knew about the murders. Daniels was so confident of his story that
he had printed it up as a pamphlet, "Correct Account of the Murder
of Generals Joseph Smith and Hyrum Smith at Carthage, on the 27th

Day of June, 1844" and had started selling copies two weeks before the trail for 25 cents apiece.

Daniels said he had ridden out of Warsaw with the militias and was present at the fateful meet-up near Golden's Point. He wrote in the pamphlet that defendant Thomas Sharp riled up the troops with a stem-winding, Mormon-hating speech, urging them to end "the mad career of the Prophet." Per Daniels, Sharp urged the assembled militias to murder the Smiths while Governor Ford was visiting Nauvoo, and "we shall then be rid of the d——ed little Governor and the Mormons, too." Daniels even reproduced the supposed text of the letter from the Carthage Greys, urging the Warsaw irregulars to storm the jail:

> Now is a delightful time to murder the Smiths. The governor has gone to Nauvoo with all the troops. The Carthage Greys are left to guard the prisoners. Five of our men will be stationed at the jail; the rest will be upon the public square. To keep up appearances, you will attack the men at the jail—a sham scuffle will ensue—their guns will be loaded with blank cartridges—they will fire in the air.

Under Lamborn's prodding, Daniels revealed even more details about the decision to attack Carthage. According to his account, Captain Jacob Davis said he would rather go home than march on Carthage. An earlier witness testified he heard Davis "say he'd be d——d if he was going to kill men confined in prison." "They called him a damned coward [and said] they would never elect him Captain again," Daniels told Lamborn.

In the pamphlet, Daniels added a few choice details to the scene at the jail. He wrote that Joseph actually killed one of the mobbers, and that defendant Levi Williams directed the assault from atop his horse. "Rush in!" Williams shouted, "There is no danger, boys—all is right!" As the wounded Joseph tumbled out the jailhouse window, Daniels recalled Williams heaping on more brimstone: "Shoot him! God d—n him! Shoot the d—d rascal!" Inconveniently, on the witness stand Daniels said that he did not see Aldrich, Sharp, or Davis at the jailhouse

An illustration from William Daniels's 1844 pamphlet "A Correct
Account of the Murders of Generals Joseph and Hyrum Smith"
Credit: Community of Christ Archives

melee. He did say that the guards were firing blanks, although he came
by this information secondhand.

But Daniels had saved his most fantastical imaginings for last.
He claimed that a young man lifted Joseph's prostrate body off the
ground and propped it against the waist-high wooden wall surrounding the jail's well. The ruffian, "bare-foot and bare-headed, having
on no coat—with his pants rolled above his knees, and shirtsleeves
above his elbows," muttered:

> This is Old Jo; I know him. I know you, Old Jo. Damn you; you are the
> man that had my daddy shot.

Supposedly the "savage" was the son of Missouri governor Lilburn
Boggs, the target of Porter Rockwell's assassination attempt.

Daniels was just warming up.

With Joseph's body slouched against the well curb, Levi Williams supposedly assembled four men to shoot the wounded prisoner at point-blank range. While the mobbers primed their muskets and raised the barrels to eye level,

> President Smith's eyes rested upon them with a calm and quiet res-
> ignation. He betrayed no agitated feelings and the expression upon
> his countenance seemed to betoken his only prayer to be, "O, Father
> forgive them, for they know not what they do."

The mobbers fired, and Joseph's body pitched forward.

Suddenly the ill-clad ruffian returned to the scene, now armed with a bowie knife. He lifted his arm, with every intention of severing Joseph's head,

> . . . when a light, so sudden and powerful, burst from the heavens
> upon the bloody scene (passing its vivid chain between Joseph and
> his murderers,) that they were struck with terrified awe and filled
> with consternation. This light, in its appearance and potency, baffles
> all powers of description.

The dazzling light stayed the hand brandishing the bowie knife. The soldiers dropped their muskets "and they all stood like marble statues, not having the power to move a single limb of their bodies."

In his written account, Daniels said the miraculous illumination had converted him to Mormonism, which in turn prompted the mountain-top visitation from Joseph.

Lamborn knew that the heavenly light story would be catnip for the defense, so he homed in on that supernatural detail: You didn't actu-ally write that pamphlet with your name on it, did you?

No, Daniels answered. The publisher Lyman Littlefield wrote the pamphlet, "though I suppose he got it from what I told him," Daniels allowed. "I suppose it will astonish you to tell you that I saw a light," he added.

Daniels declined to speculate on the source or the meaning of the light—otherworldly or otherwise. He and Lamborn quietly permitted the messianic implications to leach into the trial record.

Rising to cross examine, occasionally mopping his brow in the stiflingly hot courtroom, Orville Browning knew he had plenty of material to work with. Why, he asked, was Daniels marching out of Warsaw on an anti-Mormon mission in the first place? Daniels said that after he heard the defendants discussing the Smiths' murder in a tavern the night before, they arrested him. Yet somehow he was included on the foray to Golden's Point, where his captors disappeared. Well then, said Browning, you were in an ideal situation to ride into Carthage and warn the Mormon prisoners of the plot to kill them. No, said Daniels, that would not have worked, because the fix was in with Worrell and the Greys guarding the jail.

Browning toyed with Daniels for a while, posing a question, waiting for an answer, and then pointing out how the new version of events contradicted the written account in the pamphlet. Were Joseph's eyes open or shut when Williams's men executed him? Daniels couldn't remember. But the pamphlet he authored said Joseph gazed on his killers with "calm and quiet resignation."

Oh, Littlefield wrote that, Daniels answered.

Inevitably, Browning interrogated the miraculous vision of light:

Q: At what time did you see this marvelous light?
A: I saw it at the place after the shooting.
Q: Well, tell us about that light.
A: It was like a flash of lightning there at the moment.
Q: When [Joseph] was shot, did any person go up to him?
A: Yes, a young man attempted to get him.
Q: Had he a bowie knife in his hand?
A: I did not see that.

The "flash of lightning" supposed to have illuminated
Joseph Smith's death, reimagined by C. C. Christensen
Credit: Brigham Young University Art Museum

Littlefield had embellished that detail, Daniels testified.[*]

Now Browning successfully elicited numerous "bad facts" from Daniels, small details of his life sure to imprint themselves on the jurors' memories. What do you do for a living, Mr. Daniels? Daniels admitted that he had been making a living by exhibiting a painting of Joseph Smith's death, a painting that incorporated all the baroque details of his published "Correct Account."

"Do you tell people that the painting is inaccurate?" Browning inquired.

"When asked, I have told that it was not correct but when not asked, I said nothing," Daniels replied.

Daniels's greed, or lack thereof, came out under cross-examination. In his published pamphlet, he averred that he had come forward be-

---

[*] A second account of a miraculous light surfaced in the journal of Mary Rollins Lightner, one of Joseph Smith's plural wives. Lightner reported meeting several militiamen returning from Carthage the day after the Smiths' murder: "They told us that the Smiths were killed and that a great light appeared at their death. I said that should prove Joseph a true Prophet of God. O no, said one, it would only prove that God was well pleased with those that killed him."

cause of a spiritual revelation, but it became clear that he and Little-field were hoping to turn a quick buck with the "Correct Account." Furthermore, Daniels had bruited around town that he might be paid to testify—or stay away—from the Joseph Smith murder trial. He said that he had been offered $500 to tell his story at trial, and $2,500 to make himself scarce and *not* talk. Daniels insisted he had accepted neither proposition, but his demeanor left room for doubt.

It was 6:15 p.m. Judge Young announced that court would reconvene on Monday at 7:00 a.m. The courtroom claques scored Day One a draw. Sharp and Williams were clearly agitating for vigilante action at Golden's Point. Worrell had muddied the waters, or worse, concerning the Greys' collusion in the Smiths' deaths. And Daniels was a crazy fabulist, an obvious millstone around the prosecution's neck.

I I I

THE TRIAL LASTED THREE MORE DAYS, MUCH OF THE TIME devoted to disagreements over who saw what. Several witnesses placed Williams, Aldrich, Grover, and Sharp near the jailhouse carnage, but recollections varied concerning their involvement in the massacre. Sharp was on foot; Sharp was on horseback; Sharp was driving a buggy; Sharp and Williams were in a wagon. Grover and Davis were at the railroad shanties; unless they weren't. Williams led the attack on Carthage; no, he was already *in* Carthage. Eyewitness accounts wandered all over Hancock County.

Then Lamborn put a Mormon woman, Eliza Graham, on the stand to recount what she saw and heard on the night of the Smiths' killings. Graham worked at the Warsaw House, a tavern managed by her aunt, Mrs. Fleming. Around sunset, she said, the editor Thomas Sharp arrived at the tavern in a two-horse carriage and asked for a cup of water. "We have finished the leading men of the Mormon Church," she heard him say.

As Graham told it, defendants Davis and Grover showed up at the tavern around midnight with about sixty men, including William Voras, who had been wounded in the jailhouse shoot-out. Decompressing at the inn, the men tried to one-up each other with rival claims of having finished off "Old Jo," according to Graham. Grover claimed to have killed the Prophet, and so did Davis. On cross-examination, Browning made much of Graham's Mormon church membership and elicited her damaging admission that she had previously pled complete ignorance of the case, to avoid testifying in court.

The final prosecution witness was Benjamin Brackenbury, a young man who drove a baggage wagon with Captain Davis's militia company. Brackenbury was at Golden's Point and then followed the irregulars on the road to Carthage. Like Daniels, he said somewhere between seventy and a hundred of them left the road three or four miles outside of Carthage, to approach the jailhouse through the woods. Brackenbury saw all five defendants head into Carthage, and he saw four of them return the way they came. For the record, he also saw three of the absent defendants, William Voras, John Wills, and William Gallagher—all of them wounded—straggling back to Warsaw after the attack. Captain Grover "said he had killed Smith, that Smith was a damned stout man, and that he had went into the room where Smith was, and that Smith had struck him twice in the face."

Browning laid into Brackenbury, with mixed results. Yes, Brackenbury had partaken of some spirits on June 27, "enough to make me feel nice." You didn't actually see Captain Grover go to the jail, did you? Browning asked. No, Brackenbury answered, but when he got into my wagon afterward, "he was talking to Mr. Williams about killing the Smiths." Grover boasted that he was the first man through the jailhouse doorway and repeated his claim that Smith bashed him in the face. Browning remarked, that was odd, given that he was holding a pistol.

If you can't attack the testimony, the adage goes, attack the witness. Browning proceeded to do just that.

Q: What business do you follow?
A: Loafering.

Q: And how long have you been doing that?
A: The most of this winter.
Q: When did you commence that trade?
A: A little before last court here [October].

Brackenbury added that he had been living with the Jack-Mormon Minor Deming for several months, and he didn't know who paid for his room and board.

The prosecution rested its case.

Browning and his colleagues at the defense table spent part of Tuesday and half of Wednesday summoning sixteen witnesses, mainly to impeach Brackenbury, Graham, and Daniels. Some astonishing details emerged. Daniels apparently boasted to two acquaintances that he had personally overwhelmed Franklin Worrell at the jailhouse door, wrestled his sword from him, and threw it over a fence. One of the witnesses said Daniels had no special remorse for the Smiths' deaths, "as they richly deserved it." The defense lawyers had rounded up three of Brackenbury's fellow barrel-makers, or "brother chips," as they called themselves. They reported that Brackenbury "had quit coopering and never expected to do any more hard work" because he had tripped across a "speculation" that was going to pay him $500, that is, testifying against the men who had murdered the Smiths.

Browning likewise found several witnesses to shoot holes in Eliza Graham's testimony, including her employer at the Warsaw House, Mrs. Fleming. He rested his case, and court adjourned for lunch, with closing arguments to start at 2:00 p.m.

⁘

THAT AFTERNOON, IN HIS FINAL APPEARANCE OF THE TRIAL, THE disheveled Lamborn stood before the jury looking bereft. Walking in apparent pain and leaning on his cane, Lamborn shuffled around the courtroom, hardly the picture of a legal titan marshaling his forces for a stunning peroration.

Lamborn ended his case as he had begun it, on a note of self-pity. The defense had arrayed four talented lawyers against him, the former attorney general noted; he was a stranger from Quincy, unknown in these parts, and so on. Then he loosed a bolt of lightning like the one that Daniels had tried to exploit in his pathetic pamphlet: Lamborn abandoned the substance of his case.

Shocking his onlookers, Lamborn dumped Daniels and his artless confections overboard. Daniels, he said, "has made statements which ought to impeach his evidence before any court." His pamphlet was obviously "a tissue of falsehoods from beginning to end." "I intend to be fair and candid," Lamborn said, "and therefore exclude Daniels' evidence from the consideration of the jury." He went further. Brackenbury, who saw all of the defendants march on Carthage, was "drunk, is a loafer and perjured himself before the grand jury. I am satisfied that his evidence can be successfully impeached, and therefore withdraw it from the jury." He had only one credible witness left—the earnest Eliza Graham. Lamborn disowned her, too: "She is contradicted, and I therefore give her up."

Lamborn's awkward self-immolation wasn't over. "I have no doubt in my mind, not a particle, that [Jacob] Davis cooperated in the murder," Lamborn thundered. "But there is no legal evidence to convict him. Nor is there evidence to convict Captain Grover, although I verily believe he was at the jail with his gun."

Then he sat down.

The defense table stirred uneasily. Their opponent had just surrendered the better part of his case. What would they do? With their clients' lives hanging in the balance, they did their jobs. Three of them tore apart Lamborn and his evidence for the better part of a day and a half. Calvin Warren delivered an impassioned anti-Mormon philippic, strongly suggesting that whoever killed the Smiths had done society a favor. "If these men are guilty, then are every man, woman and child in the county guilty," Warren said. "The same evidence . . . could have been given against hundreds of others. It was public opinion that the Smiths ought to be killed, and public opinion made the laws."

On Thursday morning, Warren's colleague Onias Skinner expatiated for three hours on the legal definition of a conspiracy, explaining how his clients' actions amounted to nothing of the sort. By Thursday afternoon, there was nothing left for Browning to do but administer the coup de grâce to the state's botched prosecution. He did so, brilliantly. "No human mind can doubt but Daniels has been bribed," Browning told the jury. "He cares neither for God nor man." Neither Daniels nor Brackenbury work for a living, Browning told the jury, eleven of whom were farmers. But they "fare sumptuously . . . fed by an unseen hand." The uxorious Browning, who was very much in love with his pipe-smoking wife, Eliza, allowed that he attacked Eliza Graham's account "with reluctance," belonging as she does "to the gentler sex." Then he eviscerated her testimony.

Browning's assessment of the state's case? "You would not hang a dog on such evidence."

The next morning, Judge Young instructed the jury, and they returned a not guilty verdict immediately after lunch.

The leaders of the mob that killed Joseph Smith strode boldly out of the courtroom, free to resume their normal lives.

⁘ ⁘ ⁘

"AS WE ANTICIPATED," BRIGHAM YOUNG NOTED IN HIS JOURNAL. "It would be a new thing under the sun for Satan's Kingdom to bring to justice a man who has murdered a prophet of God." The Saints' official newspaper, the *Nauvoo Neighbor*, had barely covered the trial and "referred the case to God for a righteous judgment." John Hay felt that "there was not a man on the jury, in the court, in the county, that did not know the defendants had done the murder. But it was not proven, and the verdict of not guilty was right in law."

Had Lamborn thrown the case? Repudiating vast blocs of prosecution testimony seems unheard of, but judicial standards on the frontier circuit were often lax. Abraham Lincoln, an accomplished Illinois litigator, admitted he often placed witnesses on the stand with little idea as to what they might say. Perhaps the Carthage trial just wasn't worthy of Lamborn's best efforts, for a $100 fee and the possible risk of his life. As mentioned, Lamborn's name was never free from the whiff of corruption. A contemporary, Usher Linder, said Lamborn was "wholly destitute of principle and shamelessly took bribes" when he was Illinois's attorney general. "I know myself of his having dismissed forty or fifty indictments in the Shelbyville Court, and openly displayed the money he had received from defendants."

Or perhaps Lamborn simply wasn't up to the job. He died less than two years later, shaking his life away in an attack of delirium tremens after abandoning his wife and child.

Lamborn's equivocal commitment to punishing Joseph Smith's murderers surfaced when it came time to schedule the separate trial of Hyrum Smith's killers. Fresh from their decisive acquittals, the defendants demanded a speedy follow-up to Lamborn's courtroom debacle. Judge Young set a courtroom date for Tuesday, June 24.

Lamborn went through the motions of preparing his case. He subpoenaed ninety-three prosecution witnesses and assembled commitments from men and women who should have participated in the first trial, for example, jailer George Stigall and his wife, one of the guards under Worrell's command, and several members of the Carthage Greys.

Judge Young traveled to Carthage on June 24 to gavel the trial of Hyrum's murderers into session. Astonishingly, Lamborn never showed up. Young freed the defendants "for want of prosecution."

Governor Ford, who had appointed Lamborn and promised the Mormons justice in the courtroom, threw up his hands. "No one would be convicted of any crime in Hancock," he wrote. "Government was at an end there, and the whole community were delivered up to the dominion of a frightful anarchy."

Nauvoo Temple

PART THREE

"*Let us go to the far western shore / Where the blood-thirsty 'christians' will hunt us no more.*"

13

AFTERMATH

The death of the modern Mahomet will seal the fate of
Mormonism. They cannot get another Joe Smith. The holy
city must tumble into ruins, and the "latter-day saints" have
indeed come to the latter day.

—New York Herald, *after Joseph's death*

THE COLD-BLOODED MURDERS OF JOSEPH AND HYRUM SMITH
shocked both Mormons and Gentiles. For several months after
the killings, an uneasy calm prevailed in Hancock County. Perhaps
the anti-Mormon settlers experienced shame; whatever the case, it
took almost a full year for hostilities to resume between the Mormons
and their implacable Illinois enemies. But in the summer of 1844, the
Saints faced a more pressing problem than the simmering hatred in
Hancock County: Who would lead the church?

Joseph had built the Church of Jesus Christ of Latter-day Saints
into a formidable enterprise. For a short time in 1844, Nauvoo was
the largest city in Illinois, with more than 10,000 residents. At least
as many Saints again lived elsewhere in the United States, and in the

ever-expanding British church. All of them looked to Nauvoo, and to Joseph, for leadership and religious revelation.

Replacing the Prophet would be no easy task. Joseph had often mentioned Hyrum, the church's patriarch, as his logical successor, but Hyrum was dead. Within just days of the brothers' assassination, it became clear that Joseph had mentioned many others, too—relatives, associates, apostates, and even his unborn son—as possible successors. In the early 1830s, Joseph had said that Oliver Cowdery, one of his first scribes, or David Whitmer, an original witness to the translation of the golden plates, would be fit to take over the church. He had also named Sidney Rigdon, the fiery preacher with whom Joseph experienced several joint revelations, as a likely successor. In his own family, he had blessed his teenage son Joseph III in January 1844, and had suggested his brother Samuel and even David Hyrum, born five months after Joseph's death, as worthy prophets or revelators of the church. In fact, Joseph had delivered so many contradictory pronouncements that he had even included a zero option, prophesying in 1837 that the "keys" of the new dispensation could not be passed on until Jesus Christ returned to earth (Doctrine and Covenants 112:15).

To complicate matters, Joseph had dispatched almost all church leaders, including ten of the twelve apostles, across the United States to campaign for his presidential candidacy. The most powerful figures remaining in Nauvoo were Willard Richards, the badly wounded John Taylor, and stake president William Marks, the city's senior religious leader. Marks was also president of the church's High Council and a senior member of Joseph's secret Council of Fifty. But the most powerful person in post-assassination Nauvoo was arguably a woman: Joseph's widow, Emma Smith.

Emma enjoyed a special status in Nauvoo, partly stemming from her ceremonial role as the first lady of Mormonism and partly attributable to her benevolent intelligence and forceful personality. Emma functioned as the queen of the Mormons, attending public events attired in regal finery, riding sidesaddle on her favorite mare, or waving from a well-appointed carriage. She presided over the vast Nauvoo Mansion, the town's social and political epicenter, where Joseph conducted much of his business. Emma had organized the women of Nauvoo into a Female Relief Society, over which she presided. Originally intended to raise funds to build the Nauvoo Temple, the Relief Society took on much broader obligations, such as monitoring morality in the fast-growing city. More than once, Emma launched investigations into reports of adultery or polygamy among her peers. Inevitably, the women concerned denied the shocking accusations, which were usually true. Most of the leading figures in the Relief Society, unbeknownst to Emma, had already sealed themselves to Joseph in secret matrimony.

Paradoxically, to pursue his many furtive marriages and assignations, Joseph Smith needed Emma and the cover story of a loving, monogamous marriage to validate the conservative morality of his Old Testament religion. Even though Emma had been informed of the polygamy revelation, and briefly acquiesced to some of Joseph's secret sealings with young women, the public face of Mormonism espoused only monogamy. Thus, Joseph often declared that he had only one wife, the faithful, loving Emma. Polygamy remained a secret practice, heatedly denied in public forums. Moreover, Joseph transferred much of his wealth, most of it land owned on behalf of the church, to Emma. When he died, she immediately became one of Nauvoo's wealthiest and most influential citizens, and also extremely protective of her fortune, and of her children's legacy.

Emma hated polygamy. She hated the secrecy and of course resented the sexual humiliation visited on the first wives of all the Mormon leaders. "Secret things cost Joseph and Hyrum their lives," she told her husband's confederate William Clayton, adding, "I prophecy [sic] that it will cost you and the Twelve your lives as it has done them." For the first month and a half after Joseph's death, her loathing of plural marriage determined her preferences for a successor. Nauvoo immediately split into two rival political camps. On one side, Emma, William

Marks, and Joseph's erratic brother William Smith were lobbying for a church dominated by Joseph's relatives, free from the doctrinal baggage of the past few years: the secret councils, the secret rituals, but most of all, the secret marriages. Marks opposed polygamy when the doctrine was first introduced to the City Council in 1843, and later claimed, unconvincingly, that Joseph intended to abolish plural wifery shortly before his death.

Arrayed against Marks, Emma, and William Smith were Richards, Taylor, and William Phelps, Joseph's ghostwriter. These three were stalling for time, trying to delay key meetings and conferences until the influential apostles and their forceful president, Brigham Young, could return to Nauvoo from the campaign trail and make the case for a continuation of Joseph's policies and theology.

Stake president Marks was widely respected, but uninterested in leading the Saints. That left Joseph's two younger brothers—the ailing Samuel and the mercurial William, admittedly a fragile repository for his family's succession claims. Tall, gaunt, of almost sepulchral appearance, William had worked hard to alienate his more successful older brother. "Lusty, hot tempered and always in debt," William was among those who condemned Joseph as a "false prophet" while he was cooling his heels for six months in a Missouri jail. William opined that Joseph might do well to end his days there: "If I had the disposing of my brother, I would have hung him years ago." On another occasion, William assaulted his brother after a particularly fierce debate. Joseph wrote of the "wickedness of his brother, who Cain-like had tried to kill him." Joseph once instructed Brigham Young to excommunicate William, then thought better of it. (William would later be excommunicated by two separate Mormon churches in two years.) It was William who briefly edited the *Wasp*, the scandalous Nauvoo newspaper that accused Joseph's enemies of "buggery," and worse.

When William finally returned to Nauvoo from a mission trip to the East Coast, "He seemed determined to live up to his privilege and stand in his place," reported James Monroe, a young tutor living in Nauvoo.

William claimed to be of "royal blood" and purported to preach "the gospel according to St. William." No wonder Brigham Young ridiculed him as an "aspiring man." Both Emma and the Smiths' sixty-nine-year-old grandmother, Lucy Mack Smith, the keeper of the desiccated mummies, endorsed William, or his brother Samuel, as possible regents for the thirteen-year-old Joseph Smith III. Emma spoke up forcefully in the leadership councils. She warned Richards and Phelps "not to trample on her" and separately threatened to "do the church all the injury she could" unless William Marks or someone else "she approves of" was appointed president of the Saints.

On July 30, a month after the Carthage killings, the succession struggle took a deadly turn. Thirty-six-year-old Samuel Smith, Joseph's brother, died under mysterious circumstances. William suspected that Willard Richards had arranged for Samuel's poisoning, to ensure that no successor could be chosen before Brigham and the apostles returned to Nauvoo. Although he was nominally a victim of a "bilious fever," Samuel Smith's death has gone down in Mormon history as an ambiguous event or an unsolved crime. Samuel was an alcoholic, it was whispered. Supposedly, he suffered some grievous physical injuries in Carthage on the day his brothers were killed. But his daughter Mary confided to a cousin, "My father was undoubtedly poisoned." She recounted that her father and uncle were taking the same medication, prescribed by Nauvoo doctors. Her uncle threw the medicine in the fire, but "Father continued taking it until the last dose—he spit out and said he was poisoned. But it was too late—he died." When approached by official church historians in 1914 to describe her father's death, Mary did not repeat her allegations of foul play.

❧ ❧ ❧

BY EARLY AUGUST, SERIOUS CLAIMANTS TO JOSEPH'S MANTLE WERE closing in on Nauvoo. Brigham Young was rushing back from Boston, but in 1844, even speedy travel took days, not hours. He took a train from Boston to Albany on July 24. On July 26, he boarded a steamboat in Buffalo, bound for Detroit. Brigham sent a message to the Saints from Chicago on August 1. On August 4, he sent word that he was in Galena, Illinois, a lead-mining center north of Nauvoo on the Mississippi, only a day or two away by boat.

But Sidney Rigdon, arriving from Pittsburgh, beat Brigham to the punch. With William Law discredited and Joseph dead, Rigdon was now the only surviving member of the First Presidency. A successful revivalist preacher, Rigdon converted to Mormonism in 1830, the year the Book of Mormon was published, and often preached alongside Joseph Smith. He was erudite, book-smart, and a tad unstable. Joseph and Rigdon had feuded ferociously over the years, although Smith generally acknowledged the older man's superior intellect and preaching abilities. Rigdon's stock had been falling during the final years of Joseph's reign, primarily because of the older man's lack of enthusiasm for polygamy. Joseph had improbably accused Rigdon of conspiring with the Missouri authorities to kidnap the Prophet and tried to arrange his expulsion from the church. William Marks and other church leaders supported Rigdon and defied Joseph, who then washed his hands of his former counselor. "I have thrown him off my shoulders," Joseph declared in 1843, "and you have put him on me; you may carry him, but I will not." Joseph's ire was temporary, and soon afterward he admitted Rigdon to the secret Council of Fifty and approved his counselor's nomination for vice president on his 1844 presidential ticket.

Rigdon was excitable, and not always in a good way. It was he who urged the "war of extermination" against the Saints' enemies in Missouri—a suggestion the Missourians quickly embraced as their own—and odd reports surfaced concerning his 1844 induction into the Council of Fifty. Fellow member Jedediah Grant said Rigdon "leaped for joy, and walked the room as sprightly as a boy in his gayest frolics" in the upstairs room of Joseph Smith's store. "Joseph! Joseph! Thou servant of the most High God, I will never leave or forsake thee!" Rigdon exclaimed. Orson Hyde reported that Rigdon "began to speak, then to shout, then to dance, and threw his feet so high that he lost his balance and came well nigh falling over backwards upon the stove" at the same ceremony. "He was so extravagant in his shouting," Hyde reported, "that most of the members hung their heads."

Rigdon and his family had moved to Pittsburgh in the spring of 1844, purportedly because his vice-presidential nomination required him to live outside of Illinois; the nominees for president and vice president couldn't hail from the same state. At the same time, it was whispered that Rigdon wanted to put 1,000 miles between his attractive twenty-one-year-old daughter Nancy and the priapic Nauvoo polygamists.

Rigdon's arrival in Nauvoo immediately changed the terms of the succession debate. Addressing the Saints' Sunday service in the leafy grove on the Temple hill, Rigdon recounted a vision he experienced on June 27, the day Joseph died. Rigdon saw Joseph Smith in heaven, "on the right hand of the Son of God . . . clothed with all the power, glory, might and majesty and dominion of the celestial kingdoms." Joseph still held "the keys of the kingdom," Rigdon testified, and "would continue to hold them to all eternity . . . no man could ever take his place."

The revelation stated that there must be a guardian appointed "to build the church up to Joseph, as he had begun it." And the guardian should be me, Rigdon said: I am "the identical man that the ancient prophets had sung about, wrote and rejoiced over." Then Rigdon started to slip off the rails, preaching on one of his favorite themes, Armageddon ("one hundred tons of metal per second thrown at the enemies of God"), and reiterating a curious threat he had previously directed against Queen Victoria of England:

> I am going to fight a real bloody battle with sword and with gun . . . I will also cross the Atlantic to encounter the queen's forces, and overcome them—plant the American standard on English ground and then march to the palace of her majesty, and demand a portion of her riches

and dominions, which if she refuse, I will take the little madam by the nose and lead her out, and she shall have no power to help herself.

The Nauvoo stalwarts scorned Rigdon's high-flown rhetoric and visionary claims. Returning Apostle Parley Pratt later scoffed that Rigdon was "the identical man the prophets never sang nor wrote a word about." Future church president Wilford Woodruff mocked Rigdon's "second class vision."

‡ ‡ ‡

BRIGHAM YOUNG ARRIVED JUST TWO DAYS AFTER RIGDON AND quickly attacked the older preacher's bona fides. Just as Rigdon's stock had been gradually falling among the Saints, Brigham's had been rising. A medium-sized fireplug of a man with distinctive red hair, Young was an uneducated, areligious frontier husbandman who devoted his life to Joseph Smith from the moment the two men met. They were born not far from each other in Vermont, and both men grew up in northwestern New York. When Young and his brother traveled from New York to Ohio in 1832 to meet the Prophet Joseph, "I expected I should find him in his sanctum dispensing spiritual blessing and directions [about] how to build the Zion of God on earth," Brigham's brother recalled. Instead, they found Joseph, the most earthy of earthly prophets, chopping wood in the forest. The Young brothers grabbed axes and set to work. Brigham was enchanted by the Prophet who "took heaven . . . and brought it down to earth."

Brigham Young and Joseph Smith worked side by side for the next twelve years. Young, who lacked Joseph's charismatic appeal, possessed an organizational flair that his mentor lacked. When several thousand Saints had to cross the frozen Mississippi River in the wake of their expulsion from Missouri, Brigham asked Bishop Edward Partridge to provide aid for poor families making the grisly trek. "The poor may take care of themselves, and I will take care of myself," Partridge told him.

"If you will not help them out, I will," answered Young, who assisted in organizing the initial Mormon encampment in Quincy, Illinois.

Joseph entrusted Young and the apostles with an 1840 mission trip to England. The first Mormon missionaries had set foot in Great Britain three years earlier, but it was the 1840 mission, an astonishing religious and logistical success, that sent steamboats packed with eager Saints west across the Atlantic. An estimated 3,000 converts sailed across the ocean and then up the Mississippi to Nauvoo. The doggedly loyal Young supported Joseph in his adoption of the Masonic rites and in his self-coronation as king of the Kingdom of God. He also followed the Prophet into polygamy, a doctrine Young initially abhorred. Joseph assigned the delicate task of excommunicating William and Wilson Law, and the other *Expositor* dissidents, to a secret court presided over by Brigham Young.

Where Joseph had been dilatory, Young was assiduous. Where Joseph claimed charismatic inspiration, Young generally eschewed divine revelation. Joseph contributed 135 canonized revelations to church doctrine. In contrast, Young offered only one, concerning the organization of the exodus to Utah. "I never pretended to be Joseph Smith," Young declared. "I'm not the man that brought forth the 'Book of Mormon.'"

Brigham had his own revelation en route to Nauvoo, which convinced him that he, not Rigdon, was the true inheritor of Joseph's mantle. "By vision of the spirit," Young had learned that the Quorum of the Twelve Apostles should assume the presidency of the entire church. In a preliminary meeting with Rigdon, Young claimed not to "care who leads the church, even though it were Ann Lee," the charismatic Shaker leader who thought she was Jesus Christ. "But one thing I must know," Young said, "and that is what God says about it. I have the keys and the means of obtaining the mind of God on the subject."

The two rivals agreed to compete as verbal gladiators for the favor of the assembled church. On Thursday, August 8, the two claimants appeared in the East Grove at 10:00 a.m. for a dramatic rhetorical showdown. This was the same natural theater where several of the young religion's most dramatic scenes had already played out, including Joseph's apocalyptic King Follett sermon and his final Sunday sermon to the Saints. Five thousand onlookers gathered to hear first Rigdon, then Brigham, plead for their vote to sustain one man's leadership.

Rigdon, the fabled orator, appeared first on the rickety wooden stand in front of the assembled Saints. But a powerful wind was blowing in his face, so he walked through the audience to a buckboard wagon at the back of the crowd. The audience turned around on their benches to face him. Standing in the wagon box, he delivered the most important speech of his life.

Victors write the history, and by most accounts, Rigdon failed to mesmerize the Mormons. "He was dry as sticks in his preaching," Benjamin Ashby, age fifteen at the time, later remembered. "He made a silly, boastful speech about leading the church back to Pittsburgh, and twirling the nose of Queen Victoria." The wiry Rigdon, who suffered occasional bouts of mania, again mined the Armageddon theme, promising to "dethrone kings and emperors, and lead the armies of Israel to fight the great battle of Gog and Magog." There is no reliable record of his ninety-minute talk, during which he repeated his claim to be Joseph's spokesman and the designated guardian of the church. There is a record of Brigham Young's dramatic entrance, however. Just as Rigdon was about to ask the faithful to vote him as their leader, "Lo! To his grief and mortification, [Brigham Young] stepped upon the stand and with a word stayed all the proceedings of Mr. Rigdon," according to one of Young's allies, Apostle Orson Hyde.

"I will manage this voting for Elder Rigdon," Young shouted from the opposite end of the grove, yelling into the stiff wind. "He does not preside here. This child [i.e., Young himself] will manage this flock for a season."

Brigham had staged a theatrical reversal. While Rigdon was speaking, he had climbed up the wooden platform at the other end of the grove. When he interrupted Rigdon, the entire audience swiveled around in their seats to hear him. Then, supposedly, a miracle occurred, buttressed by many testimonies over the years. "It was Joseph's voice," reported twenty-six-year-old Benjamin Johnson, who remembered turning his gaze from the wagon to the wooden platform where Brigham was standing. "As soon as he spoke, I jumped on my feet," Johnson said. "His person, in look, attitude, dress and appearance was Joseph himself, personified, and I knew in a moment the spirit and mantle of Joseph was upon him." The apostle Hyde remembered that he was sitting in the grove with his two wives; when Brigham started talking, "One of them said: 'It is the voice of Joseph! It is Joseph Smith!'" Hyde's other wife remarked more prosaically, "I do not see him, where is he?" Curiously, Young had just alluded to the Bible passage, John 10:27: "My sheep hear my voice, and I know them, and they follow me."*

Brigham's mystical "transfiguration" deserves to be treated skeptically. Historian Richard Van Wagoner noted that Orson Hyde's dramatic testimony of the August 8 events could not be his own; on presidential assignment in "Babylon," Hyde didn't return to Nauvoo until August 13. Mormon elder John D. Lee likewise left a dramatic account ("Brigham Young arose and roared like a young lion, imitating the style and voice of Joseph the Prophet"), but he wasn't in Nauvoo, either. Lee arrived in Nauvoo on August 20.

In fact, there was hardly any similarity between Joseph and the man later to be called "the Lion of the Lord." Joseph was taller than Brigham, and he spoke in a very different, folksy cadence. The robust Brigham had long, light-red hair, whereas Joseph had dark brown locks. The epiphany later recorded by so many faithful Saints appeared in no contemporary accounts of Brigham's talk. Four apostles, including Young himself, wrote diary entries for August 8, and none mentioned Brigham speaking in the voice of Joseph. This detail

---

* One disaffected listener, S. S. Thornton, wrote to his father-in-law that "Mr. Young had tried to mimic Joseph for several years . . . and on his return from Boston after [Joseph's] martyrdom even went out to get a dentist to take out a tooth on the same side that Joseph lost one, to make myself appear as much like him as possible."

likewise eluded Nauvoo's two faith-promoting newspapers, the *Nauvoo Neighbor* and the *Times and Seasons*.

Whatever voice he was speaking in, Brigham utterly demolished Rigdon's feeble claim on the Saints' allegiance. Brigham knew his audience, fully one-third of whom were struggling immigrants from Britain. He and the apostles had converted many of them during the legendary missionary trip to Britain in 1840. "I know your feelings," Brigham boomed. "Do you want me to tell you your feelings?" He judged that the forlorn Saints were "like children without a father, and sheep without a shepherd."

Young gambled that the Saints weren't looking for a replacement prophet in the immediate aftermath of Joseph's death. God revealed prophets to his believers, and Rigdon didn't make the grade. "Do you want a spokesman?" as Rigdon claimed to be, Young taunted. "Do you want the church properly organized, or do you want a spokesman to be chief cook and bottle washer?" If Rigdon was so eager to be Joseph's spokesman, Young thundered, "he must go to the other side of the vail"—in other words, he must die—"for the Prophet is there, but Elder Rigdon is here."

The Twelve "were appointed by the finger of God," Young thundered. "Here is Brigham, have his knees ever faltered? Have his lips ever quivered?" The twelve apostles, Young insisted, have "the Keys of the Kingdom to all the whole world so help me God." The keys were the code words and signs that would allow faithful Mormons to enter heaven in the afterlife. "We have all the signs and the tokens to give to the Porter and he will let us in the quay," Young explained. Joseph had the keys, and he passed them to the Twelve, according to Young. Rigdon had nothing, save his own questionable, self-serving revelation.

Now Brigham called for a vote. Would the Saints sustain the authority of the Twelve, or elect Rigdon as their leader? As the cowed Rigdon sat slump-shouldered on the wooden stand next to Young, 5,000 hands shot into the air, unanimously choosing Brigham Young, president of the Twelve, to lead them into an uncertain future.

Unbeknownst to the Saints assembled in the Nauvoo grove, this was a signal moment in Mormon history; the faithful would never elect their church leader again. Since then, church leaders have ascended to the Quorum of the Twelve Apostles as counseled by divine revelation, and the most senior apostle has assumed the church presidency. Brigham Young, who ruled the church for thirty years, would be the last president chosen by the will of the people.

I I I

JOSEPH KNEW THAT THE MOST SERIOUS CHALLENGE TO HIS authority could come only from a rival prophet. The Saints accepted that God had spoken to, and directed the affairs of, their revelator. But suppose another prophet happened onto the scene, asserting the same claims as Joseph? Or worse, asserting the primacy of his revelations over Joseph's?

There was precedent for such a threat. In 1835, Joseph briefly embraced a character named Joshua the Jewish Minister (real name: Robert Matthews), who claimed to be the resurrected Matthias, the apostle chosen to replace Judas in the original Twelve. Matthias wandered around the Saints' Kirtland, Ohio, settlement sporting a green frock, harlequin-colored pantaloons, bound with a crimson sash with twelve tassels. Matthias had come directly to Kirtland from Sing Sing prison, where he had served a four-month term for beating his daughter. Smith initially lent an ear to Matthias's odd ravings about King Nebuchadnezzar and the prophet Daniel's dream, and even invited the itinerant felon to preach to the Saints. But Smith quickly realized that Matthias had a screw loose. After two nights in Kirtland, Joseph showed his new acquaintance the gate, saying that "his God is the Devil, and I could not keep him any longer."

Much closer to home, a ten-year-old Mormon boy named James Colin Brewster claimed to have received a visit from the angel Moroni while living in Kirtland. Brewster's claims surfaced at a time of intense conflict within the church. Joseph had just launched his short-lived, rogue banking experiment, the Kirtland Safety Society Anti-Banking Company, which would quickly bankrupt many Saints and Gentiles, and prompted Joseph to flee Ohio in the dead of night. Moroni confirmed to young James that the church was in trouble and "had not lived according to the former revelations," and that "the High Council was in transgression." Predictably, the High Council, chaired by Joseph's uncle John Smith, disfellowshipped Brewster and anyone who refused to denounce his teachings.

Brewster's career trajectory began to closely parallel that of Joseph Smith. Soon he discovered the "lost books of Esdras," an ancient Hebrew prophet. Esdras denounced the current state of the church: "Woe to the shepherds that will not feed the flock," the writings stated; "I say unto you that the enemy of all righteousness has laid snares to destroy the saints of the most high, and he hath led many away into darkness." Brewster's father, Zephaniah, who had helped him transcribe Esdras's revelations, fretted that his son might be a heretic. He brought the Esdras manuscript to Joseph Smith. "I enquired of the Lord and the Lord told me the book was not true," Joseph proclaimed. In the *Times and Seasons* newspaper, John Taylor accused young Brewster of money digging—the very charge leveled against Joseph Smith several years earlier—and called Esdras "a perfect humbug." Taylor reminded the Saints of Joseph's own revelation, canonized in the church's Doctrine and Covenants (28:2), when God said, "No one shall be appointed to receive commandments and revelations in this church excepting my servant Joseph Smith."

Brewsterism had no lasting impact on the Mormon church, and no one knows where the precocious boy prophet ended his days. But his brief career did prove that the Saints, who were predisposed to believe in angelic interventions, sacred tablets, and lost stories of Israel, might succumb to the blandishments of a new prophet, if one appeared on the horizon.

Almost immediately after Joseph Smith's death, one did. In early August 1844, at a gathering of Mormons at Florence, Michigan, a thirty-one-year-old lawyer and recent convert to the church named James J. Strang brandished a letter supposedly signed by Joseph Smith. In the letter, almost certainly a forgery, a disconsolate Joseph ("The wolves are upon the scent, and I am waiting to be offered up") related that God appeared to him and declared Strang to be Smith's lawful successor: "And now behold my servant James J. Strang hath come to there from far from truth . . . my servant James shall lengthen the cords and strengthen the stakes of Zion." Joseph ordered the Saints to gather to Strang's tiny colony in Voree, Wisconsin, about 275 miles northeast of Nauvoo, not far from Lake Michigan: "There shall my people have peace and rest and wax fat and pleasant in the presence of their enemies." Strang later claimed that an angel appeared to him at 5:30 p.m. on June 27, 1844, the very moment of Joseph's death. The angel extended his hand, anointed Strang's head with oil, and proclaimed him to be the successor prophet to Joseph Smith.

The Michigan Mormons promptly excommunicated Strang, and when word of his claims reached Nauvoo, Brigham Young and the apostles excommunicated him a second time for good measure. Two could play this game. As a purported true prophet, Strang quickly excommunicated Brigham and most of the Nauvoo apostles, for "usurping the authority belonging to the first presidency, taking to themselves the powers and duties of the high quorums, and commanding the church to go into the wilderness." He pronounced this baroque curse on the Brighamite leadership: "May their bones rot in the living tomb of their flesh; may their flesh generate from its own corruptions a loathesome life for others; may their blood swarm with a leprous life of mote-like, ghastly corruption feeding on flowing life—" and so on. The Twelve gave as good as they got, calling Strang "a successor of Judas Iscariot, Cain & Co., Envoy Extraordinary and Minister Plenipotentiary of His Most Gracious Majesty Lucifer."

Strang quickly raised the stakes. In 1845, he announced that an angel had informed him about some ancient brass plates buried not far from his home. To decipher the Michigan plates, the angel provided Strang with the same divining tools, the spectacle-like Urim and Thummim, used by Joseph Smith to translate the Book of Mormon. Like Joseph's golden tablets, these plates told the tale of an ancient nation that lived in North America and perished in a tumultuous battle that ended their civilization. Joseph's muse, the angel Moroni, provided him with the entire Book of Mormon to translate, but Rajah Manchou of the ancient civilization of Vorito left Strang only a few hundred words of evidence. Like Moroni, Rajah had survived a cataclysm, but his people had not. "My people are no more," Rajah reported. "They sleep with the mighty dead, and they rest with their fathers." In the desolate land, "The forerunner men shall kill, but a mighty prophet there shall dwell. I will be his strength, and he shall bring forth thy record." The forerunner was of course Joseph Smith, and Strang was the mighty prophet.

A few years later, an angel led Strang to the Plates of Laban, which enabled him to translate the Book of the Law of the Lord. ("A fresh plate-digger, translator and prophet has arisen in the West," the Washington-based *National Intelligencer* cynically reported.) The Book of the Law, deemed to be an Old Testament text so sacred that many Jews never knew it existed, would have reminded Mormons of Joseph's translation of the Book of Abraham and the Book of Moses, two of his canonical confections.

Like Joseph, the slight, bearded Strang was eloquent and charismatic. He wrote with panache, and his anti-polygamy tirades, as well as his broadsides aimed at the "usurper" Brigham, found an audience in Nauvoo. By the second half of 1845, the Gentiles had resumed their harassment of the Mormons in Hancock County. By fall, Young realized the Saints would have to migrate again, this time westward across the Mississippi to lands beyond the reach of the American government. Strang proffered an alternative. Don't travel to "an unexplored wilderness among savages in trackless deserts, where the footprint of the white man is not found," Strang urged the Nauvoo Saints. Instead, journey with me, to a peaceful, welcoming Mormon community in Wisconsin. Strang cannily exploited the church's split on the subject of polygamy, which he called an "abomination." "My opinions on the subject are unchanged, and I regard them as unchangeable," he wrote. "They are established on a full consideration of ALL the scriptures, both ancient and modern, and the discipline of the church shall conform thereto."

Even though Strang never set foot in Nauvoo after Joseph's death, his pamphleteering and his missionaries were finding an audience. Diarist William Clayton noted in January 1846 that "Bishop Reuben Miller reports that Strang is making heavy breaches in the church, and drawing many after him."

In one place 30 families have left the church and gone with him. It is also rumored that many of the Saints here are full of Strangism and talking hard in his favor.

That same month, Brigham Young complained that Bishop Miller was "considerably bewildered by Strang['s] new-fangled Revelation—rendered him almost devoid of Reason although apparently honest in what he was doing—& said that the word of the Lord would be decidedly satisfactorily to him." On the spot, Young obliged Miller with the following revelation:

Thus saith the Lord unto Reuben Miller through Brigham Young: that Strang is a wicked & corrupt man & that his revelations are as false as he is—therefore turn away from his folly—& never let it be said of Reuben Miller—that he ever was led away & entangled—by such nonsense.

Miller would soon abandon Young and travel east to join forces with Strang.

Strang continued to woo Saints away from Nauvoo, so God addressed the Strangite heresy a second time, now in a revelation to Apostle Orson Hyde. "Behold James J. Strang hath cursed my people by his own spirit and not by mine."

> Never at any time have I appointed that wicked man to lead my people, neither by my own voice, nor by the voice of my servant Joseph Smith, neither by the voice of mine angel: but he hath sought to deceive and Satan helpeth him.
>
> Let my saints gather up with all consistent speed and move westward. . . .

In a letter to the British church, Hyde assured the Saints that tales of Strang's mass conversions were much exaggerated. "I do not know of ten persons in Nauvoo that have joined Mr. Strang," Hyde insisted. "There are none who join him except a few Rigdonites . . . Strangism is but a second and revised edition of Rigdonism."

Hyde's fellow apostle, Heber Kimball, scoffed that "Strangism was not worth investigating—it was not worth the skin of a fart."

Even though Brigham threatened to sanction any Saint caught reading a Strangite publication or listening to one of the Wisconsin missionaries, several prominent Saints rallied to Strangism, for a time. William Marks, Emma Smith, and William Smith briefly considered themselves Strangites, as did Joseph's mother, Lucy Mack Smith, Apostle George Adams, and Martin Harris, an original witness to the creation of the Book of Mormon. Strang knew that the support of the Smith family would validate his shaky succession claim. In one exchange, Strang offered to appoint William Smith to be patriarch of his new church, *if* William relocated to Wisconsin with his mother, and with the Egyptian mummies and the famous papyrus scrolls. Strang also asked William to bring along the cadavers of his dead brothers, Joseph and Hyrum. William did travel to Voree, but no living or dead family members, and no funerary paraphernalia, accompanied him. William was one of about a thousand or so Saints who answered James Strang's call, gathering first at Voree, and then going to Beaver Island, Strang's remote fastness in the middle of Lake Michigan.

With each passing month, however, Strang revealed more of his personal eccentricities. He knew that Joseph Smith had created secret conclaves for chosen Saints, so he quickly introduced a secret organization called the Halcyon Order of the Illuminati. Strang, the order's "Imperial Primate," ordained a few dozen of his followers as chevaliers, marshals, earls, and cardinals. In the initiation rite, he escorted new members to a dark room, where he anointed them with a mysterious, luminous oil that created a halo effect above their heads. William Smith discovered that the oily mixture contained phosphorus and could set a man's hair on fire. Strang pooh-poohed the risk, likening his initiation to the miracles of Christ.

On July 8, 1850, Strang summoned his followers to an odd event inside his partly finished tabernacle on Beaver Island. Attended by seventy dignitaries wearing scarlet robes, Strang presented himself to his followers seated on a throne, wearing a long red-and-white gown. In accordance with the teaching of the Book of the Law of the Lord, the Lake Michigan prophet declared himself to be the king of Beaver Island, and beyond. A follower lowered a paper crown studded with stars onto Strang's head, while an apostle brought forth a "royal diadem" and placed it in Strang's hands. The congregation testified that "the Kingdom of God is set up on the Earth no more to be thrown down."

This was the fulfillment of Joseph Smith's prediction that the Saints would establish the Kingdom of God on earth in preparation for the Second Coming. Joseph had already secretly crowned *himself* king of the Kingdom of God, although not in public. Joseph correctly guessed that the United States wouldn't tolerate any monarch, no matter how vaporous his realm. As the leader of perhaps 20,000 not very popular Mormons adrift in an ocean of Gentiles, Joseph hid his kingship under a bushel. Strang had no such inhibitions, apparently unaware of the farcical effect of his claims. He aped Joseph in yet another sphere, baptizing dead celebrities in the chilly White River that flowed just north of Voree. Lord Byron, Oliver Cromwell, Napoleon Bonaparte, John Adams, and John Quincy Adams all became Strangite Saints in their respective afterlives.

Soon it became clear that Strang intended to copy yet another of Joseph's doctrines; he was a secret polygamist. William Marks and the Smith family rallied to Strang mainly because he publicly abjured polygamy. But Strang's private life proved to be complex indeed. For seven months starting in 1849, Strang traveled the country with his young nephew, Charley Douglass, who served as his assistant and secretary. "Douglass" was in fact a comely nineteen-year-old Mormon girl named Elvira Field, whom Strang had secretly married in the summer of 1849. At the time he was thirty-six years old, and already married to a wife who had borne him two children. Strang, who had campaigned so militantly against spiritual wifery, said the plates made him do it, specifically, the Plates of Laban, with their secret Law of the Lord. "Strang translated the plates that he claimed were genuine," a follower explained

> and found in them the principle of polygamy; and after the translation he published it, and then he indorsed the doctrine of polygamy after he was commanded to do so. . . .

"Charley Douglass's" secret wouldn't last long. One Saint raised the question of Charley's "physiological peculiarities" with Strang, who quickly answered that Charley had a look-alike sister on Beaver Island.* Around the time that Elvira delivered her first child, Strang's first wife, Mary, fled Beaver Island, for reasons one can only surmise.

---

*Following the dictates of the Plates of Laban, which forbade "every form of [women's] dress that pinches or compresses the body or limbs," Strang had a predilection for dressing women in pants and enforced a dress code on Beaver Island. Females had to wear ankle-length bloomers, which he called "Mormon dress." A visiting Gentile wrote: "I do not object to the number [of wives assigned to] each man, but the trousers I do not like."

Strang was soon openly espousing plural wifery, and eventually had five wives. Just as the Hancock County Gentiles deemed polygamy to be sinful and perverse, so did the fishermen and lumberjacks who were Strang's neighbors along the Lake Michigan shoreline. They didn't like the Mormons casting their votes en bloc, either, and they didn't like Strang's autarkic economic policies, which made lake traders unwelcome in Mormon settlements. In 1856, the man who claimed to be the next Joseph Smith died just as Joseph did, cut down by vigilante assassins who enjoyed the protection of the powers that be. Strang was killed with the connivance of the US Navy, which quickly spirited his killers away from Beaver Island, and away from prosecution. The difference between Strang and Smith was that Joseph's church continued to thrive and grow for 170 years after his death, while Strangism devolved into a comical footnote to the history of religion.

Ϯ Ϯ Ϯ

FOR BRIGHAM YOUNG, INTENT ON CONSOLIDATING HIS POWER in Nauvoo, Strangism was an annoyance and not much more. Discrediting Sidney Rigdon, an ordained "seer and revelator" and a comrade who spent three months with Joseph Smith fighting off rats in a fetid Missouri jail, took a higher priority. In a six-hour public trial just one month after the Young-Rigdon showdown, the Quorum of the Twelve excommunicated their former colleague, in absentia. "His late revelations are of the devil," William Phelps testified. "Brother Joseph said he would carry him no more," Apostle Heber Kimball chimed in. Brigham Young called Rigdon "a black hearted wretch," and the former first counselor's fate was sealed. Except for a few dissenting votes, including that of William Marks, the assembled Saints washed their hands of Joseph Smith's longtime colleague.

"President Young arose and delivered Sidney Rigdon over to the buffetings of Satan in the name of the Lord," the official church history recorded, "and all the people said, 'Amen.'"

Rigdon quickly moved back East to end his life in poverty and humiliation. In his dotage, Rigdon's mania became more acute. His family eventually forbade him to preach. "He seemed sane upon every other subject except religion," his son Wyckliffe Rigdon wrote. "When he got on that subject, he seemed to lose himself and his family would not permit him to talk in that subject, especially with strangers."

Joseph Smith's family was a separate problem. Emma and Brigham were at loggerheads. The two feuded over money. For public consumption, Joseph had affected ecclesiastic poverty. He once claimed to own a horse, two pet deer, "two old turkeys and four young ones . . . an old cow . . . a dog, his wife, children, and a little household furniture." In fact he had placed much of his property, and some church properties, in Emma's name, and Emma feared that the apostles would confiscate the Nauvoo Mansion and other assets from her, leaving her destitute. Joseph's estate was deeply in debt. His 1842 bankruptcy petition had failed, and creditors were still demanding yearly payments on his questionable property claims in Nauvoo and across the river. "There is considerable danger if the family begin to dispute about the property, that Joseph's creditors will come forward and use up all the property there is," his confidant William Clayton noted in a July 2, 1844, diary entry. "If they will keep still there is property enough to pay the debts and plenty left for other uses."

Emma and Brigham were likewise irreconcilable on polygamy, which Emma started to deny had ever existed. Brigham voiced astonishing accusations against Emma: "Twice she undertook to kill him," he charged, suggesting that she tried to poison her husband, and that she delivered him to certain death by allowing him to return to Nauvoo from his abortive flight to Montrose, Iowa. Brigham craved the legitimacy of the Smith family's approval, reacting angrily when it eluded him.

The sulfurous William became a proxy in the war between Emma and the Twelve. On the first anniversary of Joseph's death, the boys' mother, Lucy Mack Smith, promulgated a dream in which God told her that "the Presidency of the Church belongs to William, according to his lineage, he having inherited it from the family before the foundation of the world." The Twelve grudgingly appointed William to be church patriarch, a largely ceremonial position, then quickly realized their mistake. William claimed that the patriarch ruled over the Twelve, which prompted an immediate, vituperative response from Brigham and the apostles. On a day when he decided to address the Saints in the grove, William arrived to find the seats and benches smeared with feces. His challenge to the Twelve ended with his excommunication, and a long period of self-imposed exile from mainstream Mormonism. William famously observed that the Twelve "were mean enough to steal if they could get the chance even Christ's supper off his plate, or seduce the Virgin Mary, or Rob an orphan child of 25 cents. So damnable are their acts & conduct that old Judas would be a perfect gentleman to these men." After Brigham's death, William joined the Reorganized Church of Jesus Christ of Latter Day Saints, led by the Prophet's oldest son, Joseph Smith III.

Ï Ï Ï

BRIGHAM HAD CONSOLIDATED HIS GRIP ON THE NAUVOO SAINTS. But while he was shrugging off leadership challenges from Rigdon, Strang, and William Smith, the same forces that had marshaled to kill Joseph were gathering strength again. This time the "old settlers," still led by Thomas Sharp and the marauder Levi Williams, were agitating for a final solution: the expulsion of the Mormons from Illinois. Sharp, who offered "THREE CHEERS FOR THE BRAVE COMPANY WHO SHOT [Joseph Smith] TO PIECES" shortly after the murders, had never stopped waving the bloody shirt. "It is impossible that the two communities can long live together," the *Signal* editorialized shortly after Joseph's death. "They can *never* assimilate. We repeat our firm conviction that one or the other *must* leave."

Even the pusillanimous Governor Ford realized that civil society was doomed in Hancock County. In April 1845, he confided to Brigham

Young that the Mormons would always be "enemies and outcasts" in Illinois, privately suggesting that Young take the Saints elsewhere:

> Your religion is new and it surprises the people as any great novelty in religion generally does. However truly and sincerely your own people may believe in it, the impression on the public mind everywhere is that your leading men are impostors and rogues and that the others are dupes and fools. . . .
>
> If you can get off by yourselves, you may enjoy peace; but, surrounded by such neighbors, I confess that I do not see the time when you will be permitted to enjoy quiet.

The artificial peace that followed the killings at the Carthage jail effectively ended with the trial, and its summary acquittals. The message was clear: No anti-Mormon depredation would ever be punished in Illinois. The old settlers were free to act as they pleased.

In the early fall of 1845, Levi Williams and his Warsaw vigilantes began to systematically attack Mormon farms and settlements outside Nauvoo. The attacks began in Morley's Settlement, twenty-five miles south of Nauvoo. "The mob is upon us," two Mormons reported. "They have burned six buildings already. . . . They are in number about two hundred. They shoot at every brother they see." Over the course of several weeks, Williams and his "regulators" attacked Mormon enclaves in Lima, Bear Creek, Camp Creek, and La Harpe, destroying about two hundred homes and farms and torching innumerable mills and hay ricks. By September 16, Brigham had had enough. For the fourth time in recent Mormon history, their leader backed away from a shooting war with the Gentiles, saving untold lives in the process. Young issued a "Proclamation to Col. Levi Williams and Mob Party," informing his enemies that "it is our intention to leave Nauvoo and the country next spring." The Mormons soon hammered out an understanding with a committee of distinguished Illinoisans, including Joseph's friend Stephen Douglas, that they would plant no new crops in Nauvoo and depart the area "as soon as the grass is green and the water runs." That implied that they would leave around March, when the Mississippi ice floes would start breaking up, and their teams of horse and oxen could graze on the Iowa plains during their journey westward.

Unbeknownst to the Gentiles, and even to most Mormons, Brigham and the Twelve had decided to move to the Rocky Mountains, to one of two vast and uninhabited tracts of land: the Great Salt Lake Valley or Utah Valley, just to the north. "Uninhabited," though, was a figure of speech; several Native American tribes frequented both valleys, which formally belonged to Mexico's California holdings. But Mexico was busy losing a war to the United States, and Young and the Twelve correctly surmised that it would be several years before anyone bothered to lay claim to these arid, intermontane expanses. Getting there would be quite a trick. From Nauvoo, the trail led more or less due west, for 1,300 miles along the course of the Missouri, Platte, and Sweetwater Rivers. The last few hundred miles of the journey would require arduous mountain trekking, some of it through passes and along ranges known only to a small coterie of scouts and mountain men.

If the Saints knew anything about the land enclosed by the Rockies, they knew it was bleak. But once the Twelve announced their relocation plans, the church-owned *Nauvoo Neighbor* began publishing upbeat excerpts from the journals of legendary explorer John C. Fremont:

> The Rocky Mountains . . . instead of being desolate and impassable . . . embosom beautiful valleys, rivers, and parks, with lakes and mineral springs, rivaling and surpassing the most enchanting parts if the Alpine regions of Switzerland. The Great Salt Lake, one of the wonders of the world . . . and the Bear River Valley, with its rich bottoms, fine grass, walled up mountains . . . is for the first time described.

The biblical nature of the proposed journey was lost on no one. Speaking to a general conference of the church in the fall of 1845, Apostle

A famous painting by Lynn Fausett depicting the Saints'
first departures from Nauvoo to the Iowa Territory. In the
background, the Nauvoo Temple is fully completed.
Credit: Utah State Historical Society

Heber Kimball announced that "the time of our exodus is come; I have
looked for it for many years." He continued:

> We want to take you to a land, where the white man's foot never trod,
> not a lion's whelps, nor the devil's; and there we can enjoy it, with no
> one to molest us and make us afraid; and we will bid all the nations
> welcome, whether Pagans, Catholics or Protestants.

Young stalled for time with the Saints' tormentors, in part to prepare for the daunting journey west—the Mormons built 3,400 wagons that winter—but also to complete the prophesied construction
of the Nauvoo Temple. The Twelve had promised that Joseph's secret temple endowment ritual, heretofore administered on the second floor of his general store, would be available to any Saint in good
standing when the Temple was completed. The feverish construction finally ended in December, and the long-awaited "temple work"

began. Husbands and wives were sealed in eternal marriage; plural wives were sealed to men "for time"; dead relatives were baptized and assured eternal life; and the Twelve introduced a ceremony of spiritual adoption, in which church leaders sealed friends and distant relatives to themselves as children. Most Saints were desperate to receive the basic endowment ritual and don their temple garments, which Joseph and the Twelve taught they would need to meet Jesus Christ in the final days, and to enjoy the prophesied exaltation. Over 5,000 Saints received their temple blessings in November and December 1845, with Brigham Young, Heber Kimball, and other apostles sometimes working twenty consecutive hours to process believers through the elaborate rites. By February 1, the temple work had ended, and the first Mormon companies assembled at the base of Parley Street to be ferried across the Mississippi to Iowa. The river was flowing, although it would freeze up later in the month, easing the way for the hundreds of wagons wending their way west.

On February 15, Brigham Young and his brother Joseph led a company of fifteen wagons down to the water's edge. The Mormons were running six ferries, operating simultaneously, across the frigid river. Willard Richards and his eight wives filled two of the wagons lined up directly behind Brigham. Like many Saints, Young had failed to sell his Nauvoo home. The Mormons' Hancock County tormentors often didn't bother to bid on properties they knew would fall into their hands as soon as the Saints left the state. Brigham carefully maneuvered his oxen onto a broad flatboat, helped pole his worldly possessions out into the roiling current, and led the Mormons west, into the mainstream of American history.

14

THIS WORLD AND THE NEXT

> Their innocent blood, with the innocent blood of all the
> martyrs under the altar that John saw, will cry unto the
> Lord of Hosts till he avenges that blood on the earth.
>
> —*Doctrine and Covenants of the Church of*
> *Jesus Christ of Latter-day Saints, Section 135*

MORMONS HAVE A FERVENT, OFTEN BLOODY-MINDED, FAITH in retributive justice. Here is a letter sent to Nauvoo by James Sloan, a leading Saint missionary in England:

The Marquis of Downshire, who oppressed the Saints at Hillsborough in Ireland, has had the pleasure of his son, Lord William, being killed by his horse at a hunt in England, a few weeks past, and Mr. Reilly, his agent, who aided in their abuse, has received the third attack of some paralytic affliction and obliged to resign his office; his son again, who headed a mob to annoy the Saints and prevent preaching, has gone to Cork in bad health; *So much for them.* [Emphasis in original.]

So much for them, indeed. Why wouldn't the Saints hope that God would square accounts with their oppressors? No one else would. Missouri simply expelled them by the thousands, killing dozens of Saints and confiscating hundreds of farms and homes without even a gesture of restitution. When Joseph Smith and his followers sought succor from the federal government, the leading politicians of the time told him, orotundly, to go to hell. The charade in the Carthage courthouse proved yet again that justice would elude the Saints in this world. So they hoped that God would act where man had failed them.

Apostle Heber Kimball wrote in his diary that "ever since Joseph's death," he and "seven to twelve persons . . . had met together every day to pray . . . and will never rest . . . until those men who killed Joseph & Hyrum have been wiped out of the earth." In the feverish final months at the Nauvoo Temple, the more than 5,000 Saints who received the sacred endowment ritual also pledged Brigham Young's oath of vengeance. "We are now conducted into another secret room," one communicant wrote of the ceremony,

> in the centre of which is an altar with three books on it—the Bible, Book of Mormon, and Doctrine and Covenants (Joseph's Revelations). We are required to kneel at this altar, where we have an oath administered to us to this effect; that we will avenge the blood of Joseph Smith on this nation, and teach our children the same. They tell us that the nation has winked at the abuse and persecution of the Mormons, and the murder of the Prophet in particular; Therefor the Lord is displeased with the nation, and means to destroy it.*

Eliza Snow, the Mormons' leading occasional poet, who was a plural wife of both Joseph Smith and Brigham Young, wrote a poem in 1862 explaining that the raging Civil War was God's revenge on the United

---

* In 1903, Utah's first Senator-elect, Reed Smoot, repeatedly denied that he had taken the Oath of Vengeance, which remained in the temple ritual until 1927.

States. Writing from Salt Lake City, she intended to rebuke William Cullen Bryant's widely circulated, pro-Union call to arms, "Our Country's Call," with her lines:

> Its fate is fixed—its destiny
> Is sealed—its end is sure to come;
> Why use the wealth of poesy
> To urge a nation to its doom?
> . . . It must be so, to avenge the blood
> That stains the walls of the Carthage jail.

"Salt Lake is to be and remain the single cheering oasis amid the universal National desolation in the years to come," was the *New York Times*'s sardonic comment on Snow's verses.

Snow would have been aware of Joseph Smith's remarkable "Civil War prophecy," delivered on Christmas Day, 1832, during the Nullification Crisis, a furious dispute between South Carolina and Andrew Jackson's federal government:

> 1 Verily, thus saith the Lord concerning the wars that will shortly come to pass, beginning at the rebellion of South Carolina, which will eventually terminate in the death and misery of many souls;
>
> 2 And the time will come that war will be poured out upon all nations, beginning at this place.
>
> 3 For behold, the Southern States shall be divided against the Northern States, and the Southern States will call on other nations, even the nation of Great Britain, as it is called. . . .

In 1843, Joseph made another prediction that came true. He prophesied that his friend Stephen Douglas would later aspire to the presidency, adding: "If you ever turn your hand against me or the Latter-day Saints, you will feel the weight of the hand of Almighty God upon you." In 1857, Senator Douglas did turn his hand against the Saints, now openly practicing polygamy in the Utah Territory. Douglas called Mormonism "a disgusting cancer" that "should be cut out by the roots." Douglas lost the presidency to Abraham Lincoln in 1860 and died the following year.

There was no statute of limitations for a crime against heaven—the killing of a prophet who claimed to converse with God, with the Savior, and with the seers of the Old Testament. In 1901, fifty-seven years after Joseph's death, a small newspaper in the Mormon enclave of Lamoni, Iowa, reprinted a brief obituary from Petaluma, California, and then added its own commentary. The original item reported that "Robert Lomax, the man who led the Illinois raiders in 1844, when Joseph Smith, the Mormon prophet was killed is dead." (Lomax's name appears in none of the lists of mobbers assembled after the killings.) The California paper reported that Smith died after "a hard fight," conveniently forgetting that he and his brother were murdered in cold blood.

The events were fresher in the mind of the *Lamoni Chronicle* writer, who correctly recalled that "there was no assembly of the Mormons in [Carthage] and no fight there." The Iowa newspaper concluded:

> If Mr. Lomax was there and a leader of that band engaged in the unlawful and unholy work, the reckoning of justice for him and his work lies with the courts on the other side.

I I I

IN THE NINETEENTH AND TWENTIETH CENTURIES, POWERFUL legends sprang up concerning God's vengeance on the mobbers who killed Joseph and Hyrum. In 1952, church archivist N. B. Lundwall gathered the many legends into an entertaining book, *Fate of the Persecutors of the Prophet Joseph Smith,* which for many years enjoyed the status of most-stolen book in the Salt Lake City public library system.

Numerous diarists recorded instances of "the Mormon curse," a rotting of the flesh that struck down the men who had lifted their hands against the Prophet. (Perhaps the curse fulfilled Joseph's recorded prophecy five days before his death that his tormentors "will be smitten with the scab &.") The Indians reported that a man named Jack Reed, who supposedly helped kill Joseph, was so deformed that no white woman could look at him:

> He was literally eaten alive by worms. His eye balls had fallen out, the flesh on his cheeks and neck had fallen off, and though he could breathe he could take nourishment only through an opening in his throat.
>
> Pieces of flesh as large as two hands had reputedly fallen from different parts of his body.

Of Corporal James Belton, who bragged of taking a shot at Joseph Smith during the events of June 27, it was reported that "he died from a cancer in his eye, and when his meals were brought to him, the pus from his eye would drop in his plate."

Like Lomax, the names of neither Belton nor Reed appear on the lists of the alleged mobbers compiled by Willard Richards, Jacob Backenstos, and William Clayton.

A crippled, elderly mobber who boasted that "I saw the last bullet shot into the old boy," that is, Joseph, was said to be sharing a cabin with his abusive son in Coalville, Utah. The son used his father as a pack horse to carry sacks filled with coal and flayed him with a belt when the old man tarried in his work. Eventually, their cabin burned down with the father inside. Somehow, the elderly, charred parent didn't die; local well-wishers put together a collection for some medicine, sending the son into Park City to fetch the healing lotion. Instead, the son drank the money away in a dingy saloon, and his unrepentant father-mobber succumbed in his absence.

Much wishful thinking likewise attended the fates of the principals in *People v. Levi Williams, et al.* But in the main, the "respectable set of men" who murdered Joseph and Hyrum thrived in the middle of the nineteenth century. Mark Aldrich moved to Tucson and served as president of the Arizona territorial legislature. Jacob Davis, a state senator in 1844, later became a congressman. William Grover was appointed US attorney for the eastern district of Missouri. *Nauvoo Expositor* collaborator Chauncey Higbee lived a long life in Pittsfield, Illinois, where he worked as a judge, a banker, and a state senator. He had a high school named after him in 1908. Robert F. Smith, the Carthage Greys captain who sealed Joseph Smith's fate, became a colonel in the Illinois militia and served with distinction in the Civil War. He rose to the rank of brigadier general and became military governor of conquered Savannah, Georgia.

William Law and his family moved first to northern Illinois, and then to Shullsburg, Wisconsin, where he practiced medicine until his death in 1892 at age eighty-three. His wife, Jane, and his brother, Wilson, who farmed in the area, died in 1883 and 1877, respectively. Five years before his death, the elderly, white-haired doctor spoke at length about Joseph Smith and the Saints with German journalist Wilhelm Wyl. "The greatest mistake of my life was my having anything to do with Mormonism," Law told his visitor. "I feel it to be a very deep disgrace and never speak of it when I can avoid it." Jane had long ago set fire to their only copy of the Book of Mormon, and the family had abandoned the faith. "It never was a church of Christ, but a most wicked blasphemous humbug, gotten up for the purpose of making money," Law said. "I have no doubt thousands of honest, virtuous people joined the Church not knowing anything of the wicked workings of the leaders, and thousands (probably in ignorance) still cling to the delusion."

His wizened hands trembling, Law heaped abused on Joseph Smith: "He was naturally base, corrupt and cruel . . . a raveling wolf. . . . He claimed to be a god, whereas he was only a servant of the Devil, and as such met his fate." Law cared just as little for Emma, whom he called "a full accomplice of Joseph's crimes. She was a large, coarse woman, as deep a woman as there was, always full of schemes and smooth as oil. They were worthy of each other, she was not a particle better than he."

After Joseph Smith's death, the fortunes of the hate-mongering Thomas Sharp soared. He won three terms as mayor of Warsaw, and four terms as an elected judge. Lionized at the 1870 meeting of the Hancock County Pioneer Association, Sharp offered some judicious, albeit unapologetic, comments on the "troublous times" of 1844. "I know there are members of this association who view the occurrences from a different standpoint from what I do," he told the pioneers, "and it is not my desire to say anything that may wound the feelings of any here present.

> In those days the blood of the people who were so unfortunate to have their homes here, was hot with excitement. Some things were undoubtedly done by the Old Settlers, and approved by them, that had better not have been done; but it must be remembered, that great excitements are always the result of great provocations, and that . . . angelic propriety of conduct is not always to be expected.

"Everybody loved Judge Sharp," according to an "In Memoriam" note published upon his death in 1890. "His heart was always warm, cheerful, and bright, as it were in the enjoyment of the spring time of life, his clear, loud and hearty laugh was heard even in his affliction, and sounded as sweet and joyful as the song of the birds at early dawn."

The astute Orville Browning, who ably defended the Smiths' assassins, went on to help found the Republican Party with his friend Abraham Lincoln. Browning remained close to President Lincoln while he was in the White House and Browning was serving out a Senate term vacated by the death of Stephen Douglas. Browning became President Andrew Johnson's secretary of the interior, then returned to Quincy, Illinois, to amass a fortune as a railroad lawyer. He invested his considerable gains in fraudulent mining schemes promoted by his son-in-law. Both Browning and his widow died penniless.

Trial judge Richard M. Young also had an unfortunate end. The former senator lived out his days at the Government Hospital for the Insane in Washington, DC, where he died in 1861.

Mormons have taken a morbid delight in chronicling the desultory fate of Governor Thomas Ford. In 1850, just four years after retiring as governor, he was penniless, with five children to support. His law practice had failed. Dying of alcoholism or tuberculosis, or both, he hoped to enrich his family by publishing his *History of Illinois.* That didn't work. Ford and his wife died within two weeks of each other in 1850, leaving their five orphans a legacy of $100 each. The children "were taken by different philanthropic citizens of Peoria," according to chronicler John F. Snyder, "and properly raised and educated." Two of the daughters led more or less normal lives. The third, Mrs. Davies, died at age seventy-two after living for several years as a "county charge" in a Peoria hospital. She was "a desolate, heart-broken woman, whose past was a sealed book of bitter memories and disappointments," according to Snyder, who noted that her predeceased husband was "a brilliant man, but like too many others he looked too often upon the wine when it was red." One of Thomas Ford's sons lost an arm fighting in the Civil War. His brother was hung as a horse thief in Kansas after the war, possibly the victim of mistaken identity.

Ford was initially consigned to a pauper's grave, but the Illinois legislature appropriated $500 to build an eighteen-foot-tall marble obelisk above his final resting place in 1853. A windstorm blew it down in 1858. One Mormon historian took especial glee in reporting that "weeds, tall grass and brush have luxuriated thick and rank" over Ford's untended grave in Peoria. "Occasionally there has been talk of raising a subscription for the purpose from the citizens of Peoria, but nobody has taken the initiative." As recently as 1994, Mormon church president Gordon B. Hinckley repeated the grim details of Ford's "troubled destiny" at a ceremony marking the 150th anniversary of the Carthage slayings. Ford suffered a life "of unrelieved poverty and defeat," Hinckley told his audience. "Such is the sad story of the man who violated his pledge to Joseph and Hyrum Smith. Such is the sad story of his family after him."

God works in mysterious ways, sometimes aided by human hands. When anti-Mormon agitation started up in Hancock County a few months after the assassins' trial in 1845, the Mormon-elected sheriff, Jacob Backenstos, became a target of the old settlers' wrath. Backenstos tried to defend the outlying Mormon settlements from Levi Williams and like-minded marauders. Franklin Worrell, who "guarded" the Carthage jail, professed to be infuriated by Backenstos's election. "I am *Mad, Mad*," Worrell wrote to the *Upper Mississippian* newspaper, "yes mad as the devil—Damn Such a Set of Miscreants as we have in this county."

Threatened with violence at his Carthage home, Backenstos resolved to move his family to Nauvoo. In mid-September, the sheriff left town in a buggy and noticed that a small band of armed men was following him. After overnighting in Warsaw, heading north on the Nauvoo road, he saw Worrell and seven other armed men pursuing him on horseback, with a rifle-filled wagon trailing behind. Near Golden's Point, Backenstos happened upon two Mormons, Return Jackson Redden and Orrin Porter Rockwell, who were helping a family of burned-out Saints move back into Nauvoo. With his pursuers just 150 yards behind him, Backenstos cried out for help. Rockwell galloped to his aid, and Backenstos ordered his pursuers to stop. They continued to ride toward him. The sheriff ordered Rockwell to fire, and Joseph Smith's childhood friend raised his rifle and shot Worrell squarely in the torso, catapulting him four feet off his saddle onto the ground.

At the sound of the shots, Jacob Baum, a Mormon farmer, ran up to find out what was happening on his property.

"I got him," Rockwell said.

"Got who?"

"Worrell. I was afraid my rifle wouldn't reach him, but it did, thank God."

The terrified mobbers reined in, loaded Worrell's corpse into their wagon, and rode back to Carthage. Worrell died on the way.

The Saints' prayers had been answered.

Backenstos and Rockwell were both indicted for the Worrell killing, which took place in broad daylight. Both were acquitted.

Rockwell himself lived for another thirty-three years, traveling with the Saints to Utah, where he became a notorious enforcer and bodyguard for church president Brigham Young. He married four times, but never polygamously; Joseph's "principle" was not for him. Toward the end of both of their lives—Young would die in 1877, Rockwell in 1878—Young apparently tired of Rockwell's hard-drinking ways and exiled him to Fish Lake in central Utah to "colonize the straggling bands of natives in the vicinity [and] teach them honesty, industry, morality and religion."

The hardened mountain man who had shared a bottle of moonshine with the British explorer Sir Richard Burton in a remote Utah canyon quickly tired of missionary work. He returned to Salt Lake City, where he collapsed of heart failure after an early-hours visit to a local saloon. Rockwell died while under federal indictment for a murder he may well have committed; we will never know. The *Salt Lake Tribune*—the city had become large and diverse enough to sustain a non-Mormon newspaper—knew he *was* guilty and exulted in Rockwell's death: "Thus the gallows was cheated of one of the fittest candidates that ever cut a throat or plundered a traveler." "A fanatical devotee of the Prophet," the paper continued,

> He killed fellow Saints who held secrets that menaced the safety of their fellow criminals in the priesthood. He killed Apostates who dared to wag their tongues about the wrongs they had endured. And he killed mere sojourners in Zion merely to keep his hand in.

"The recollection of his evil deeds haunted him," the *Tribune* insisted, and to gain escape from this fiery torment he sought the intoxicating bowl, and whenever he appeared in the streets of Salt Lake, it was generally in the character of a vociferating maniac.

A thousand Saints jammed the Fourteenth Ward assembly rooms in Salt Lake for Rockwell's funeral. Eulogist Joseph F. Smith, Hyrum's son and a future church president, allowed that the deceased "had his little faults, but Porter's life on earth, taken altogether, was one worthy of example, and reflected honor upon the Church."

A "fitting tribute of one outlaw to the memory of another," the *Tribune* sneered.

Rockwell's name lived on in more than one cowboy ballad, including this one:

> Have you heard of Porter Rockwell, the Mormon Triggerite,
> They say he hunts down outlaws when the moon is shining bright.
> So if you rustle cattle, I'll tell you what to do,
> Get the drop on Porter Rockwell, or he'll get the drop on you.

❊ ❊ ❊

THE TWENTY-TWO-YEAR-OLD EMMA HALE, WHO FIRST MET JOSEPH Smith when he came to dig for money on her father's Pennsylvania farm, was deemed to be quite a catch: five feet, nine inches tall, vivacious, with distinctive hazel eyes set off by her olive complexion. Most of her life she wore her hair long, brushing it to a dark sheen, with her tresses gathered in twin braids at the nape of her neck.

In the winter of 1879, Emma was seventy-four years old, still tall, and wore her gray hair combed in two soft waves over her temples. "Her face was thin; her nose lean, aquiline and pointed," recalled one of the many visitors Emma received at the Nauvoo Mansion that she had shared with Joseph and his multiple wives some forty years previously. Another visitor called her "a picture of a fine woman, stranded on the lee-shore of age . . . among people who did not appreciate her intellect or her innate refinement." After a brief period of exile in upstate Illinois, she had moved back to the mansion in 1847. On December 23 of that year—that day that would have been Joseph Smith's forty-second birthday—she married businessman Lewis Bidamon in a Methodist ceremony. Bidamon was a drinker, a bon vivant, and an adventurer; eighteen months after their wedding, he ran off to the California gold rush. He managed to remain Emma's somewhat loyal companion for thirty-two years. At the end of her life, Emma was keeping tavern at the mansion in an awkward ménage à trois with Bidamon and his mistress, Nancy Abercrombie, the mother of Bidamon's illegitimate son, Charles. On her deathbed, Emma asked Nancy and Lewis to marry, to spare Charles the indignity of bastardy. They did so, and lived as man and wife until Bidamon died twelve years later.

Rumors that Emma had abandoned her husband's church were untrue. On the other hand, she steadfastly refused repeated overtures from the "Brighamites" to relocate to Salt Lake and confer dynastic legitimacy on their church. Emma famously remarked to one of Young's ambassadors that "she could go to Heaven without going to the Mountains." Despairing of Emma ("literally the most wicked woman in this earth"), Brigham trained his charm offensive on her son Joseph Smith III, who likewise spurned the siren call of the Utah polygamists. In 1860, young Joseph accepted the presidency of the Reorganized Church of Jesus Christ of Latter Day Saints, which, inconveniently for Brigham, established its headquarters in Independence, Missouri, the true Zion, as revealed to Joseph the Prophet.

In this February of 1879, a few months before Emma's death, two of her three surviving sons, Alexander and Joseph Smith III, traveled through the deep snow from Plano, Illinois, to Nauvoo, to interview their mother. (Their thirty-five-year-old brother, David, was feeble-minded and would spend most of his adult life in a mental institution.) This was to be no ordinary colloquy. Ever since his father's death, Joseph III found himself bedeviled by the question of polygamy. Improbably, he ascribed David's mental torments to the latter's misguided belief that their father had more than one wife: "I am convinced that insidiously there was inculcated into my brother's mind the idea that his father was either a polygamist in practice or that he was the spiritual author of the Utah plural marriage philosophy." A certain irony attends David's supposed institutionalization for believing the truth, whereas Joseph III enjoyed a full and prosperous life while nurturing his misguided idée fixe.

For decades, abetted by his mother's distortions, Joseph III had refused to believe that the Prophet had taken wives other than Emma, and that he had preached the "principle" so warmly embraced in Salt Lake City. Joseph and the editors of the *Saints' Herald*, the Reformed Mormons' newspaper, felt he should set the record straight with his mother, once and for all. As Joseph later explained, he had been urged to make this trip more than once: "It had been frequently stated to us: 'Ask your mother, she knows.' 'Why don't you ask your mother; she dare not deny these things.' 'You do not dare to ask your mother!'"

He did dare. In the mansion's capacious sitting room, with his stepfather looking on,* Joseph unfolded the two pages of questions he had prepared back in Plano. He eased gently into the talk.

Who married you and Joseph? he asked. Sidney Rigdon? A Presbyterian minister?

No, Emma answered, a local squire married us. "My folks were bitterly opposed," she recalled.

Did you and father quarrel? Joseph asked.

---

* Melissa Lott Wiles, young Joseph's "Aunt Melissa" and one of the Prophet's young plural wives, later told Joseph III that Emma was forced to deceive him in this famous interview: "You took your mother before Mr. Bidamon, a bitter enemy of our people, and then asked such questions of her as you wished . . . I have no doubt that your mother told you the truth so far as she could under the circumstances; but if you had taken her by herself . . . and asked your questions, she would probably have answered you as I have done." Melissa shocked Joseph III by admitting that she was the Prophet's wife "in very deed."

"No," Emma replied. "There was no necessity for any quarreling. He knew that I wished for nothing but what was right; and, as he wished for nothing else, we did not disagree."

Joseph then asked a series of pointed questions about the creation of the Book of Mormon. Emma was one of her husband's scribes; she and Oliver Cowdery wrote out the entire manuscript. Was the Prophet reading from a book, or another manuscript? Joseph asked. No, his mother answered. "If he had had anything of the kind he could not have concealed it from me."

Joseph pressed the question: "Could not father have dictated the Book of Mormon to you, Oliver Cowdery and the others who wrote for him, after having first written it, or having first read it out of some book?"

No, Emma insisted, "Joseph Smith could neither write nor dictate a coherent and well-worded letter, let alone dictate a book like the Book of Mormon." It was "a marvel and a wonder," she added.

What about the golden plates? young Joseph asked.

"The plates often lay on the table without any attempt at concealment," his mother answered, "wrapped in a small linen tablecloth, which I had given him to fold them in."

> I once felt of the plates, as they thus lay on the table, tracing their outline and shape. They seemed to be pliable like thick paper, and would rustle with a metallic sound when the edges were moved by the thumb, as one does sometimes thumb the edges of a book.

Why didn't you unwrap them? Joseph asked.

"I did not attempt to handle the plates, other than I have told you, nor uncover them to look at them," Emma answered. "I was satisfied that it was the work of God, and therefore did not feel it to be necessary to do so."

Bidamon jumped in: Did your husband forbid you from touching the plates?

I don't think so, Emma replied; I "was not specially curious about them. I moved them from place to place on the table, as it was necessary in doing my work."

"What of the truth of Mormonism?" Joseph asked.

"I know Mormonism to be the truth;" Emma answered,

and believe the Church to have been established by divine direction. I have complete faith in it. In writing for your father I frequently wrote day after day, often sitting at the table close by him, he sitting with his face buried in his hat, with the stone in it, and dictating hour after hour with nothing between us.

These were all interesting questions, but they were not really the purpose of the trip. No Mormon, Reformed or Brighamite, questioned the divine inspiration of the Book of Mormon. It was polygamy, the doctrine of many wives, that cleaved the Saints down the middle, in 1844 and in 1879.

Q: What about the revelation on polygamy? Did Joseph Smith have anything like it? What of spiritual wifery?

A: There was no revelation on either polygamy or spiritual wives. There were some rumors of something of the sort, of which I asked my husband. He assured me that all there was of it was, that, in a chat about plural wives, he had said, "Well, such a system might possibly be, if everybody was agreed to it, and would behave as they should; but they would not; and besides, it was contrary to the will of heaven."

No such thing as polygamy or spiritual wifery was taught, publicly or privately, before my husband's death, that I have now, or ever had any knowledge of.

Q: Did he not have other wives than yourself?

A: He had no other wife but me; nor did he to my knowledge ever have.

Joseph chose not to publish this exchange in his memoirs, which he dedicated "To my mother, Emma Hale, whom my father, Joseph Smith, married on January 18, 1827, and who was his only wife."

⚰ ⚰ ⚰

ON JUNE 27, 1854, HUNDREDS OF SAINTS GATHERED IN SALT LAKE City's low-slung, adobe-walled tabernacle, to observe the tenth anniversary of what was now called the "martyrdom." The bullet-riddled John Taylor was among the first to call Joseph a martyr, in his famous hymn, "O Give Me Back My Prophet Dear." Joseph himself occasionally compared his fate to that of the persecuted Jesus. In a famous letter from the Liberty, Missouri, jail, Joseph called himself a "lamb" being prepared for "slaughter," a trope he resurrected in June 1844. Immediately after Joseph's assassination, poetess Eliza Snow compared Carthage to the "Calvary scene": "For never since the Son of God was slain / Has blood so noble flowed from human vein."

The audience in the tabernacle was sweltering; the high desert plain of the Saints' new Zion was scorching hot. Brigham Young ordered the bishops in the audience to haul fifty buckets of cool water from nearby City Creek into the gabled building, and he provided ladles so the crowd could drink.

The Saints had again founded a new Zion, one outside the borders of the formally settled United States that had so bedeviled them in Missouri and Illinois. The leading citizens of Hancock County had hoped to extinguish Mormonism by killing its founding prophet. The opposite occurred. Brigham Young proved to be more forceful, more fervent, and better organized than Joseph Smith. He arranged for over 10,000 Saints to trek from Illinois to Utah, while continuing the energetic missionary work that swelled the gathering to the new Zion. Young reigned supreme over the burgeoning theodemocracy. He briefly governed a territory called Deseret, larger than present-day France, which included Utah, Nevada, and Arizona, and portions of six other states. Since 1852, Deseret had been officially polygamous, prompting no end of denunciations from the faraway US government. Washington confiscated vast swaths of Young's domain, but Young still ruled over about 20,000 Saints spread across the expanse of today's Utah.

Young opened the tenth anniversary celebration, testifying "by all the power that I am in possession of that Brother Joseph Smith was a true man of God, a true prophet of the Lord [and] a true apostle of Jesus Christ." He reminded the Saints why so many of them loved Joseph; how "the brethren would complain of Joseph that he was rude, wild; he was not as sober, gracious, so dead long-faced, and religious as he ought to be."

> You recollect what he used to tell the people once? "Why," says he, "brethren and sisters if I was as pure, as holy, and sanctified as you wish me to be, I could not be in your society. The Lord would not let me stay here."

A most jolly and human prophet, to be sure.

But the featured speaker, the star of the show as it were, was Apostle John Taylor, now forty-five years old. Taylor's presence at the tabernacle was nothing short of miraculous. Just ten years before, the mobbers had riddled him with bullets and left him for dead underneath a filthy mattress in the Carthage jail. He survived two impromptu operations without anesthesia. But like Mormonism itself, Taylor had not merely survived, he had prevailed. The Canadian convert had opposed Brigham's one-man rule, incurring Young's wrath for his lack of fealty. Young thought Taylor was uppity, claiming that he said of the Quorum of the Twelve, "You are my niggers & you shall black my boots." He wanted Taylor "to bow down and confess that [he was] not Brigham Young," something Taylor refused to do.

Brigham may not have revered Taylor, but the Saints did. On this day, he enjoyed a special status as the only survivor of the Carthage massacre; Willard Richards had died just three months previously. Joseph and Hyrum's uncle, John Smith, who visited the four prisoners the night before their deaths, died on May 23. Taylor would live thirty-three more years and assume the church presidency upon Brigham's death. A feisty and erudite leader, he died with a price on his head, hiding from federal deputies who were chasing down polygamists in the refractory Utah Territory. He spent his last days on a farm north of Salt Lake City, "in the DO," as the Saints called their constantly moving underground headquarters. (The word comes from being "on the dodge.")

Willard Richards's successor as church historian, George Smith, had decided to compile a formal history of the martyrdom, and Taylor's remarks in the tabernacle would begin that process. Two years later, Taylor would retreat to Westport, Connecticut, to produce a ninety-six-page account—perhaps the definitive work—on the events of June 27, 1844. The first person to print Taylor's dramatic tale was none other than the British explorer Sir Richard Burton, whom Porter Rockwell successfully charmed in Salt Lake City. Burton published Taylor's martyrdom memoir as an appendix to his best-selling account of his Utah adventures, *The City of the Saints*, in 1862.

At the tenth-anniversary celebration at the tabernacle, Taylor began his remarks by talking about the advent of polygamy. Returning from a mission trip to England, Taylor learned about "spiritual wifery" from Brigham Young and Heber Kimball. "It tried our minds and feelings," Taylor recalled. "We saw it was something going to be heavy upon us. It was something that harried up our feelings." Conflating some facts, Taylor told the story of the *Nauvoo Expositor*, and the City Council's fateful decision to destroy the newspaper.

"We knew we were right and did it," he explained.

Taylor described Joseph's last journey eastward across the prairie from Nauvoo to Carthage.

Somebody asked him as we were journeying to Carthage, says they: "Joseph, what will be the upshot of this matter?"

"Well," says he, "I do not know anything about it. Do not talk to me about matters now. I have given up my office and calling for the time being . . . I do not profess to guide this people now while I am in the hands of officers. Somebody else must do it."

This is the body of the meaning, the spirit of the words, if not the exact words.

Taylor then regaled his audience with a lengthy, first-person account of the prisoners' final nights in the jailhouse. Except for Willard Richards's curt memorandum published in the church newspaper immediately after the killings, this was the first attempt to narrate the last days of the Smith brothers in all their agonizing detail—Governor Ford's perfidy, Captain Robert Smith's double-dealing, and the ghastly, final shootout: "They leaned against the door. Someone fired a gun through the keyhole. A ball came through the door and struck [Hyrum] in the face. . . ."

"They have not hurt Joseph or Hyrum," Taylor told the tabernacle audience, "But they have hurt themselves. They are damned and we shall see it."

"I know there are hundreds in this congregation who would have been glad to have been where we were," he said. "I know Joseph and Hyrum lived and died men of God and will live for evermore."

ACKNOWLEDGMENTS

PREPARING TO WRITE THIS BOOK I HAD THE PRIVILEGE OF meeting many of the greatest living historians of the Latter-day Saints, who provided me with valuable counsel. Richard Bushman, D. Michael Quinn, Scott Kenney, Gary Bergera, and John Turner all spent time with me. Todd Compton, Stephen LeSueur, and Lori Stromberg agreed to read portions of my manuscript and each made important suggestions. Brigham Young University historian Michael Hicks and my friend the writer Katherine Powers both read the entire final draft and provided valuable input.

In Salt Lake City, Ronald Barney of the Mormon Historical Society provided continual encouragement and a host of valuable sources for me to pursue. Robin Jensen and Alex Smith at the Latter-day Saints' Church History Library answered many of my questions and Bill Slaughter helped me with illustrations, as he has helped so many other writers. I would also like to thank CHL staffers Brittany Chapman and Anna Bybee. Trevor Weight at the Brigham Young University Art Gallery and Douglas Misner at the Utah State Historical Archive furnished illustrations for me, as did Carol Nielson at The Daughters of Utah Pioneers museum.

Steven Lindeman, Sharon Kessinger, and Chelsea Robarge also helped me enormously in Utah. Katrina Haglund and Ron Scott shared advice and contacts with me from Boston.

Sherry Morain, executive director of the John Whitmer Historical Association, took an early interest in this book and introduced me to many of the leading historians of the Nauvoo period. She also arranged with Lachlan Mackay, director of Historic Sites for the Community of Christ (formerly the Reorganized Church of Latter Day Saints) for me to spend several nights in Nauvoo in a house once occupied by William Marks, a determined foe of polygamy. Sherry and Lachlan led me to Joseph Johnstun, an expert on 1840s Nauvoo, and to historian William Shepard, who graciously shared many of his research materials with me. Jan Marshall unlocked many an obscure John Whitmer Historical Association document for me.

Historian and cartographer John Hamer created two attractive maps for my Frontispiece, for which much thanks.

John Hallwas, one of the preeminent scholars of the Mormon experience in Illinois, arranged for me to visit his archive at Western Illinois University, where I was assisted by librarian Kathy Nichols. Historians Rodney Davis, Lavina F. Anderson, Roger Launius, Grant Palmer, Bryon Andreason, Adam Christing, Dan Vogel, and Vickie Cleverly Speek also provided help and counsel along the way.

Librarians and archivists are the unacknowledged legislators of the universe, but here I acknowledge them: at the Yale Beinecke Rare Book and Manuscript Library, Todd Fell and Eva Wrightson helped me assemble documents. So did Cindy Brightenburg at Brigham Young University's Harold B. Lee Library, Susan Forbes at the Kansas State Historical Society, and Janet Holtman, from the Hancock County Historical Society. I am grateful that W. V. Smith digitized so many nineteenth-century Mormon journals, autobiographies, and B. H. Roberts's entire church history at the Book of Abraham Project website, www. boap.org. I made extensive use of Massachusetts's interlibrary loans, aided by Elinor Hernon, Karen Fischer, and Paula Lawrence at the Newton Free Library. My friends and former colleagues at the *Boston Globe*, Lisa Tuite and Jeremiah Manion, stayed with me for the duration. Tom Wolf helped me prepare my manuscripts. Thanks to all.

It's wonderful to have friends. Ron Koltnow, Roger Lowenstein, Charles Pierce, Joseph Finder, Steven Stark, John Burgess, David Taylor,

Acknowledgments

James Parker, Mark Feeney, David Warsh, and Jennifer Schuessler cheered me on for several years. My friend of over forty years, Michael Carlisle, heard that a young editor named Benjamin Adams dreamed of commissioning a book on the historic but little understood assassination of Joseph Smith. Ben got his book, and he provided superb editorial guidance from beginning to end. I cherish my relations with Ben and his colleagues at PublicAffairs, with whom I have now collaborated three times. Susan Weinberg, Clive Priddle, and my *droog* from another lifetime, Peter Osnos, have always supported my work; marketing director Lisa Kaufman edited my last two books. Special thanks again to Jaime Leifer and Lindsay Fradkoff, for marketing and promotional support. Managing editor Melissa Raymond is the firm hand on the production tiller, aided for this project by Rachel King and the indefatigable and erudite copy editor Michele Wynn.

One of the underpinnings of Joseph Smith's theology was his belief that families would meet again after death and live together for all eternity. I would like nothing more than to spend the remains of my days, and more, with my wife and three sons, who have been my constant friends and supporters for most of my life. I owe them a huge debt. Kirsten, Christopher, Eric, and Michael—I love you.

CHRONOLOGY

December 23, 1805: Joseph Smith is born in Sharon Township, Windsor County, Vermont.

January 18, 1827: Joseph elopes and marries Emma Hale.

Spring 1830: Publication of the Book of Mormon, establishment of the Church of Christ in upstate New York.

February 1831: Joseph moves the seat of his church government to Kirtland, Ohio.

May 1834: The church is renamed The Church of the Latter Day Saints.

January 1838: Joseph flees Kirtland after Mormon bank failure, reestablishes the church in Missouri. The church is renamed The Church of Jesus Christ of Latter-day Saints.

October 1838: Missouri Governor Boggs issues anti-Mormon Extermination Order, closely followed by the massacre of seventeen Saints at Haun's Mill, Missouri.

Winter 1838–1839: Joseph imprisoned; Mormons flee across the Mississippi River to Illinois.

May 1839: Joseph joins the Mormons in their new town of Nauvoo, Hancock County, Illinois.

Spring 1841: Joseph cautiously unveils doctrine of "plural marriage" to his inner circle, marries Louisa Beaman, age twenty-six.

June 1841: "Anti-Mormon" political party founded in Hancock County.

Chronology

May 28, 1843: Joseph seals his marriage to Emma "for time and eternity." He now has approximately twenty-five other wives.

June 24, 1843: Missouri sheriffs arrest Joseph in Dixon, Illinois. Renowned Whig lawyer Cyrus Walker wins Smith's freedom in return for the promise of Mormon votes in the forthcoming congressional election. Guided by revelation, the Saints vote en masse for Walker's opponent, alienating both Whigs and Democrats.

January 29, 1844: Joseph announces his candidacy for president of the United States.

April 7, 1844: Joseph delivers the King Follett Discourse, explaining that "God himself was once as we are now" and that humans can aspire to divinity. Smith adds, "I don't blame anyone for not believing my history. If I had not experienced what I have, I could not have believed it myself."

April 21, 1844: Joseph's former confidant William Law organizes the breakaway True Church of Jesus Christ of Latter-day Saints, decrying the heretical doctrines of the plurality of gods, and polygamy.

June 7, 1844: Law and fellow dissidents publish the *Nauvoo Expositor* newspaper, accusing Joseph Smith of "a perversion of sacred things."

June 10, 1844: Acting on Smith's instructions, the Nauvoo City Council orders the destruction of the *Expositor* newspaper and its printing press.

June 14, 1844: Thomas Sharp's Warsaw, Illinois, *Signal* calls for "a war of extermination" against the Mormons.

June 18, 1844: In full military regalia, Lieutenant General Joseph Smith declares martial law in Nauvoo, telling the 2,000-man Nauvoo Legion that "I have unsheathed my sword."

June 23, 1844: Joseph Smith flees Nauvoo, crossing the Mississippi River to Iowa.

June 24, 1844: Smith returns to Nauvoo, agrees to travel to Carthage, Illinois, to face riot charges.

June 27, 1844: A mob storms the Carthage jail, killing Joseph and his brother Hyrum.

August 8, 1844: Brigham Young assumes control of the Mormon Church.

February 6, 1846: Young leads a small wagon train across the ice-choked Mississippi River, bound for the Mormons' new home in the Utah Territory.

NOTES

1. FLIGHT

2   Orrin Porter Rockwell . . . "shaggy and dangerous": Fawn Brodie, *No Man Knows My History: The Life of Joseph Smith the Mormon Prophet* (New York: Vintage Books, 1995), p. 330.

3   Finally discerning his friend: Harold Schindler, *Orrin Porter Rockwell: Man of God, Son of Thunder* (Salt Lake City: University of Utah Press, 1966), p. 109.

4   "had shewn unto us the plates": Book of Mormon: A Reader's Edition (Springfield: University of Illinois Press, 2003), p. 632.

4   "If you will write the revelation": Gary James Bergera, "'Illicit Intercourse,' Plural Marriage, and the Nauvoo Stake High Council, 1840–1844," *John Whitmer Historical Association Journal* 23 (2003), p. 83ff.

5   "The whole of America is Zion": D. Michael Quinn, *The Mormon Hierarchy: Origins of Power* (Salt Lake City: Signature Books, 1994), p. 124.

6   "People coming to Nauvoo expected": William Wyl, *Mormon Portraits* (Salt Lake City: Tribune Printing, 1886), p. 26.

6   "I love that man better": Ibid., p. 378.

6   "I investigated the case": Brodie, *No Man Knows*, p. 289.

7   "I am the only man that has ever": B. H. Roberts, ed., *History of the Church of Jesus Christ of Latter-day Saints*, 2nd ed., rev., vol. 6 (Salt Lake City: Deseret Book Company, 1978), p. 409.

8   "I am above the kingdoms of the world": Roger Launius and John Hallwas, eds., *Kingdom on the Mississippi Revisited: Nauvoo in Mormon History* (Urbana and Chicago: University of Illinois Press, 1996), p. 154.

8   "When I look into the Eastern papers": Scott H. Faulring, ed., *An American Prophet's Record: The Diaries and Journals of Joseph Smith* (Salt Lake City: Signature Books, 1989), p. 456.

9   "we would not be surprised to hear": *Warsaw Signal* (IL), May 29, 1844.

2. KING JOSEPH

14   "Come on! ye prosecutors!": B. H. Roberts, ed., *History of the Church of Jesus Christ of Latter-day Saints*, 2nd ed., rev., vol. 6 (Salt Lake City: Deseret Book Company, 1978), p. 408.

15   "A mad mix of doctrines": Harold Bloom, *The American Religion* (New York: Simon and Schuster, 1992), p. 111.

15   Nor was meeting Jesus a unique occurrence: Fawn Brodie, *No Man Knows My History: The Life of Joseph Smith the Mormon Prophet* (New York: Vintage Books, 1995), p. 22.

16   Hale reviled the money-digging expedition: E. D. Howe, *Mormonism Unvailed* (Painesville, NY, 1834), p. 263.

16   "glorious beyond description": *Millennial Star* 42, p. 190.

18   the stock phrase, "It came to pass": Mark Twain, *Roughing It* (New York: Harper Brothers, 1918), p. 110.

21   He didn't claim to be a full-time preacher: Roberts, ed., *History of the Church*, vol. 5, p. 265.

21   they expected "to find him in his sanctum": John G. Turner, *Brigham Young, Pioneer Prophet* (Cambridge: Harvard University Press, 2012), p. 31.

22   "Newel K. Whitney! Thou art the man!": Roberts, ed., *History of the Church*, vol. 6, p. 1.

22   lodging with the Whitneys: George D. Smith, *Nauvoo Polygamy* (Salt Lake City: Signature Books, 2011), p. 136.

22   "about 70 of the brethren": Scott H. Faulring, ed., *An American Prophet's Record: The Diaries and Journals of Joseph Smith* (Salt Lake City: Signature Books, 1989), p. 307.

23   a young Gentile woman from Portsmouth: Charlotte Haven, "A Girl's Letters from Nauvoo," *Overland Monthly* 16 (December 1890).

23   "He has unlimited influence": John Hallwas and Roger Launius, *Cultures in Conflict: A Documentary History of the Mormon War in Illinois* (Logan: Utah State University Press, 1995), p. 34.

24   converted . . . Campbellite preacher Sidney Rigdon: Richard Van Wagoner, *Sidney Rigdon: A Portrait of Religious Excess* (Salt Lake City: Signature Books, 1994), p. 127.

24   "He had all the weaknesses": Brigham Young, *Journal of Discourses*, vol. 4 (Liverpool and London: F. D. and S. W. Richards, 1854), p. 78, rpt. 78, available online at http://contentdm.lib.byu.edu/cdm/compoundobject/collection/JournalOfDiscourses3/id/9599/rec/1.

25   "Since this order has been preached": Matthew Bowman, *The Mormon People* (New York: Random House, 2012), p. 76.

26 "Universal satisfaction manifested": Richard Lyman Bushman, *Joseph Smith: Rough Stone Rolling* (New York: Alfred A. Knopf, 2005), p. 450.

27 "We were washed and anointed": Turner, *Brigham Young*, p. 86.

27 postulants donned a special white garment: Brodie, *No Man Knows*, pp. 280–281.

27 adapted and perverted the . . . Masonic ritual: David John Buerger, "The Development of the Mormon Temple Endowment Ceremony," *Dialogue—A Journal of Mormon Thought* 20 (4).

28 "The secret of masonry is": Roberts, ed., *History of the Church*, vol. 6, p. 59.

28 he had many secrets to keep: D. Michael Quinn, *The Mormon Hierarchy: Origins of Power* (Salt Lake City: Signature Books, 1994), p. 112.

28 preached the most famous sermon of his life: Bushman, *Rough Stone Rolling*, p. 534.

29 "We suppose that God was God": For text of King Follett sermon, see Roberts, ed., *History of the Church*, vol. 6, p. 302ff.

29 "some of the most blasphemous doctrines": Lyndon W. Cook, *William Law: Biographical Essay; Nauvoo Diary; Correspondence; Interview* (Orem, UT: Grandin Book, 1994), p. 49.

30 decided to run for the presidency: Michael Marquardt, *The Rise of Mormonism* (Xulon Press, 2005), p. 625.

30 "pardon every convict": Susan Easton Black, "Nauvoo Neighbor: The Latter-day Saint Experience at the Mississippi River, 1843–1845," *BYU Studies* 51 (3) (2012), p. 150.

30 "General Smith is the greatest": Roberts, ed., *History of the Church*, vol. 6, p. 361.

31 a different steamboat sounding: Black, "Nauvoo Neighbor," p. 150.

31 they dispatched surrogates: Roberts, ed., *History of the Church*, vol. 6, p. 157.

32 "governor of a new religious territory": *New York Herald*, July 3, 1841.

32 "purpose was . . . to govern the entire world": *Times and Seasons*, May 1, 1844, and Roberts, ed., *History of the Church*, vol. 6, p. 292.

33 president pro tem of the world: Grant H. Palmer, "Did Joseph Smith Commit Treason in His Quest for Political Empire in 1844?" *John Whitmer Historical Association Journal* 32 (2) (Fall/Winter 2012), p. 54.

33 sounding out the Russians: Faulring, *American Prophet's Record*, p. 290.

34 expeditions are "attended with much expense": Quinn, *Mormon Hierarchy*, p. 132.

3. Zion, Illinois

37 "The citizens responded to the call": Wandle Mace, "Autobiography (1809–1846)," typescript, Harold B. Lee Library, Provo, Utah, p. 13.

37   neither medical training nor legal education: Susan Easton Black, "Isaac Galland: Both Sides of the River," *Nauvoo Journal* (Fall 1996).

38   "No man of understanding": Maurine Carr Ward, "John Needham's Nauvoo Letter: 1843," *Nauvoo Journal* (Spring 1996).

38   "the honored instrument": Black, "Isaac Galland," p. 5.

39   "signifies a beautiful situation": B. H. Roberts, ed., *History of the Church of Jesus Christ of Latter-day Saints,* 2nd ed., rev., vol. 4 (Salt Lake City: Deseret Book Company, 1978), p. 268.

39   "literally a wilderness": Ibid., vol. 3, p. 375.

39   it was pestilential: Robert Bruce Flanders, *Nauvoo: Kingdom on the Mississippi* (Urbana and Chicago: University of Illinois Press, 1965), p. 54.

40   "soon expect to see flocking": Roberts, ed., *History of the Church,* vol. 4, p. 213.

40   "a sufficient quantity of 'honey comb'": Lyndon W. Cook, "Isaac Galland— Mormon Benefactor," *BYU Studies* 19 (3) (Spring 1979).

41   "wealthy immigrant from the slave States": Thomas Ford, *A History of Illinois, from Its Commencement as a State in 1818 to 1847* (Chicago: S. C. Griggs, 1845), p. 280.

41   "unambitious of wealth": Ibid.

41   "long, lank, lean, lazy": Ibid., p. 281.

42   "the abominable doctrine": Allan Nevins, ed., *The Diary of Philip Hone, 1828–1851,* 2 vols. (New York: Dodd, Mead, 1927), p. 155.

42   "increasing disregard of law": D. Michael Quinn, ed., *The New Mormon History* (Salt Lake City: Signature Books, 1992), p. 99.

43   "We would rather be shot": Ford, *A History of Illinois,* p. 249.

44   it did issue honorary degrees: Susan Easton Black, "The University of Nauvoo, 1841–45," *Religious Educator* 10 (3) (2009).

44   its distinctive court system: Flanders, *Nauvoo: Kingdom on the Mississippi,* p. 98.

45   "growing like a mushroom": John Hallwas and Roger Launius, *Cultures in Conflict: A Documentary History of the Mormon War in Illinois* (Logan: Utah State University Press, 1995), p. 15.

47   "We are a curiosity": John G. Turner, *Brigham Young, Pioneer Prophet* (Cambridge: Harvard University Press, 2012), p. 301.

47   built his two-story redbrick store: Roger Launius and Mark McKiernan, "Joseph Smith Jr.'s Red Brick Store," *Western Illinois Monograph Series,* no. 5, Herald Publishing House, 2005, p. 17.

48   secret rituals administered upstairs: Ibid., p. 31.

50   "Mother found installed in the keeping-room": Joseph Smith III, *Joseph Smith III and the Restoration* (Independence, MO: Herald Publishing House, 1952), p. 74.

50 Lifting the trick stairs: Ibid., p. 25.

51 The mummies, "frightfully disfigured": Henry Caswall, *The City of the Mormons, or, Three Days at Nauvoo in 1842* (London: Rivington, 1842), p. 28.

51 "up a short, narrow stairway": Charlotte Haven, "A Girl's Letters from Nauvoo," *Overland Monthly* 16 (December 1890).

52 "trim looking old lady": Eudocia Baldwin Marsh, "Mormons in Hancock County: A Reminiscence," ed. Douglas L. Wilson and Rodney O. Davis, *Journal of the Illinois State Historical Society* 64 (1) (Spring 1971), p. 38.

52 "But serpents don't have legs": Haven, "A Girl's Letters."

53 Bostonians Charles Francis Adams and Josiah Quincy: Josiah Quincy, "Joseph Smith at Nauvoo," in *Figures of the Past* (Boston: Roberts Bros., 1896).

53 "too much power to be safely trusted": Ibid.

4. Everybody Hates the Mormons

56 "sound of a rushing mighty wind": B. H. Roberts, ed., *History of the Church of Jesus Christ of Latter-day Saints*, 2nd ed., rev., vol. 2 (Salt Lake City: Deseret Book Company, 1978), p. 428.

57 "The several companies presented": Wandle Mace, "Autobiography (1809–1846)," typescript, Harold B. Lee Library, Provo, Utah; Norton Jacobs, "Autobiography and Diary," typescript, Harold B. Lee Library, Provo, Utah.

57 "Smith had always shown great favor": Eudocia Baldwin Marsh, "Mormons in Hancock County: A Reminiscence," ed. Douglas L. Wilson and Rodney O. Davis, *Journal of the Illinois State Historical Society* 64 (1) (Spring 1971).

57 "I am a son": B. H. Roberts, *The Rise and Fall of Nauvoo* (Salt Lake City: Deseret News, 1900), p. 107.

58 a mammoth success: Roberts, ed., *History of the Church*, vol. 4, p. 326ff.; also see Marsh, "Mormons in Hancock County"; Linda King Newell and Valeen Tippetts Avery, *Mormon Enigma: Emma Hale Smith* (Champaign: University of Illinois Press, 1994), p. 93; Glen Leonard, *Nauvoo: A Place of Peace, a People of Promise* (Salt Lake City: Deseret Book Company, 2002), p. 234; and Richard E. Bennett, Susan Easton Black, and Donald Q. Cannon, *The Nauvoo Legion in Illinois: A History of the Mormon Militia, 1841–1845* (Norman, OK: Arthur Clark, 2010).

60 "I lived at Spunky Point": William Roscoe Thayer, *The Life and Letters of John Hay* (Boston: Houghton Mifflin, 1915), p. 6.

60 The novice newspaper owner Sharp: John Hallwas, "Thomas Gregg: Early Illinois Journalist and Author," *Western Illinois Monograph Series*, no. 2, Western Illinois University, Macomb, 1983, p. 44; Daniel Walker Howe, *What Hath God Wrought: The Transformation of America, 1815–1848* (New York: Oxford University Press, 2007), p. 598.

61 "the mean hypocritical human": Jacobs, "Autobiography and Diary."

61 Sharp would prove . . . a formidable enemy: Thomas Gregg, *History of Hancock County, Illinois, together with an outline history of the State, and a digest of State laws,* vol. 2 (Chicago: Chapman, 1880), p. 750.

63 "Come, Josey, fork over": Marshall Hamilton, "Thomas Sharp's Turning Point: Birth of an Anti-Mormon," *Sunstone* (October 1989), p. 21.

63 "make us feel right bad": Warsaw *Signal,* June 9, 1841.

63 "How *military* these people are": Ibid., July 21, 1841.

64 a powerful voting bloc: Ibid., June 23, 1841.

64 "Mormon Joe and his Danite seraglio": Ibid., July 31, 1844, and August 25, 1846.

64 William entered the fray: D. Michael Quinn, *The Mormon Hierarchy: Origins of Power* (Salt Lake City: Signature Books, 1994), p. 220.

65 the first issue of the Nauvoo *Wasp:* For accounts of April 6, see Jerry C. Jolley, "The Sting of the Wasp: Early Nauvoo Newspaper—April 1842 to April 1843," *BYU Studies* 22 (4) (1982); Marshall Hamilton, "Thomas Sharp's Turning Point: Birth of an Anti-Mormon," *Sunstone* (October 1989); Annette Hampshire, "Thomas Sharp and Anti-Mormon Sentiment in Illinois, 1842–1845," *Journal of the Illinois State Historical Society* 72 (May 1979); Fawn Brodie, *No Man Knows My History: The Life of Joseph Smith the Mormon Prophet* (New York: Vintage Books, 1995), p. 288.

67 "We care not a fig": *Times and Seasons,* December 10, 1841.

67 "He is not as fit as my dog": New York *Sun,* July 28, 1840.

68 Cyrus Walker, "the greatest criminal lawyer": Roberts, ed., *History of the Church,* vol. 5, p. 431ff.; Brodie, *No Man Knows,* p. 348.

68 perfidious Missouri sheriffs: Lyman Omer Littlefield, *Reminiscences of Latter-day Saints* (Logan: Utah Journal, 1888), p. 128.

69 "I understand the gospel": Roberts, ed., *History of the Church,* vol. 5, p. 472.

69 Hyrum Smith . . . made a startling announcement: John Hallwas and Roger Launius, *Cultures in Conflict: A Documentary History of the Mormon War in Illinois* (Logan: Utah State University Press, 1995), p. 87.

70 "Brother Hyrum tells me this morning": Roberts, ed., *History of the Church,* vol. 5, p. 526.

71 "From this time forth": Thomas Ford, *A History of Illinois, from Its Commencement as a State in 1818 to 1847* (Chicago: S. C. Griggs, 1845), p. 329.

71 Mormons had become political orphans: Roger Launius, "American Home Missionary Society Ministers and Mormon Nauvoo: Selected Letters," *Western Illinois Regional Studies* (Spring 1985).

72 "Mormonism is exerting a great . . . influence": Clyde Buckingham, "Mormonism in Illinois," *Journal of the Illinois State Historical Society* 32 (2) (June 1939).

72   "most dangerous and virulent enemies": Matthew Bowman, *The Mormon People* (New York: Random House, 2012), p. xvi.

72   "the pretended prophet": Warsaw *Message*, September 13, 1843.

72   penchant for "consecrated thieving": Michael S. Riggs, "From the Daughters of Zion to 'The Banditti of the Prairies': Danite Influence on the Nauvoo Period," *Restoration Studies* 7 (1998), p. 96.

73   Joseph condemned stealing: Two excellent sources on Mormon stealing are ibid., and William Shepard, "Stealing at Mormon Nauvoo," *John Whitmer Historical Association Journal* (2003).

73   accusations of counterfeiting: Quinn, *The Mormon Hierarchy*, p. 127.

74   "an excellent specimen of base coin": Joseph Jackson, *Adventures and Experiences of Joseph Jackson: Disclosing the Depths of Mormon Villainy in Nauvoo* (Warsaw, IL, 1846), p. 11ff.

75   "We cannot talk about spiritual things": Leonard Arrington, *Great Basin Kingdom: An Economic History of the Latter-Day Saints, 1830–1900* (Cambridge: Harvard University Press, 1958), p. 425.

75   Nauvoo's autarkic civil government: George Moore, "Diary, 1842–1844," *Western Illinois Regional Studies* 5 (1982), p. 175.

76   detailing Joseph's inglorious past: Marshall Hamilton, "MONEY-DIGGERSVILLE— The Brief Turbulent History of the Mormon Town of Warren," *John Whitmer Historical Association Journal* 9 (1989).

77   Joseph responded with a tirade: Roberts, ed., *History of the Church*, vol. 4, p. 486ff.

5. POLYGAMY AND ITS DISCONTENTS

82   Joseph explained to Mary: Mary Rollins's story is told in Todd Compton, *In Sacred Loneliness: The Plural Wives of Joseph Smith* (Salt Lake City: Signature Books, 1997), chap. 8; Linda King Newell and Valeen Tippetts Avery, *Mormon Enigma: Emma Hale Smith* (Champaign: University of Illinois Press, 1994), p. 65ff.

84   the original polygamy revelation of 1831: Newell and Avery, *Mormon Enigma*, p. 65.

85   Joseph had been confiding his thoughts: Richard Van Wagoner, "Mormon Polyandry in Nauvoo," *Dialogue—A Journal of Mormon Thought* 18 (Fall 1985).

86   Polygamy was not an idea that: Richard Bushman, *Joseph Smith: Rough Stone Rolling* (New York: Alfred A. Knopf, 2005), p. 275.

86   "wonderful lustful spirit": George D. Smith, *Nauvoo Polygamy* (Salt Lake City: Signature Books, 2011), p. 532.

88   Emma "did not believe a word": Smith, George D., ed., *An Intimate Chronicle: The Journals of William Clayton* (Salt Lake City: Signature Books, 1995), p. 110; Newell and Avery, *Mormon Enigma*, p. 152.

88   Emma "was more bitter": Newell and Avery, *Mormon Enigma*, p. 144.

88   "blood would flow": Smith, *An Intimate Chronicle*, August 16, 1843.

88   Despite her many humiliations: D. Michael Quinn, *Early Mormonism and the Magic World View* (Salt Lake City: Signature Books, 1998), p. 163.

89   "I felt of the plates": Newell and Avery, *Mormon Enigma*, p. 25.

89   During his nine-month-long jail term: Ibid., pp. 144, 170.

89   raven-haired poetess Eliza Snow: Fawn Brodie, *No Man Knows My History: The Life of Joseph Smith the Mormon Prophet* (New York: Vintage Books, 1995), p. 471; Newell and Avery, *Mormon Enigma*, p. 134.

89   "Straight from hell, madam": Newell and Avery, *Mormon Enigma*, p. 171.

89   Emma Smith's horrified reaction: J. Lewis Taylor, "John Taylor: Family Man," in *Champion of Liberty: John Taylor*, ed. Mary Jane Woodger (Provo, UT: Religious Studies Center, Brigham Young University, 2009).

90   "very repugnant to my feelings": Leonard Arrington, *The Mormon Experience: A History of the Latter-Day Saints* (Urbana and Chicago: University of Illinois Press, 1992), p. 222.

91   Jennetta, died just two years later: Devery Anderson, "'I Could Love Them All,' Nauvoo Polygamy in the Marriage of Willard and Jennetta Richards," *Sunstone* 171 (June 2013).

91   Smith eventually married dozens of wives: Compton, *In Sacred Loneliness*, p. 616.

93   Nauvoo required a girl to be fourteen: John S. Dinger, ed., *The Nauvoo City and High Council Minutes* (Salt Lake City: Signature Books, 2011), p. 65.

93   "I would never have been sealed to Joseph": Smith, *Nauvoo Polygamy*, p. 198ff.

93   People change: Helen Mar Whitney, *Why We Practice Plural Marriage* (Salt Lake City: Office of the Juvenile Instructor, 1884).

94   adventure . . . befell Apostle Orson Pratt: Marvin Hill, *Quest for Refuge: The Mormon Flight from American Pluralism* (Salt Lake City: Signature Books, 1989), p. 118.

94   the Twelve excommunicated both Pratts: Richard Van Wagoner, "Sarah M. Pratt: The Shaping of an Apostate," *Dialogue—A Journal of Mormon Thought* 19 (Summer 1986), p. 77.

95   "You must not be a doctor here": *Salt Lake Tribune*, July 31, 1887.

95   "No man could be better fitted": Lyndon W. Cook, *William Law: Biographical Essay; Nauvoo Diary; Correspondence; Interview* (Orem, UT: Grandin Book, 1994).

96   Law brothers led a flying squad: B. H. Roberts, ed., *History of the Church of Jesus Christ of Latter-day Saints*, 2nd ed., rev., vol. 5 (Salt Lake City: Deseret Book Company, 1978), p. 431ff.

96   "a honest upright man": Cook, *William Law*, p. 55.

96   "All hail to our Chief!": *Times and Seasons*, February 15, 1843.

96   "If an angel from heaven": Cook, *William Law*, p. 37.

97   "He would have shot": Ibid., p. 133.

97   "endeavored to seduce my wife": Ibid., p. 128.

99   "Poor, weak woman!": Charlotte Haven, "A Girl's Letters from Nauvoo," *Overland Monthly* 16 (December 1890).

99   "Whether we view Joseph": Roberts, ed., *History of the Church*, vol. 6, p. 42.

99   "a delightful habitation": Scott H. Faulring, ed., *An American Prophet's Record: The Diaries and Journals of Joseph Smith* (Salt Lake City: Signature Books, 1989), p. 308.

100   "we began here first": Robert Bruce Flanders, *Nauvoo: Kingdom on the Mississippi* (Urbana and Chicago: University of Illinois Press, 1965), p. 188.

100   Foster arrived home one evening: Brodie, Fawn. *No Man Knows My History: The Life of Joseph Smith the Mormon Prophet.* (New York: Vintage Books, 1995), p. 371.

100   "'You,' shaking his fists": Scott H. Faulring, ed., *An American Prophet's Record: The Diaries and Journals of Joseph Smith* (Salt Lake City: Signature Books, 1989), p. 474.

101   "I have seen him steal": *Times and Seasons*, May 15, 1844.

101   Foster pulled a pistol: Richard Bushman, *Joseph Smith: Rough Stone Rolling* (New York: Alfred A. Knopf, 2005), p. 532.

101   "notorious in this city": Wagoner, "Sarah M. Pratt," p. 77.

101   "too indelicate for the public eye": *Times and Seasons*, May 15, 1844

101   Chauncey had been severed from the church: Dinger, *The Nauvoo City and High Council Minutes*, p. 415.

102   extraordinary tirade against Chauncey Higbee: Rocky O'Donovan, "The Abominable and Detestable Crime Against Nature: A Brief History of Homosexuality and Mormonism, 1840–1980," in *Multiply and Replenish: Mormon Essays on Sex and Family*, ed. Brent Corcoran (Salt Lake City: Signature Books, 1994).

102   Joseph accused Harrison Sagers: Dinger, *The Nauvoo City and High Council Minutes*, p. 478.

102   "walked up and down the streets": Roberts, ed., *History of the Church*, vol. 6, p. 46.

103   "we have lately been credibly informed": *Times and Seasons*, February 1, 1844.

103   "one or two disaffected individuals": Roberts, ed., *History of the Church*, vol. 6, p. 378.

104   "Do you solemnly swear": James Wesley Scott, "The Jacob and Sarah Warnock Scott Family: 1779–1910," online history and genealogy available at http://www.scottcorner.org/JACOB%20&%20SARAH%20SCOTT.pdf,

p. 79; Horace H. Cummings, "Conspiracy of Nauvoo," August 8, 1932, typescript submitted note, BYU Library, Provo, Utah.

104 "I kept a detective": Cook, *William Law,* p. 118.

105 Attacks of a very different kind: Andrew F. Ehat, "Joseph Smith's Introduction of Temple Ordinances and the 1844 Mormon Succession Question," master's thesis in history, Brigham Young University, December 1982, p. 77.

6. "THE PERVERSION OF SACRED THINGS"

109 plans to publish a new, independent newspaper: Marvin Hill, *Quest for Refuge: The Mormon Flight from American Pluralism* (Salt Lake City: Signature Books, 1989), p. 144.

110 *Expositor* was "a hazardous enterprise": Macomb *Eagle,* May 22, 1875.

110 not a cautious enterprise: B. H. Roberts, ed., *History of the Church of Jesus Christ of Latter-day Saints,* 2nd ed., rev., vol. 6 (Salt Lake City: Deseret Book Company, 1978), p. 43.

111 "You have trampled upon": Lyndon W. Cook, *William Law: Biographical Essay; Nauvoo Diary; Correspondence; Interview* (Orem, UT: Grandin Book, 1994), p. 30.

111 "I had prepared some manuscript": Ibid.

113 "the perversion of sacred things": Brotherton's letter appeared in the St. Louis *Bulletin,* July 15, 1842, and elsewhere. Details of the case appear in Fawn Brodie, *No Man Knows My History: The Life of Joseph Smith the Mormon Prophet* (New York: Vintage Books, 1995), p. 307, and George D. Smith, *Nauvoo Polygamy* (Salt Lake City: Signature Books, 2011), p. 264ff.

116 *Expositor* flew out the doors: B. Carmon Hardy, *Doing the Works of Abraham: Mormon Polygamy: Its Origin, Practice, and Demise* (Norman, OK: Arthur H. Clark, 2007), p. 69.

117 the eager-to-please council: George D. Smith, ed. *An Intimate Chronicle: The Journals of William Clayton* (Salt Lake City: Signature Books, 1995), p. 133; John S. Dinger, ed., *The Nauvoo City and High Council Minutes* (Salt Lake City: Signature Books, 2011), p. 215.

117 passed several special ordinances: Dinger, ed., *Nauvoo City and High Council Minutes,* p. 188.

117 inveighing against their enemies: Ibid., p. 238ff, has a complete record of the council's Saturday session.

118 "the wickedest man on earth": Hyrum L. Andrus and Helen Mae Andrus, *They Knew the Prophet* (Salt Lake City: Bookcraft, 1974), p. 148.

118 a raucously unreliable memoir: Dinger, ed., *Nauvoo City and High Council Minutes*; and Joseph Jackson, *Adventures and Experiences of Joseph Jackson: Disclosing the Depths of Mormon Villainy in Nauvoo* (Warsaw, IL, 1846).

119 "Free People of Color": *Evening and Morning Star Extra,* July 16, 1833.

119 an angry mob killed . . . abolitionist editor: Thomas Ford, *A History of Illinois, from Its Commencement as a State in 1818 to 1847* (Chicago: S. C. Griggs, 1845), p. 244ff.

120 "a greater nuisance than": Dinger, *Nauvoo City and High Council Minutes,* p. 250ff, has the complete record of the council's Monday session.

120 "quote Blackstone and other authors": George W. Givens and Sylvia Givens, *Five Hundred Little-Known Facts About Nauvoo* (Springville, UT: Bonneville Books, 2010), p. 36.

120 "Whatsoever unlawfully annoys": William Blackstone and Cyrus Sprague, *Blackstone Commentary Abridged* (London, 1899), p. 290.

121 methodically trashed the interior: Roberts, ed., *History of the Church,* vol. 6, p. 490.

122 "work of destruction and desperation": Warsaw *Signal,* June 11, 1844.

122 "I gave them a short address": Scott H. Faulring, ed., *An American Prophet's Record: The Diaries and Journals of Joseph Smith* (Salt Lake City: Signature Books, 1989), p. 498.

122 "The work of Joseph's agents": *Salt Lake Tribune,* July 31, 1887, William Wyl interview.

123 Missionary Isaac Scott wrote: Letter, June 16, 1844, in James Wesley Scott, "The Jacob and Sarah Warnock Scott Family: 1779–1910," online genealogy available at http://www.scottcorner.org/JACOB%20&%20SARAH%20 SCOTT.pdf.

124 "War and extermination is inevitable!": *Warsaw Signal,* June 12, 1844.

124 Smith had yet again escaped arrest: Roberts, ed., *History of the Church*, vol. 6, p. 458.

125 "Such an excitement": Ibid., p. 463.

125 "violated the highest privilege": Ibid.

7. "CRUCIFY HIM! CRUCIFY HIM!"

127 "Two brethren come": Scott H. Faulring, ed., *An American Prophet's Record: The Diaries and Journals of Joseph Smith* (Salt Lake City: Signature Books, 1989), p. 491.

128 According to Morley's letter: B. H. Roberts, ed., *History of the Church of Jesus Christ of Latter-day Saints,* 2nd ed., rev., vol. 6 (Salt Lake City: Deseret Book Company, 1978), p. 482.

128 "Instruct the companies": Ibid.

128 examining Benjamin West's famous painting: Noel A. Carmack, "Of Prophets and Pale Horses: Joseph Smith, Benjamin West, and the American Millenarian Tradition," *Dialogue—A Journal of Mormon Thought* (Fall 1996).

130 "I thought I was riding out": Roberts, ed., *History of the Church,* vol. 6, p. 461.

130 "I looked out of the pit": Ibid.

131 his fiery, final sermon: The entire sermon can be found in ibid., p. 473ff.

134 Smith dispatched another letter: Ibid., p. 466.

8. ENTER PONTIUS PILATE

136 "DOUGLAS is a *master spirit*": Glen Leonard, *Nauvoo: A Place of Peace, a People of Promise* (Salt Lake City: Deseret Book Company, 2002), p. 296; and Richard Lyman Bushman, *Joseph Smith: Rough Stone Rolling* (New York: Alfred A. Knopf, 2005), p. 426.

136 "like a man weary of human nature": B. W. Richmond, *Deseret News*, November 27, 1875.

136 Illinois governorship . . . "was feeble": Thomas Ford, *A History of Illinois, from Its Commencement as a State in 1818 to 1847* (Chicago: S. C. Griggs, 1845), p. 104.

136 Tyler "accidentally became president": Ibid., p. 271.

137 "so wholly wanting in self-confidence": Robert Howard, *Mostly Good and Competent Men: The Illinois Governors, 1818–1988* (Springfield: Illinois State Historical Society, 1988); and Rodney Davis, "Introduction" to Ford, *A History of Illinois*; John Francis Snyder, "Governor Ford and His Family," *Journal of the Illinois Historical Society* 3 (1910).

137 Ford supported the vigilante "regulators": Rodney O. Davis, "Judge Ford and the Regulators, 1841–1842," in *Selected Papers in Illinois History* (Springfield: Illinois State Historical Society, 1981).

138 "no money in the treasury whatever": Ford, *A History of Illinois*, p. 446.

139 "The early settlers": Ibid., p. 406.

139 "they all hold meetings": John Hallwas, "Thomas Gregg: Early Illinois Journalist and Author," *Western Illinois Monograph Series*, no. 2, Western Illinois University, Macomb, 1983, p. 22.

140 Fraim's execution: Dallin Oaks and Marvin Hill, *Carthage Conspiracy* (Urbana and Chicago: University of Illinois Press, 1979), p. 3.

140 "2 Brothers arrived from Carthage": Scott H. Faulring, ed., *An American Prophet's Record: The Diaries and Journals of Joseph Smith* (Salt Lake City: Signature Books, 1989), p. 493.

141 "A rumor is afloat": Warsaw *Signal*, June 19, 1844.

141 He sent a young Mormon: "Autobiography of Gilbert Belnap," available at http://www.boap.org/LDS/Early-Saints/GBelnap.html.

142 "I can assure that": George Rockwell, Letters, letter addressed to "Parents," 1844, Harold B. Lee Library, Provo, Utah, and Kansas State Historical Society.

143 Legion drilled every morning: Richard E. Bennett, Susan Easton Black, and Donald Q. Cannon, *The Nauvoo Legion in Illinois: A History of the Mormon Militia, 1841–1845* (Norman, OK: Arthur Clark, 2010), p. 241.

143 guard the waterfront and station pickets: Leonard, *Nauvoo,* p. 370; Bennett, Black, and Cannon, *Nauvoo Legion,* p. 241.

144 "We have never violated the laws": "The Last Speech of President Smith to the Legion," in B. H. Roberts, ed., *History of the Church of Jesus Christ of Latter-day Saints,* 2nd ed., rev. (Salt Lake City: Deseret Book Company, 1978), vol. 6, p. 498ff.

146 "filled with a perfect set of rabble": B. H. Roberts, *The Rise and Fall of Nauvoo* (Salt Lake City: Deseret News, 1900), p. 418.

146 "You have no idea": Leonard, *Nauvoo,* p. 368; S. O. Williams letter to John Prickett, July 10, 1844, in John Hallwas and Roger Launius, *Cultures in Conflict: A Documentary History of the Mormon War in Illinois* (Logan: Utah State University Press, 1995), p. 222.

146 a vast military bivouac: S. O. Williams letter to John Prickett.

146 "about six acres of ground": B. W. Richmond, *Deseret News,* November 27, 1875.

147 "scene of great bustle and excitement": Eudocia Baldwin Marsh, "Mormons in Hancock County: A Reminiscence," ed. Douglas L. Wilson and Rodney O. Davis, *Journal of the Illinois State Historical Society* 64 (1) (Spring 1971).

147 Ford addressed the restive militias: Ford, *A History of Illinois,* p. 332.

147 letter to President John Tyler: Roberts, ed., *History of the Church,* p. 508.

148 "Your conduct in the destruction": Ibid., p. 533ff.

148 Smith answered immediately: Ibid., p. 538ff.

149 "He gave us a full description": Brian Cannon, "John C. Calhoun, Jr., Meets the Prophet Joseph Smith Shortly Before the Departure for Carthage," *BYU Studies* 33 (4) (1993).

149 Repairing to his upstairs study: Roberts, ed., *History of the Church,* vol. 6, p. 545ff; Linda King Newell and Valeen Tippetts Avery, *Mormon Enigma: Emma Hale Smith* (Champaign: University of Illinois Press, 1994), p. 185.

9. SURRENDER

151 "I do not know where": Linda King Newell and Valeen Tippetts Avery, *Mormon Enigma: Emma Hale Smith* (Champaign: University of Illinois Press, 1994), p. 186.

152 "Some were tried": Ronald K. Esplin, "Life in Nauvoo, June 1844: Vilate Kimball's Martyrdom Letters," *BYU Studies* 19 (2) (1979).

152 "Mind your own business": Newell and Avery, *Mormon Enigma,* p. 187.

152 "I believed the governor to be": Wandle Mace, "Autobiography (1809–1846)," typescript, Harold B. Lee Library, Provo, Utah, p. 49; Dan Jones, "The Martyrdom of Joseph Smith and His Brother Hyrum," *BYU Studies* 24 (Winter 1984).

Notes

153 "You always said": B. H. Roberts, ed., *History of the Church of Jesus Christ of Latter-day Saints,* 2nd ed., rev., vol. 6 (Salt Lake City: Deseret Book Company, 1978), p. 545ff; Newell and Avery, *Mormon Enigma,* p. 187ff.

154 "It is of no use to hurry": Fawn Brodie, *No Man Knows My History: The Life of Joseph Smith the Mormon Prophet* (New York: Vintage Books, 1995), p. 386; Roberts, ed., *History of the Church,* vol. 6, p. 551.

154 "If anything should happen": Newell and Avery, *Mormon Enigma,* p. 189.

154 "I go as a lamb": Ibid., p. 190.

155 "This is the loveliest place": Roberts, ed., *History of the Church,* vol. 6, p. 554.

156 "I saw a large, well dressed": B. W. Richmond, "The Prophet's Death," *Deseret News,* November 27, 1875.

157 "write out the best blessing": Newell and Avery, *Mormon Enigma,* p. 191.

157 "Hodge, there are the boys": Roberts, ed., *History of the Church,* vol. 6, p. 558.

157 "Where is the damned prophet?": Ibid., pp. 559–560.

158 "No one could close his ears": George Turnbull Moore Davis, *The Autobiography of the late Col. Geo. T.M. Davis* (New York: Jenkins and McCowan, 1891).

160 "The Greys commenced": John Hallwas and Roger Launius, *Cultures in Conflict: A Documentary History of the Mormon War in Illinois* (Logan: Utah State University Press, 1995), p. 224.

160 "a hundred men loaded to shoot": Susan Easton Black, "Esquire James Weston Woods: Legal Counsel to Joseph Smith," *Mormon Historical Studies* (Fall 2003).

160 "No!" they cried: Warsaw *Signal,* June 29, 1844.

161 "It was evident": John S. Fullmer, *Assassination of Joseph and Hyrum Smith, the Prophet and Patriarch of the Church of Jesus Christ of Latter-day Saints* (Liverpool, England: F. D. Richards, 1855).

161 "such bare-faced, illegal": Roberts, ed., *History of the Church,* vol. 6, p. 570.

162 "General Smith asked them": B. H. Roberts, *The Rise and Fall of Nauvoo* (Salt Lake City: Deseret News, 1900), p. 302.

162 Richmond "told him plainly": *Deseret News,* November 27, 1875.

163 "I have had an interview": Roberts, ed., *History of the Church,* vol. 6, p. 565.

164 "Bless this little man!": Jones, "Martyrdom," p. 88.

164 "make us as comfortable": Kenneth W. Godfrey, "Correspondence Between William R. Hamilton and Samuel H. B. Smith Regarding the Martyrdom of Joseph and Hyrum Smith," *Nauvoo Journal* (Fall 1999).

164 saved a foundering ship: Jones, "Martyrdom," p. 100.

165 several Greys left their posts: Roberts, ed., *History of the Church,* vol. 6, p. 592.

165 "great bulwark": Ibid., p. 579ff.

166 "It's all nonsense!": Robert Bruce Flanders, *Nauvoo: Kingdom on the Mississippi* (Urbana and Chicago: University of Illinois Press, 1965), p. 323.

166 Joseph "walked boldly": Roberts, ed., *History of the Church*, vol. 6, p. 595.

166 "Now Old Joe": Jones, "Martyrdom," p. 101.

166 "committed to jail": Colonel J. W. Woods, "The Mormon Prophet," *Ottawa Democrat* (Ohio), May 13, 1885.

167 "like to see my family again": Ibid.

10. "THE PEOPLE ARE NOT THAT CRUEL"

169 "grown up with weeds and brambles": B. H. Roberts, ed., *History of the Church of Jesus Christ of Latter-day Saints,* 2nd ed., rev., vol. 6 (Salt Lake City: Deseret Book Company, 1978), p. 610.

170 "We have had too much trouble": Dan Jones, "The Martyrdom of Joseph Smith and His Brother Hyrum," *BYU Studies* 24 (Winter 1984).

171 "women, inoffensive young persons": Thomas Ford, *Message of the Governor of the State of Illinois in Relation to the Disturbances in Hancock County* (Springfield, IL: Walters and Weber, December 21, 1844), p. 12.

171 "foul fiend Flibbertigibbet": John Hay, "The Prophet's Tragedy," *Atlantic Monthly* (December 1869).

172 "they were the elite": Ford, *Message of the Governor,* pp. 13–14.

172 "prisoners' lives are in grave danger": B. H. Roberts, *The Rise and Fall of Nauvoo* (Salt Lake City: Deseret News, 1900), p. 309.

172 "traitors, and midnight assassins": Roberts, ed., *History of the Church*, vol. 6, p. 607.

173 "were determined to kill Joe": Jones, "Martyrdom," p. 91.

173 You may need that gun: Roberts, ed., *History of the Church*, vol. 6, p. 608.

173 "Governor continues his courtesies": Ibid., p. 605ff.

175 "went out in high glee": Hay, "Prophet's Tragedy."

175 father-son team . . . continued terrorizing: Dallin Oaks and Marvin Hill, *Carthage Conspiracy* (Urbana and Chicago: University of Illinois Press, 1979), p. 59.

176 "threw out considerable threats": Dean Jessee, "Return to Carthage: Writing the History of Joseph Smith's Martyrdom," *Journal of Mormon History* 9 (1981).

177 "After supper": Roberts, ed., *History of the Church*, vol. 6, p. 615ff.

178 Fourteen-year-old William: Hamilton's account was published in Foster Walker's "The Mormons in Hancock County," *Dallas City Review*, January 29, 1903.

179 "Come on, you cowards": Eudocia Baldwin Marsh, "Mormons in Hancock

County: A Reminiscence," ed. Douglas L. Wilson and Rodney O. Davis, *Journal of the Illinois State Historical Society* 64 (1) (Spring 1971).

179 While the Greys fussed: Roberts, *The Rise and Fall of Nauvoo*, p. 455.

181 "cutting away a piece of flesh": Roberts, ed., *History of the Church*, vol. 6, p. 620.

182 "You are the damned old Chieftain": LaJean Purcell Carruth, transcriber, "John Taylor's June 27, 1854, Account of the Martyrdom," *BYU Studies* 50 (3) (2011), note 6.

182 "Stop, Doctor": Hamilton letter to Foster Walker, December 24, 1902, in John Hallwas and Roger Launius, *Cultures in Conflict: A Documentary History of the Mormon War in Illinois* (Logan: Utah State University Press, 1995), p. 228.

183 faked confrontation with the guards: Willard Richards and John Taylor left detailed accounts of the attack on the jailhouse. Eudocia Baldwin's memoir appeared in Wilson and Davis, eds., "Mormons in Hancock County." Greys lieutenant Samuel O. Williams, John Fullmer, and Cyrus Wheelock, and Joseph Smith's lawyer J. W. Woods (Col. J. W. Woods, "The Mormon Prophet," *Ottawa Democrat* [Ohio], May 13, 1885) also left useful accounts of the Carthage events, as did John Hay.

184 in a tut-tutting mood: Roberts, ed., *History of the Church*, vol. 6, p. 623.

184 painstakingly carved: David E. Miller and Della S. Miller, *Nauvoo: The City of Joseph* (Santa Barbara and Salt Lake City: Peregrine Smith, 1974), p. 116.

185 Ford's account differs: Thomas Ford, *A History of Illinois, from Its Commencement as a State in 1818 to 1847* (Chicago: S. C. Griggs, 1845), p. 336.

185 patrolled the prairies: Thomas Barnes trial testimony, *Illinois v. Williams: Trial of the Persons Indicted in the Hancock County Circuit Court for the Murder of Joseph Smith at the Carthage Jail, on the 27th of June, 1844* (Warsaw, IL, 1845).

186 Taylor lay in agony: Roberts, *The Rise and Fall of Nauvoo*, p. 446ff.

186 "nerves like the devil": Stanley B. Kimball, "Thomas L. Barnes—Coroner of Carthage," *BYU Studies* 11 (2) (Winter 1971).

187 "Joseph and Hyrum are dead": Roberts, ed., *History of the Church*, vol. 6, p. 621.

018700 "Joseph is killed!": Harold Schindler, *Orrin Porter Rockwell: Man of God, Son of Thunder* (Salt Lake City: University of Utah Press, 1966), p. 135.

11. JOSEPH'S HOMECOMING

189 "proceeded with all convenient haste": George Turnbull Moore Davis, *The Autobiography of the late Col. Geo. T.M. Davis* (New York: Jenkins and McCowan, 1891).

190 "Will you be tied": John Taylor's excellent memoir of the Carthage events is an appendix in B. H. Roberts, *The Rise and Fall of Nauvoo* (Salt Lake City: Deseret News, 1900), p. 404ff.

190 "There's a good lady": Ibid.

190 "I ought to be killed": Ibid., p. 455.

191 "The inhabitants were all out": Donna Hill, *Joseph Smith: The First Mormon* (Salt Lake City: Signature Books, 1998); and Susan Easton Black, "The Tomb of Joseph," in *The Disciple as Witness: Essays on Latter-day Saint History and Doctrine in Honor of Richard Lloyd Anderson* (Provo, UT: Maxwell Institute, 2000).

191 "The weeping was communicated": B. W. Richmond, "The Prophet's Death," *Deseret News*, November 27, 1875.

192 "she extended her trembling hand": Lavina F. Anderson, *Lucy's Book* (Salt Lake City: Signature Books, 2001), contextual note Chapter 6.

192 "How could they kill": *Deseret News*, November 27, 1875; Marvin Hill, *Quest for Refuge: The Mormon Flight from American Pluralism* (Salt Lake City: Signature Books, 1989), p. 153.

192 "when I entered the room": Richard Lyman Bushman, *Joseph Smith: Rough Stone Rolling* (New York: Alfred A. Knopf, 2005), p. 8.

192 "the people with one united voice": B. H. Roberts, ed., *History of the Church of Jesus Christ of Latter-day Saints*, 2nd ed., rev., vol. 6 (Salt Lake City: Deseret Book Company, 1978), p. 626.

193 "shot in the right breast": Ibid., p. 627.

193 "She trembled at every step": Richmond, "The Prophet's Death."

194 "every business forgotten": Dan Jones, "The Martyrdom of Joseph Smith and His Brother Hyrum," *BYU Studies* 24 (Winter 1984).

194 "the neck and face forming": Richmond, "The Prophet's Death."

195 prayer of vengeance "upon the murderers": William Shepard, "The Concept of a 'Rejected Gospel' in Mormon History," vol. 4, parts 1 and 2, *Journal of Mormon History* (2008), p. 140; Davis Bitton, "The Martyrdom of Joseph Smith in Early Mormon Writings," *John Whitmer Historical Association Journal* 3 (1983), p. 8.

196 Levi "told me to place": Shepard, "Concept of a 'Rejected Gospel,'" p. 142.

196 "Their dead bodies": "Journal of Allen Stout, for the Period 1815–1848," typescript in Harold B. Lee Library, Provo, Utah, available online at http://www.boap.org/LDS/Early-Saints/AStout.html.

196 "oath of vengeance": Samuel Morris Brown, *In Heaven As It Is on Earth* (New York: Oxford University Press, 2012), p. 291.

198 "All the field officers": Thomas Ford, *Message of the Governor of the State of Illinois in Relation to the Disturbances in Hancock County* (Springfield, IL: Walters and Weber, December 21, 1844).

198 "I seemed paralyzed": Bitton, "Martyrdom," p. 8.

199 "the papers were full of News": Heber Kimball, *On the Potter's Wheel: The Diaries of Heber C. Kimball*, ed. Stanley B. Kimball (Salt Lake City: Signature Books, 1987), chap. 4, available online at http://signaturebookslibrary .org/?p=1771.

200 "Thus Ends Mormonism!": *New York Herald*, July 8, 1844.

200 Invoking the "noble blood": John Hay, "The Prophet's Tragedy," *Atlantic Monthly* (December 1869).

201 "If the public understood": George Rockwell, Letters, letter to "Parents," August 3, 1844, Harold B. Lee Library, Provo, Utah, and Kansas State Historical Society.

201 "recent disgraceful affair at Carthage": Ford, *Message of the Governor*.

202 "He called at a grog shop": Rockwell, letter to "Parents."

202 future Church . . . might swell: Thomas Ford, *A History of Illinois, from Its Commencement as a State in 1818 to 1847* (Chicago: S. C. Griggs, 1845), p. 359.

203 Phelps . . . impassioned, incendiary speech: Richard Van Wagoner and Steven C. Walker, "The Joseph Smith/Hyrum Smith Funeral Sermon," *BYU Studies* 23 (1) (1983).

205 "We will petition Sister Emma": "General Conference," *Millennial Star*, October 8, 1845.

205 Emma arranged . . . midnight burial: Linda King Newell and Valeen Tippetts Avery, *Mormon Enigma: Emma Hale Smith* (Champaign: University of Illinois Press, 1994), pp. 197, 213; Black, "Tomb of Joseph."

206 "The Utah cousins": Brown, *In Heaven*, p. 302.

12. TRIAL BY JURY

208 "They would have murdered": John Taylor, "The John Taylor Nauvoo Journal, January 1845–September 1845," *BYU Studies* 23 (3) (1983), p. 45.

209 "one of the most able": *The Bench and Bar of Illinois: Historical and Reminiscent*, vol. 1, ed. John McAuley Palmer (Chicago: Lewis Publishing Company, 1899), p. 181.

210 Browning . . . "ablest speaker in the state": Most biographical details of the trial participants come from Dallin Oaks and Marvin Hill, *Carthage Conspiracy* (Urbana and Chicago: University of Illinois Press, 1979), a near-definitive account of the trial. The Church History Library in Salt Lake City offers a digital copy of George Darling Watt's famous shorthand record of the trial for a nominal fee ("Report of the Trial of the Murderers of Joseph Smith, 1845").

211 "vomited at the feet": In Lavina F. Anderson, *Lucy's Book* (Salt Lake City: Signature Books, 2001), p. 728.

212 "a respectable set of men": Oaks and Hill, *Carthage Conspiracy*, p. 22.

212 "the finest looking man": Ibid., p. 76.

212 Muskets and sidearms: Ibid., p. 113; *Daily Missouri Republican*, May 27, 1845.

212 wild anti-Mormon onlookers: Thomas Ford, *A History of Illinois, from Its Commencement as a State in 1818 to 1847* (Chicago: S. C. Griggs, 1845), p. 368.

213 "The eyes of the whole country": All trial quotes come from Watt's "Report of the Trial of the Murderers of Joseph Smith, 1845."

214 Lamborn pressed Peyton: Oaks and Hill, *Carthage Conspiracy*, p. 118.

216 "difficult to imagine anything cooler": John Hay, "The Prophet's Tragedy," Atlantic Monthly (December 1869).

217 Daniels said he had ridden: William Daniels, "Correct Account of the Murder of Generals Joseph Smith and Hyrum Smith at Carthage, on the 27th Day of June, 1844."

226 "As we anticipated": John G. Turner, *Brigham Young, Pioneer Prophet* (Cambridge: Harvard University Press, 2012), p. 122; and Hay, "The Prophet's Tragedy."

227 "wholly destitute of principle": Oaks and Hill, *Carthage Conspiracy*, p. 174.

227 "No one would be convicted": Ford, *A History of Illinois*, p. 369.

13. Aftermath

233 "Secret things cost Joseph": George D. Smith, ed., *An Intimate Chronicle: The Journals of William Clayton* (Salt Lake City: Signature Books, 1995), p. 144.

234 "Lusty, hot tempered": Fawn Brodie, *No Man Knows My History: The Life of Joseph Smith the Mormon Prophet* (New York: Vintage Books, 1995), p. 245.

234 "wickedness of his brother": Vicki Cleverley Speek, *"God Has Made Us a Kingdom": James Strang and the Midwest Mormons* (Salt Lake City: Signature Books, 2006), p. 43.

234 "He seemed determined": D. Michael Quinn, *The Mormon Hierarchy: Origins of Power* (Salt Lake City: Signature Books, 1994), p. 152.

235 victim of a "bilious fever": Ibid., p. 153.

236 "I have thrown him off": B. H. Roberts, ed., *History of the Church of Jesus Christ of Latter-day Saints*, 2nd ed., rev., vol. 6 (Salt Lake City: Deseret Book Company, 1978), p. 49.

236 Rigdon "leaped for joy": Andrew F. Ehat, "Joseph Smith's Introduction of Temple Ordinances and the 1844 Mormon Succession Question," master's thesis in history, Brigham Young University, December 1982, p. 102.

237 Rigdon saw Joseph Smith in heaven: Richard Van Wagoner, "The Making of a Mormon Myth: The 1844 Transfiguration of Brigham Young," *Dialogue—A Journal of Mormon Thought* 28 (4) (Spring 2001), p. 163.

237   there must be a guardian appointed: Ibid.

238   The Nauvoo stalwarts scorned: Leonard Arrington, *Brigham Young: American Moses* (Urbana and Chicago: University of Illinois Press, 1986), p. 112.

238   "I expected I should find him": John G. Turner, *Brigham Young, Pioneer Prophet* (Cambridge: Harvard University Press, 2012), p. 33.

238   poor families making the grisly trek: Roberts, ed., *History of the Church*, vol. 3, p. 247.

239   Joseph assigned the delicate task: Lyndon W. Cook, *William Law: Biographical Essay; Nauvoo Diary; Correspondence; Interview* (Orem, UT: Grandin Book, 1994), p. 19.

239   "never pretended to be Joseph Smith": Turner, *Brigham Young*, p. 114.

239   Brigham had his own revelation: Van Wagoner, "Making of a Mormon Myth," p. 165.

240   "He was dry as sticks": Lynne Watkins Jorgensen, "The Mantle of the Prophet Joseph Passes to Brother Brigham: A Collective Spiritual Witness," *BYU Studies* 36 (4) (1996–1997), p. 154.

240   Brigham Young's dramatic entrance: Richard Van Wagoner, *Sidney Rigdon: A Portrait of Religious Excess* (Salt Lake City: Signature Books, 1994), p. 339.

240   "I will manage this voting": Jorgensen, "Mantle of the Prophet," p. 165.

241   Orson Hyde's dramatic testimony: Van Wagoner, "Making of a Mormon Myth," p. 168.

242   "I know your feelings": Ibid.

242   "Do you want a spokesman?": Van Wagoner, *Sidney Rigdon*, pp. 340–341.

243   Matthias had a screw loose: Richard Lyman Bushman, *Joseph Smith: Rough Stone Rolling* (New York: Alfred A. Knopf, 2005), p. 275.

243   boy named James Colin Brewster: An excellent account of Brewster's ministry can be found in Dan Vogel, "James Colin Brewster: The Boy Prophet Who Challenged Mormon Authority," in *Differing Visions: Biographical Essays on Mormon Dissenters,* ed. Roger D. Launius and Linda Thatcher (Urbana and Chicago: University of Illinois Press, 1994).

245   "behold my servant James J. Strang": Speek, *"God Has Made Us a Kingdom,"* p. 22.

245   Strang . . . excommunicated Brigham: Ibid., p. 34; Milo M. Quaife, *The Kingdom of Saint James: A Narrative of the Mormons* (New Haven: Yale University Press, 1930), p. 43.

245   "successor of Judas Iscariot": *Millennial Star*, vol. 8, p. 123.

246   Strang . . . raised the stakes: Speek, *"God Has Made Us a Kingdom,"* p. 46.

247   "Bishop Reuben Miller reports": Entry for January 23, 1846, George D. Smith, ed., *An Intimate Chronicle: The Journals of William Clayton* (Salt Lake City: Signature Books, 1995).

247 Bishop Miller was "considerably bewildered": January 30, 1846, Brigham Young, *Journal of Discourses* (Liverpool and London: F. D. and S. W. Richards, 1854), available online at http://contentdm.lib.byu.edu/cdm /compoundobject/collection/JournalOfDiscourses3/id/9599/rec/1.

248 "Behold James J. Strang hath cursed": *Millennial Star*, vol. 7, p. 157.

248 "I do not know of ten persons": Quinn, *Mormon Hierarchy*, p. 211.

248 prominent Saints rallied to Strangism: Linda King Newell and Valeen Tippetts Avery, *Mormon Enigma: Emma Hale Smith* (Champaign: University of Illinois Press, 1994), p. 232.

249 Halcyon Order of the Illuminati: Speek, *"God Has Made Us a Kingdom,"* pp. 47, 53.

249 Strang summoned his followers: Ibid., pp. 121–122.

250 the plates made him do it: Ibid., p. 164.

251 Discrediting Sidney Rigdon: Roberts, ed., *History of the Church*, vol. 7, p. 269.

252 "He seemed sane": Van Wagoner, *Sidney Rigdon*, pp. 356, 399.

252 had placed much of his property: B. H. Roberts, *The Rise and Fall of Nauvoo* (Salt Lake City: Deseret News, 1900), p. 111.

252 "Presidency . . . belongs to William": John Taylor, "The John Taylor Nauvoo Journal, January 1845–September 1845," *BYU Studies* 23 (3) (1983).

253 "mean enough to steal": Devery Anderson and Gary Bergera, *Joseph Smith's Quorum of the Anointed, 1842–1845: A Documentary History* (Salt Lake City: Signature Books, 2005), p. 162.

254 "enemies and outcasts": Arrington, *Brigham Young,* p. 123.

254 "The mob is upon us": Brigham Young, "Proclamation to Col. Levi Williams and Mob Party," available online at http://archive.org/stream /proclamationtoco00unse#page/n0/mode/2up.

255 publishing upbeat excerpts: *Nauvoo Neighbor*, September 17, 1845.

256 "time of our exodus": Glen Leonard, *Nauvoo: A Place of Peace, a People of Promise* (Salt Lake City: Deseret Book Company, 2002), p. 544.

14. THIS WORLD AND THE NEXT

259 "The Marquis of Downshire": *Journal History (Church of Jesus Christ of Latter-Day Saints),* April 10, 1844.

260 "We are now conducted": Robert Wicks and Fred Foister, *Junius and Joseph: Presidential Politics and the Assassination of the First Mormon Prophet* (Logan: Utah State University Press, 2005), p. 237.

261 "Its fate is fixed": *New York Times*, January 20, 1862.

262 most-stolen book: Debra J. Marsh, "Respectable Assassins: A Collective Biography and Socio-Economic Study of the Carthage Mob," master's thesis, University of Utah, December 2009, p. 4.

263 "the Mormon curse": B. H. Roberts, ed., *History of the Church of Jesus Christ of Latter-day Saints,* 2nd ed., rev., vol. 6 (Salt Lake City: Deseret Book Company, 1978), p. 532.

264 "naturally base, corrupt and cruel": *Salt Lake Tribune,* July 31, 1887.

265 Sharp offered some judicious: Minutes, Hancock County Pioneer Association, August 1, 1870.

265 "Everybody loved Judge Sharp": "In Memoriam," from Huntington Library, Pasadena, California; other cites from Dallin Oaks and Marvin Hill, *Carthage Conspiracy* (Urbana and Chicago: University of Illinois Press, 1979), p. 218ff.

266 desultory fate of Governor . . . Ford: John Francis Snyder, "Governor Ford and His Family," *Journal of the Illinois Historical Society* 3 (1910), and by the same author, "Death of Governor Ford's Daughter," *Journal of the Illinois Historical Society* 3 (1910).

266 "weeds, tall grass and brush": N. B. Lundwall, *The Fate of the Persecutors of the Prophet Joseph Smith* (Salt Lake City: Private edition, 1952), p. 301.

266 Ford's "troubled destiny": "Joseph the Seer," Hinckley remarks, June 26, 1994, available online at https://www.lds.org/ensign/1994/09/joseph-the -seer?lang=eng.

267 "I am *Mad*": Annette Hampshire, "Thomas Sharp and Anti-Mormon Sentiment in Illinois, 1842–1845," *Journal of the Illinois State Historical Society* 72 (May 1979), p. 93.

267 Backenstos resolved to move: Harold Schindler, *Orrin Porter Rockwell: Man of God, Son of Thunder* (Salt Lake City: University of Utah Press, 1966), p. 146; and Thomas Gregg, *History of Hancock County, Illinois, together with an outline history of the State, and a digest of State laws* (Chicago: Chapman, 1880), p. 341.

268 "the gallows was cheated": *Salt Lake Tribune,* June 11, 1878.

269 Rockwell's funeral: Schindler, *Orrin Porter Rockwell,* p. 363ff.

269 more than one cowboy ballad: Ibid., p. 359ff.

269 "Her face was thin": Linda King Newell and Valeen Tippetts Avery, *Mormon Enigma: Emma Hale Smith* (Champaign: University of Illinois Press, 1994), pp. 296–297.

270 "she could go to Heaven": Glen Leonard, *Nauvoo: A Place of Peace, a People of Promise* (Salt Lake City: Deseret Book Company, 2002), p. 635.

271 "I am convinced": Paul Edwards, "The Sweet Singer of Israel: David Hyrum Smith," *BYU Studies* 12 (2) (1972), p. 6.

271 two pages of questions: This interview can be found in "Last Testimony of Sister Emma," *Saints' Herald* 26 (October 1, 1879).

275 tenth anniversary celebration: LaJean Purcell Carruth, transcriber, "John Taylor's June 27, 1854, Account of the Martyrdom," *BYU Studies* 50 (3) (2011), p. 39.

Notes

275 the featured speaker . . . Apostle John Taylor: For the full transcription of his remarks that day, see John G. Turner, *Brigham Young, Pioneer Prophet* (Cambridge: Harvard University Press, 2012), p. 172.

276 a ninety-six-page account: Mark H. Taylor, "John Taylor: Witness to the Martyrdom of the Prophet Joseph Smith," in *Champion of Liberty: John Taylor,* ed. Mary Jane Woodger (Provo, UT: Religious Studies Center, Brigham Young University, 2009).

GLOSSARY

Bishop: Ward manager, monitors tithing by church members, distributes donated goods to immigrants and needy families.

Bogus making: Counterfeiting.

Council of Fifty: A secret body, appointed by Joseph Smith, intended to rule over Christ's *Kingdom of God* after the Second Coming.

Danites: Mormon vigilante force, formed in response to anti-Mormon violence in Missouri.

Disfellowship; excommunication: Church punishment for religious transgressions.

Elder: A male church member who has received the priesthood endowment.

Endowment: A temple ritual, introduced in Nauvoo, required for men and women to become full members of the church.

Exaltation: Highest degree of glory in the eternal Mormon afterlife.

General Authorities: Church leaders, including the *First Presidency,* the church's ruling triumvirate, composed of Joseph Smith and a first and a second counselor. Other General Authorities are *The Quorum of the Twelve Apostles*, led by Brigham Young.

Gentiles: All non-Mormons, except for Jews and "Lamanites," a Book of Mormon race.

Golden tablets; Book of Mormon: Joseph Smith said he created the Book of Mormon from golden plates found in upstate New York. Other sacred Mormon texts include The Pearl of Great Price, a collection of scripture, and Doctrine and Covenants, Smith's revelations.

Jack-Mormon: A Gentile who sympathized with the Mormons. Today, it means a lapsed Mormon.

Keys, or the keys of the priesthood: The right to exercise power in the church.

Mormon War of 1838: Missourians' successful attempt to expel the state's 5,000 Mormons.

Nauvoo City Council, Nauvoo High Council: Two bodies that, respectively, managed the city's temporal and spiritual affairs.

Nauvoo Expositor: Mormon dissident newspaper, destroyed by Joseph Smith.

Nauvoo Legion: The standing Mormon militia in Illinois, about 2,000–3,000 strong.

Old settlers: In both Missouri and Illinois, the preexisting populations—not Native Americans—who were generally hostile to Mormons.

Saints, or the Latter-day Saints: Followers of Joseph Smith, also known as the Mormons.

Second Anointing: Temple rite introduced in Nauvoo, assuring select couples eternal life.

"Spiritual wife" doctrine; "plural wife" doctrine: Polygamy, also called the "principle." Wives and husbands were "sealed for time," meaning united in this life, or "sealed for time and eternity."

Stake, ward: Ecclesiastical districts, roughly equivalent to dioceses and parishes.

Temple: Holy place of Mormon worship, larger, more grandiose, and more spiritually significant than a church. Gentiles may enter a Mormon church, but not a temple.

Temple garments: Light underclothes worn by Mormons who have received their endowment.

Tithing: Voluntary donations, generally fixed at 10 percent of income or net worth, to the church.

BIBLIOGRAPHY

Adams, Henry, Jr., ed. "Charles Francis Adams Visits the Mormons in 1844." *Massachusetts Historical Society Proceedings* 68 (1952): 267–300.

Allman, John Lee. "Policing in Mormon Nauvoo." Illinois Historical Journal 89 (2) (July 1, 1996).

Anderson, Devery. "'I Could Love Them All': Nauvoo Polygamy in the Marriage of Willard and Jennetta Richards." *Sunstone* 171 (June 2013).

———, and Gary Bergera. *Joseph Smith's Quorum of the Anointed, 1842–1845: A Documentary History*. Salt Lake City: Signature Books, 2005.

Anderson, Lavina F. *Lucy's Book*. Salt Lake City: Signature Books, 2001.

Anderson, Richard Lloyd. "Joseph Smith and the Millenarian Time Table." *BYU Studies* 3 (3–4) (1961).

Andreasen, Bryon C. "High Noon in Hancock County: Sheriff Minor Deming and the Anti-Mormons." Unpublished monograph, courtesy of the author.

Andrus, Hyrum L., and Helen Mae Andrus. *They Knew the Prophet*. Salt Lake City: Bookcraft, 1974.

Arrington, Leonard. *Brigham Young: American Moses*. Urbana and Chicago: University of Illinois Press, 1986.

———. *Great Basin Kingdom: An Economic History of the Latter-Day Saints, 1830–1900*. Cambridge: Harvard University Press, 1958.

———. "James Gordon Bennett's 1831 Report on 'The Mormonites.'" *BYU Studies* 10 (3) (1970).

———. *The Mormon Experience: A History of the Latter-Day Saints*. Urbana and Chicago: University of Illinois Press, 1992.

"Autobiography of Gilbert Belnap." Available at http://www.boap.org/LDS/Early -Saints/GBelnap.html.

Bates, Irene. "William Smith, 1811–93: Problematic Patriarch." *Dialogue—A Journal of Mormon Thought* 16 (2) (1983).

Baugh, Alexander. "'For This Ordinance Belongeth to My House': The Practice of Baptism for the Dead Outside the Nauvoo Temple." *Mormon Historical Studies* (Spring 2002).

Baxter, Maurice G. *Orville H. Browning: Lincoln's Friend and Critic*. Bloomington: Indiana University Press, 1957.

Beecher, Maureen Ursenbach. "'All Things Move in Order in the City': The Nauvoo Diary of Zina Diana Huntington Jacobs." *BYU Studies* 19 (3) (1979).

——, Linda King Newell, and Valeen Tippetts Avery. "Emma and Eliza and the Stairs." *BYU Studies* 22 (1) (1982).

Bennett, Richard E., Susan Easton Black, and Donald Q. Cannon. *The Nauvoo Legion in Illinois: A History of the Mormon Militia, 1841–1845*. Norman, OK: Arthur Clark, 2010.

Bentley, Melissa K. "A Masonic Martyrdom: Freeman Involvement in the Martyrdom of Joseph and Hyrum Smith." Selections from the Religious Education Student Symposium 2006. Religious Studies Center, Brigham Young University, 2006.

Bergera, Gary James. "'Illicit Intercourse,' Plural Marriage, and the Nauvoo Stake High Council, 1840–1844." *John Whitmer Historical Association Journal* 23 (2003).

——. "Joseph Smith and the Hazards of Charismatic Leadership." *John Whitmer Historical Association Journal* 6 (1986).

Bernauer, Barbara Hands. "Still 'Side by Side': The Final Burial of Joseph and Hyrum Smith." *John Whitmer Historical Association Journal* 11 (1991).

Biographical Review of Hancock County. Chicago: Hobart Publishing, 1907.

Bishop, M. Guy. "'What Has Become of Our Fathers?' Baptism for the Dead at Nauvoo." *Dialogue—A Journal of Mormon Thought* 23 (1990).

Bitton, Davis. "The Martyrdom of Joseph Smith in Early Mormon Writings." *John Whitmer Historical Association Journal* 3 (1983).

Black, Susan Easton. "Artois Hamilton: A Good Man in Carthage?" *Journal of Mormon History* (2005), Utah State University.

——. "Esquire James Weston Woods: Legal Counsel to Joseph Smith." *Mormon Historical Studies* (Fall 2003).

——. "Isaac Galland: Both Sides of the River." *Nauvoo Journal* (Fall 1996).

——. "Nauvoo Neighbor: The Latter-day Saint Experience at the Mississippi River, 1843–1845." *BYU Studies* 51 (3) (2012).

——. "The Tomb of Joseph." In *The Disciple as Witness: Essays on Latter-day Saint History and Doctrine in Honor of Richard Lloyd Anderson*. Provo, UT: Maxwell Institute, 2000.

——. "The University of Nauvoo, 1841–45." *Religious Educator* 10 (3) (2009).

Blackstone, William, and Cyrus Sprague. *Blackstone Commentary Abridged*. London, 1899.

Bibliography

Blake, Reed. "Twenty-four Hours to Martyrdom." Salt Lake City: Bookcraft, 1973.

Bonney, Edward. *The Banditti of the Prairies*. Philadelphia: T. B. Peterson & Bros., 1855.

Book of Mormon: A Reader's Edition. Springfield: University of Illinois Press, 2003.

Bowman, Matthew. *The Mormon People*. New York: Random House, 2012.

Brodie, Fawn. *No Man Knows My History: The Life of Joseph Smith the Mormon Prophet*. New York: Vintage Books, 1995.

Brown, Samuel Morris. *In Heaven As It Is on Earth*. New York: Oxford University Press, 2012.

Buckingham, Clyde. "Mormonism in Illinois." *Journal of the Illinois State Historical Society* 32 (2) (June 1939).

Buerger, David John. "The Development of the Mormon Temple Endowment Ceremony." *Dialogue—A Journal of Mormon Thought* 20 (4).

Burton, Richard. *The City of the Saints: Among the Mormons and Across the Rocky Mountains to California*. New York: Harper, 1862.

Bushman, Richard Lyman. "The Character of Joseph Smith." *BYU Studies* 42 (2) (2003).

———. *Joseph Smith: Rough Stone Rolling*. New York: Alfred A. Knopf, 2005.

———. *Mormonism: A Very Short Introduction*. New York: Oxford University Press, 2008.

———. "The Visionary World of Joseph Smith." *BYU Studies* 37 (1) (1997).

———. "What's New in Mormon History, a Reply to Jan Shipps." *Journal of American History* 94 (2) (September 2007).

Cannon, Brian. "John C. Calhoun, Jr., Meets the Prophet Joseph Smith Shortly Before the Departure for Carthage." *BYU Studies* 33 (4) (1993).

Card, Brigham Y., et. al, eds. *The Mormon Presence in Canada*. Logan: Utah State University Press, 1990.

Carmack, Noel A. "Of Prophets and Pale Horses: Joseph Smith, Benjamin West, and the American Millenarian Tradition." *Dialogue—A Journal of Mormon Thought* (Fall 1996).

Carruth, LaJean Purcell, transcriber. "John Taylor's June 27, 1854, Account of the Martyrdom." *BYU Studies* 50 (3) (2011).

Caswall, Henry. *The City of the Mormons, or, Three Days at Nauvoo in 1842*. London: Rivington, 1842.

———. *The Prophet of the Nineteenth Century; or The Rise, Progress and Present State of the Mormons*. London: Rivington, 1843.

Caton, John Dean. *Early Bench and Bar in Illinois*. Chicago: Chicago Legal News, 1893.

Compton, Todd. *In Sacred Loneliness: The Plural Wives of Joseph Smith*. Salt Lake City: Signature Books, 1997.

Cook, Lyndon W. "Brother Joseph Is Truly a Wonderful Man." *BYU Studies* 20 (2) (Summer 1980).

———. "Isaac Galland—Mormon Benefactor." *BYU Studies* 19 (3) (Spring 1979).

———. *William Law: Biographical Essay; Nauvoo Diary; Correspondence; Interview.* Orem, UT: Grandin Book, 1994.

———. "William Law, Nauvoo Dissenter." *BYU Studies* 22 (Winter 1982).

Cummings, Horace H. "Conspiracy of Nauvoo." August 8, 1932. Typescript submitted note. BYU Library, Provo, Utah.

Daniels, William. "Correct Account of the Murder of Generals Joseph Smith and Hyrum Smith at Carthage, on the 27th Day of June, 1844." John Taylor, Nauvoo, 1845.

Davis, David Brion. "The New England Origins of Mormonism." *New England Quarterly* 26 (2) (June 1953).

Davis, George Turnbull Moore. *The Autobiography of the late Col. Geo. T.M. Davis.* New York: Jenkins and McCowan, 1891.

———. *Massacre of Joseph Smith; The Mormon Prophet, and Hyrum, his Brother Together with a Brief History of the Rise and Progress of Mormonism. And all the circumstances which led to their Death.* St. Louis: Chambers & Knapp, 1844.

Davis, Rodney. Introduction to *History of Illinois.* Urbana and Chicago: University of Illinois Press, 1995.

Davis, Rodney O. "Judge Ford and the Regulators, 1841–1842." In *Selected Papers in Illinois History.* Springfield: Illinois State Historical Society, 1981.

Dinger, John S., ed. *The Nauvoo City and High Council Minutes.* Salt Lake City: Signature Books, 2011.

Dirck, Brian. *Lincoln the Lawyer.* Urbana and Chicago: University of Illinois Press, 2007.

The Doctrine and Covenants of The Church of Jesus Christ of Latter-day Saints Containing Revelations Given to Joseph Smith, the Prophet with Some Additions by His Successors in the Presidency of the Church. Available online at https://www.lds.org/scriptures/dc-testament.

Edwards, Paul. "The Sweet Singer of Israel: David Hyrum Smith." *BYU Studies* 12 (2) (1972).

Edwards, Paul M. "William B. Smith: The Persistent Pretender." *Dialogue—A Journal of Mormon Thought* 18 (2) (1985).

Ehat, Andrew F. "It Seems Like Heaven Began on Earth: Joseph Smith and the Constitution of the Kingdom of God." *BYU Studies* 20 (3) (1980).

———. "Joseph Smith's Introduction of Temple Ordinances and the 1844 Mormon Succession Question." Master's thesis in history, Brigham Young University, December 1982.

Enders, Donald. "The Steamboat Maid of Iowa: Mormon Mistress of the Mississippi." *BYU Studies* 19 (3) (1979).

Esplin, Ronald K. "Joseph, Brigham and the Twelve: A Succession of Continuity." *BYU Studies* 21 (3) (1981).

———. "Life in Nauvoo, June 1844: Vilate Kimball's Martyrdom Letters." *BYU Studies* 19 (2) (1979).

Faulring, Scott H., ed. *An American Prophet's Record: The Diaries and Journals of Joseph Smith*. Salt Lake City: Signature Books, 1989.

Flanders, Robert Bruce. "Dream and Nightmare: Nauvoo Revisited." In *The New Mormon History*. Edited by D. Michael Quinn. Salt Lake City: Signature Books, 1992.

———. *Nauvoo: Kingdom on the Mississippi*. Urbana and Chicago: University of Illinois Press, 1965.

Ford, Thomas. *A History of Illinois, from Its Commencement as a State in 1818 to 1847*. Chicago: S. C. Griggs, 1845.

———. *Message of the Governor of the State of Illinois in Relation to the Disturbances in Hancock County*. Springfield, IL: Walters and Weber, December 21, 1844.

Foster, Lawrence. "James J. Strang: The Prophet Who Failed." *Church History* 50 (2) (1981).

———. "The Psychology of Religious Genius: Joseph Smith and the Origins of New Religious Movements." *Dialogue—A Journal of Mormon Thought* 26 (4) (1993).

———. *Religion and Sexuality: Three American Communal Experiments of the Nineteenth Century*. New York: Oxford University Press, 1981.

Fullmer, John S. *Assassination of Joseph and Hyrum Smith, the Prophet and Patriarch of the Church of Jesus Christ of Latter-day Saints*. Liverpool, England: F. D. Richards, 1855.

Gardner, Hamilton. "The Nauvoo Legion, 1840–1845—A Unique Military Organization." *Journal of the Illinois State Historical Society* 54 (2) (Summer 1961).

Gayler, George R. "The Mormons and Politics in Illinois." *Journal of the Illinois State Historical Society* 49 (1) (Spring 1956).

Givens, George W. "In Old Nauvoo: Everyday Life in the City of Joseph." Salt Lake City: Deseret Book Company, 1990.

———, and Sylvia Givens. *Five Hundred Little-Known Facts About Nauvoo*. Springville, UT: Bonneville Books, 2010.

Godfrey, Kenneth W. "Correspondence Between William R. Hamilton and Samuel H. B. Smith Regarding the Martyrdom of Joseph and Hyrum Smith." *Nauvoo Journal* (Fall 1999).

———. "Crime and Punishment in Mormon Nauvoo, 1839–1846." *BYU Studies* 32 (1–2) (1992).

———. "Joseph Smith and the Masons." *Journal of the Illinois State Historical Society* 64 (Spring 1971).

———. "Non-Mormon Views of the Martyrdom: A Look at Some Early Published Accounts." *John Whitmer Historical Association Journal* 7 (1987).

Gregg, Thomas. *Biographical Review of Hancock County*. Chicago: Hobart Publishing, 1907.

———. *History of Hancock County, Illinois, together with an outline history of the State, and a digest of State laws*. Chicago: Chapman, 1880.

Grimsted, David. *American Mobbing, 1828–1861: Toward Civil War*. New York: Oxford University Press, 1998.

Hallwas, John. "Thomas Gregg: Early Illinois Journalist and Author." *Western Illinois Monograph Series*, no. 2, Western Illinois University, Macomb, 1983.

———, and Roger Launius. *Cultures in Conflict: A Documentary History of the Mormon War in Illinois*. Logan: Utah State University Press, 1995.

Hamilton, Marshall. "From Assassination to Expulsion: Two Years of Distrust, Hostility and Violence." *BYU Studies* 32 (1–2) (1992).

———. "Money-Diggersville—The Brief Turbulent History of the Mormon Town of Warren." *John Whitmer Historical Association Journal* 9 (1989).

———. "Thomas Sharp's Turning Point: Birth of an Anti-Mormon." *Sunstone* (October 1989).

Hampshire, Annette. *Mormonism in Conflict, the Nauvoo Years*. Lewiston, NY: Edwin Mellen Press, 1985.

———. "Thomas Sharp and Anti-Mormon Sentiment in Illinois, 1842–1845." *Journal of the Illinois State Historical Society* 72 (May 1979).

Hardy, B. Carmon. *Doing the Works of Abraham: Mormon Polygamy: Its Origin, Practice, and Demise*. Norman, OK: Arthur H. Clark, 2007.

Haven, Charlotte. "A Girl's Letters from Nauvoo." *Overland Monthly* 16 (December 1890).

Hay, John. "The Prophet's Tragedy." *Atlantic Monthly* (December 1869).

Hill, Donna. *Joseph Smith: The First Mormon*. Salt Lake City: Signature Books, 1998.

Hill, Marvin. "Carthage Conspiracy Reconsidered: A Second Look at the Murder of Joseph and Hyrum Smith." *Journal of the Illinois Historical Society* 97 (2) (Summer 2004).

———. Foreword to *The Essential Joseph Smith*. Salt Lake City: Signature Books, 1995.

———. *Quest for Refuge: The Mormon Flight from American Pluralism*. Salt Lake City: Signature Books, 1989.

Homer, Michael. "Similarity of Priesthood in Masonry: The Relationship Between Freemasonry and Mormonism." *Dialogue—A Journal of Mormon Thought* 27 (3) (Fall 1994).

Hovey, Joseph. "Autobiography, 1812–1847." Typescript. Harold B. Lee Library, Provo, Utah.

Bibliography

Howard, Robert. *Mostly Good and Competent Men: The Illinois Governors, 1818–1988.* Springfield: Illinois State Historical Society, 1988.

Howe, Daniel Walker. *What Hath God Wrought: The Transformation of America, 1815–1848.* New York: Oxford University Press, 2007.

Huntress, Keith. "Governor Thomas Ford and the Murderers of Joseph Smith." *Dialogue—A Journal of Mormon Thought* (Summer 1969).

Jackson, Joseph. *Adventures and Experiences of Joseph Jackson: Disclosing the Depths of Mormon Villainy in Nauvoo.* Warsaw, IL, 1846.

Jacob, Norton. "Autobiography and Diary." Typescript. Harold B. Lee Library, Provo, Utah.

Jennings, Warren A. "The Lynching of an American Prophet." *BYU Studies* 40 (1) (2001).

Jensen, Richard L. "Transplanted to Zion: The Impact of British Latter-day Saints Immigration upon Nauvoo." *BYU Studies* 31 (1) (1991).

Jessee, Dean. "Howard Coray's Recollections of Joseph Smith." *BYU Studies* 17 (3) (1977).

———. "Return to Carthage: Writing the History of Joseph Smith's Martyrdom." *Journal of Mormon History* 9 (1981).

Johnson, Philo. "Journal of Philo Johnson, 1894." BYU Special Collections, Provo, Utah. Available online at http://www.rootcellar.us/johnsnph.htm.

Johnstun, Joseph D. "'To Lie in Yonder Tomb': The Tomb and Burial of Joseph Smith." *Mormon Historical Studies* (Fall 2005).

Jolley, Jerry C. "The Sting of the Wasp: Early Nauvoo Newspaper—April 1842 to April 1843." *BYU Studies* 22 (4) (1982).

Jones, Dan. "The Martyrdom of Joseph Smith and His Brother Hyrum." *BYU Studies* 24 (Winter 1984).

Jorgensen, Lynne Watkins. "The Mantle of the Prophet Joseph Passes to Brother Brigham: A Collective Spiritual Witness." *BYU Studies* 36 (4) (1996–1997).

Kimball, Heber. *On the Potter's Wheel: The Diaries of Heber C. Kimball.* Edited by Stanley B. Kimball. Salt Lake City: Signature Books, 1987.

Kimball, Stanley B. "Thomas L. Barnes—Coroner of Carthage." *BYU Studies* 11 (2) (Winter 1971).

Launius, Roger. "American Home Missionary Society Ministers and Mormon Nauvoo: Selected Letters." *Western Illinois Regional Studies* (Spring 1985).

——— "Anti-Mormonism in Illinois: Thomas C. Sharp's Unfinished History of the Mormon War, 1845." *Journal of Mormon History* 15 (1989).

———. *Joseph Smith II: Pragmatic Prophet.* Urbana and Chicago: University of Illinois Press, 1988.

———. "The Murders in Carthage: Non-Mormon Reports of the Assassination of the Smith Brothers." *John Whitmer Historical Association Journal* 15 (1995).

——, and John Hallwas, eds. *Kingdom on the Mississippi Revisited: Nauvoo in Mormon History.* Urbana and Chicago: University of Illinois Press, 1996.

——, and Mark McKiernan. "Joseph Smith Jr.'s Red Brick Store." *Western Illinois Monograph Series,* no. 5, Herald Publishing House, 2005.

Leonard, Glen. *Nauvoo: A Place of Peace, a People of Promise.* Salt Lake City: Deseret Book Company, 2002.

——. "Picturing the Nauvoo Legion." *BYU Studies* 35 (2) (1995).

Littlefield, Lyman Omer. *Reminiscences of Latter-day Saints.* Logan: Utah Journal, 1888.

Lundwall, N. B. *The Fate of the Persecutors of the Prophet Joseph Smith.* Private edition, Salt Lake City, 1952.

Lyne, Thomas. *A True and Descriptive Account of the Assassination of Joseph & Hiram Smith.* New York: C. A. Calhoun, 1844.

Lyon, Joseph L., and David W. Lyon. "Physical Evidence at Carthage Jail and What It Reveals About the Assassination of Joseph and Hyrum Smith." *BYU Studies* 47 (4) (2008).

Lyon, T. Edgar. "Doctrinal Development of the Church During the Nauvoo Sojourn, 1839–1846." *BYU Studies* 15 (4) (1975).

Mace, Wandle. "Autobiography (1809–1846)." Typescript. Harold B. Lee Library, Provo, Utah. Available online at http://www.boap.org/LDS/Early-Saints/WMace.html.

Madsen, Carol Cornwall. *In Their Own Words: Women and the Story of Nauvoo.* Salt Lake City: Deseret Books, 1994.

Marquardt, Michael. *The Rise of Mormonism.* Xulon Press, 2005.

——. "Some Interesting Notes on Succession at Nauvoo in 1844." *Restoration Studies* 5 (January 1986).

Marsh, Debra J. "Respectable Assassins: A Collective Biography and Socio-Economic Study of the Carthage Mob." Master's thesis, University of Utah, December 2009.

Marsh, Eudocia Baldwin. "Mormons in Hancock County: A Reminiscence," ed. Douglas L. Wilson and Rodney O. Davis. *Journal of the Illinois State Historical Society* 64 (1) (Spring 1971).

Merrill, Timothy. "'Will the Murderers Be Hung?' Albert Brown's 1844 Letter and the Martyrdom of Joseph Smith." *BYU Studies* 45 (2) (2006).

Miller, David E., and Della S. Miller. *Nauvoo: The City of Joseph.* Santa Barbara and Salt Lake City: Peregrine Smith, 1974.

Monroe, James. Nauvoo Diary, April, May 1845. Microfilm. Beinecke Rare Book and Manuscript Library, Yale University, New Haven, Connecticut.

Moore, George. "Diary, 1842–1844." *Western Illinois Regional Studies* 5 (1982).

Mulder, William. "Nauvoo Observed." *BYU Studies* 32 (1–2) (1992).

Nevins, Allan, ed. *The Diary of Philip Hone, 1828–1851.* 2 vols. New York: Dodd, Mead, 1927.

Newell, Linda King, and Valeen Tippetts Avery. *Mormon Enigma: Emma Hale Smith.* Urbana and Chicago: University of Illinois Press, 1994.

Oaks, Dallin. "The Suppression of the 'Nauvoo Expositor.'" *Utah Law Review* 9 (1965).

———, and Joseph Bentley. "Joseph Smith and the Legal Process: In the Wake of the Steamboat Nauvoo." *BYU Studies* 19 (2) (1979).

———, and Marvin Hill. *Carthage Conspiracy.* Urbana and Chicago: University of Illinois Press, 1979.

O'Donovan, Rocky. "The Abominable and Detestable Crime Against Nature: A Brief History of Homosexuality and Mormonism, 1840–1980." In *Multiply and Replenish: Mormon Essays on Sex and Family.* Edited by Brent Corcoran. Salt Lake City: Signature Books, 1994.

Palmer, Grant H. "Did Joseph Smith Commit Treason in His Quest for Political Empire in 1844?" *John Whitmer Historical Association Journal* 32 (2) (Fall/Winter 2012).

———. "Why William and Jane Law Left the LDS Church in 1844." *John Whitmer Historical Association Journal* 32 (2) (Fall/Winter 2012).

Palmer, John McAuley, ed. *The Bench and Bar of Illinois: Historical and Reminiscent.* Vol. 1. Chicago: Lewis Publishing Company, 1899.

Park, Benjamin E., and Robin Scott Jensen. "Debating Succession, March 1846: John E. Page, Orson Hyde, and the Trajectories of Joseph Smith's Legacy." *Journal of Mormon History* 39 (Winter 2013).

Partridge, George F., ed. "The Death of a Mormon Dictator: Letters of Massachusetts Mormons, 1843–1848." *New England Quarterly* 9 (December 1936).

Peterson, Paul. "An Historical Analysis of the Word of Wisdom." Brigham Young University, master's thesis, August 1972.

Poll, Richard D. "Joseph Smith and the Presidency, 1844." *Dialogue—A Journal of Mormon Thought* 3 (Autumn 1968).

Poulsen, Robert E. "Fate of the Persecutors of Joseph Smith: Transmutations of an American Myth." *Dialogue—A Journal of Mormon Thought* 11 (4) (1978).

Quaife, Milo M. *The Kingdom of Saint James: A Narrative of the Mormons.* New Haven: Yale University Press, 1930.

Quincy, Josiah. "Joseph Smith at Nauvoo." In *Figures of the Past.* Boston: Roberts Bros., 1896.

Quinn, D. Michael. *Early Mormonism and the Magic World View.* Salt Lake City: Signature Books, 1998.

———. *The Mormon Hierarchy: Origins of Power.* Salt Lake City: Signature Books, 1994.

Bibliography

———. "The Mormon Succession Crisis of 1844." *BYU Studies* 16 (Winter 1976).

———, ed. *The New Mormon History*. Salt Lake City: Signature Books, 1992.

———. "The Practice of Rebaptism at Nauvoo." *BYU Studies* 18 (2) (1978).

Richmond, B. W. "The Prophet's Death." *Deseret News*, November 27, 1875.

Riggs, Michael S. "From the Daughters of Zion to 'The Banditti of the Prairies': Danite Influence on the Nauvoo Period." *Restoration Studies* 7 (1998).

Roberts, Alasdair. *America's First Great Depression: Economic Crisis and Political Disorder After the Panic of 1837*. Ithaca and London: Cornell University Press, 2012.

Roberts, B. H., ed. *History of the Church of Jesus Christ of Latter-day Saints*. 7 vols., 2nd ed., rev. Salt Lake City: Deseret Book Company, 1978.

———. *The Rise and Fall of Nauvoo*. Salt Lake City: Deseret News, 1900.

Robertson, Margaret. "The Campaign and the Kingdom: The Activities of the Electioneers in Joseph Smith's Presidential Campaign." *BYU Studies* 39 (3) (2000).

Rockwell, George. Letters: Extracts, 1843–1846. Harold B. Lee Library, Provo, Utah, and Kansas State Historical Society.

Romig, Ronald E. *Lucy's Nauvoo*. Independence, MO: John Whitmer Books, 2009.

Rowley, Dennis. "Nauvoo: A River Town." *BYU Studies* 18 (2) (1978).

Schindler, Harold. *Orrin Porter Rockwell: Man of God, Son of Thunder*. Salt Lake City: University of Utah Press, 1966.

Scott, James Wesley. "The Jacob and Sarah Warnock Scott Family: 1779–1910." Online history and genealogy. Available at http://www.scottcorner.org/JACOB%20&%20SARAH%20SCOTT.pdf.

Sharp, Thomas. "Minutes, Hancock County Pioneer Association, 1 August, 1870." Abraham Lincoln Library, Springfield, Illinois.

Shepard, William. "The Concept of a 'Rejected Gospel' in Mormon History." Parts 1 and 2. *Journal of Mormon History* 34 (3) (2008).

———. "Stealing at Mormon Nauvoo." *John Whitmer Historical Association Journal* 23 (2003).

Smith, Alex D. "The Book of the Law of the Lord." *Mormon History Journal* 38 (Fall 2012).

Smith, George D., ed. *An Intimate Chronicle: The Journals of William Clayton*. Salt Lake City: Signature Books, 1995.

———. *Nauvoo Polygamy*. Salt Lake City: Signature Books, 2011.

Smith, Joseph III. *Joseph Smith III and the Restoration*. Independence, MO: Herald Publishing House, 1952.

Smith, Mrs. Robert F. "Mrs. Robert F. Smith's Story." Undated manuscript. Abraham Lincoln Presidential Library, Springfield, Illinois.

Snyder, John Francis. "Death of Governor Ford's Daughter." *Journal of the Illinois Historical Society* 3 (1910).

———. "Governor Ford and His Family." *Journal of the Illinois Historical Society* 3 (1910).

Speek, Vicki Cleverley. *"God Has Made Us a Kingdom": James Strang and the Midwest Mormons.* Salt Lake City: Signature Books, 2006.

Taylor, J. Lewis. "John Taylor: Family Man." In *Champion of Liberty: John Taylor.* Edited by Mary Jane Woodger. Provo, UT: Religious Studies Center, Brigham Young University, 2009.

Taylor, John. "The John Taylor Nauvoo Journal, January 1845–September 1845." *BYU Studies* 23 (3) (1983).

Taylor, Mark H. "John Taylor: Witness to the Martyrdom of the Prophet Joseph Smith." In *Champion of Liberty: John Taylor.* Edited by Mary Jane Woodger. Provo, UT: Religious Studies Center, Brigham Young University, 2009.

Taylor, Samuel. *The Kingdom or Nothing: The Life of John Taylor, Militant Mormon.* New York: Macmillan, 1976.

Thayer, William Roscoe. *The Life and Letters of John Hay.* Boston: Houghton Mifflin, 1915.

Trial of the Persons Indicted in the Hancock County Circuit Court for the Murder of Joseph Smith at the Carthage Jail, on the 27th of June, 1844. Warsaw, IL: Warsaw Signal, 1845.

Tullidge, Edward William. *Life of Joseph the Prophet.* New York: Tullidge and Crandall, 1878.

Turner, John G. *Brigham Young, Pioneer Prophet.* Cambridge: Harvard University Press, 2012.

Turner, Jonathan. *Mormonism in All Ages.* New York: Platt and Peters, 1842.

Vogel, Dan. "James Colin Brewster: The Boy Prophet Who Challenged Mormon Authority." In *Differing Visions: Biographical Essays on Mormon Dissenters.* Edited by Roger D. Launius and Linda Thatcher. Urbana and Chicago: University of Illinois Press, 1994.

Wagoner, Richard Van. "The Making of a Mormon Myth: The 1844 Transfiguration of Brigham Young." *Dialogue—A Journal of Mormon Thought* 28 (4) (Spring 2001).

———. "Mormon Polyandry in Nauvoo." *Dialogue—A Journal of Mormon Thought* 18 (Fall 1985).

———. "Sarah M. Pratt: The Shaping of an Apostate." *Dialogue—A Journal of Mormon Thought* 19 (Summer 1986).

———. *Sidney Rigdon: A Portrait of Religious Excess.* Salt Lake City: Signature Books, 1994.

———, and Steven C. Walker. "The Joseph Smith/Hyrum Smith Funeral Sermon." *BYU Studies* 23 (1) (1983).

Ward, Maurine Carr. "John Needham's Nauvoo Letter: 1843." *Nauvoo Journal* (Spring 1996).

Bibliography

Waterman, Bryan. *The Prophet Puzzle: Interpretive Essays on Joseph Smith*. Salt Lake City: Signature Books, 1999.

Watkins, Jordan, and Steven C. Harper. "'It Seems That All Nature Mourns': Sally Randall's Response to the Murder of Joseph Smith and Hyrum Smith." *BYU Studies* 46 (1) (2007).

Watt, George Darling. "Report of the Trial of the Murderers of Joseph Smith, 1845." Digital copy from Church History Library, Salt Lake City.

Weeks, Zebulun Q. "The Last Days of Joseph and Hyrum Smith: A Chronology." *By Common Consent Papers* 6 (2) March 2011. Available at http://bycommonconsent.com/2011/03/14/bcc-papers-6–2-weeks-last-days/.

Weston, William. Letters, 1844–1845. Manuscript Collection, Newberry Library, Chicago.

Whitman, Omer, and James Varner. "Sheriff Jacob Backenstos, 'Defender of the Saints.'" *Journal of Mormon History* 29 (1) (2004).

Whitney, Helen Mar. *Why We Practice Plural Marriage*. Salt Lake City: Office of the Juvenile Instructor, 1884.

Wicks, Robert, and Fred Foister. *Junius and Joseph: Presidential Politics and the Assassination of the First Mormon Prophet*. Logan: Utah State University Press, 2005.

Williams, Mentor. "A Tour of Illinois in 1842." *Journal of the Illinois State Historical Society* 42 (3) (September 1949).

Woods, Fred E. "Gathering to Nauvoo: Mormon Immigration 1840–46." Mormon Historical Studies, *Nauvoo Journal* (Fall 1999).

Woods, Colonel J. W. "The Mormon Prophet: A True Version of His Martyrdom." *Ottawa Democrat*, May 13, 1885.

Wyl, William. *Mormon Portraits*. Salt Lake City: Tribune Printing, 1886.

Young, Brigham. *Journal of Discourses*, vol. 4. Liverpool and London: F. D. and S. W. Richards, 1854. Available online at http://contentdm.lib.byu.edu/cdm/compoundobject/collection/JournalOfDiscourses3/id/9599/rec/1.

INDEX

Index

Smith, Robert F., 70, 160–161, 166, 167, 170, 171, 172, 179, 183, 264

Smith, Samuel, 189, 190, 191, 232, 234, 235

Smith, William, 102
    Mormonism, criticism of and, 64–65
    Smith, Joseph succession and, 234–235, 248–249, 252–253

Smoot, Reed, 260n

Snow, Eliza, 89, 90, 105, 260–261, 274

Snow, Erastus, 120

Snow, Lorenzo, 83

Snyder, Adam, 135

Snyder, John F., 137, 266

Sodomy, 102

Solomon, King, 84, 85

Song of Solomon, 7

Spain, 5, 34

Speaking in tongues, 56, 81

Spencer, Augustine, 161

Spiritual wifery, 86, 89, 250, 273, 276
    See also Polygamy

St. Louis *Bulletin*, 115

St. Louis, Mo., 1

Stigall, George, 163, 164, 165, 176, 179, 181–182, 207, 227

Stout, Allen, 196

Stout, Hosea, 58

Strang, James J., 245–251

Styles, George P., 120

Superstition, 16

Taxation, 30

Taylor, John, 48, 66, 90, 92, 109, 147, 163
    Carthage jailhouse lynching and, 176–182, 186, 190–191, 208, 274–277
    Expositor affair and, 145–146
    polygamy and, 276

Smith, Joseph, death of and, 197–198

Smith, Joseph succession and, 232, 234

    surrender of, 164

    Young, Brigham and, 275–276

Taylor, Leonora, 189, 190

Ten Commandments, 84

Texas, 5, 30, 32, 34

Theodemocracy, 31

Theology, 9, 20, 88, 98, 116, 120, 234, 281

Thieving, 72–73, 77

Thompson, John, 15–16

Thornton, S. S., 241

Times and Seasons newspaper, 35, 58, 59, 63, 65, 66, 96, 101, 109, 242, 244

Tithing, 20–21, 22, 56, 94

True Church of Latter-day Saints, 103–104

Turner, Jonathan, 72

Twain, Mark, 18

Tyler, John, 31, 136, 147–148, 150

United States, 14, 33

Urim and Thummim, 17, 18, 246

U.S. government. *See* Government

Utah, 25, 48, 49, 93, 154n, 239, 255, 262, 268, 270, 271, 274–276

Van Buren, Martin, 2, 31, 67, 95

Van Wagoner, Richard, 241

Vermont, 6, 8, 14, 15, 206, 238

Vigilantism, 2, 36, 42–43, 128, 137, 171, 222, 251, 254

Voorhis, William, 181–182

Voras, William, 208, 222–223

Walker, Cyrus, 68–69, 70

Walker, Lucy, 48, 198–199

Warren, Calvin, 76–77, 211, 225–226

ALEX BEAM writes columns for the *Boston Globe* and for the *International Herald Tribune*. He is the author of two works of nonfiction, *Gracefully Insane* and *A Great Idea at the Time*. He has also written for the *Atlantic Monthly*, *Slate*, and *Forbes/FYI*. He lives in Newton, Massachusetts, with his wife and three sons.

PublicAffairs is a publishing house founded in 1997. It is a tribute to the standards, values, and flair of three persons who have served as mentors to countless reporters, writers, editors, and book people of all kinds, including me.

I. F. STONE, proprietor of *I. F. Stone's Weekly*, combined a commitment to the First Amendment with entrepreneurial zeal and reporting skill and became one of the great independent journalists in American history. At the age of eighty, Izzy published *The Trial of Socrates*, which was a national bestseller. He wrote the book after he taught himself ancient Greek.

BENJAMIN C. BRADLEE was for nearly thirty years the charismatic editorial leader of *The Washington Post*. It was Ben who gave the *Post* the range and courage to pursue such historic issues as Watergate. He supported his reporters with a tenacity that made them fearless and it is no accident that so many became authors of influential, best-selling books.

ROBERT L. BERNSTEIN, the chief executive of Random House for more than a quarter century, guided one of the nation's premier publishing houses. Bob was personally responsible for many books of political dissent and argument that challenged tyranny around the globe. He is also the founder and longtime chair of Human Rights Watch, one of the most respected human rights organizations in the world.

. . .

For fifty years, the banner of Public Affairs Press was carried by its owner Morris B. Schnapper, who published Gandhi, Nasser, Toynbee, Truman, and about 1,500 other authors. In 1983, Schnapper was described by *The Washington Post* as "a redoubtable gadfly." His legacy will endure in the books to come.

Peter Osnos, *Founder and Editor-at-Large*